Essential Guide to Metals and Manufacturing

Essential Guide to Metals and Manufacturing

Krishan Katyal

Copyright © 2019 by Krishan Katyal.

Library of Congress Control Number:		2019904040
ISBN:	Hardcover	978-1-7960-2555-2
	Softcover	978-1-7960-2554-5
	eBook	978-1-7960-2574-3

All rights reserved. No part of this book may be reproduced or transmitted in any form or by any means, electronic or mechanical, including photocopying, recording, or by any information storage and retrieval system, without permission in writing from the copyright owner.

The views expressed in this work are solely those of the author and do not necessarily reflect the views of the publisher, and the publisher hereby disclaims any responsibility for them.

Any people depicted in stock imagery provided by www.pexels.com and such images are being used for illustrative purposes only.
Certain stock imagery© www.pexels.com.

Print information available on the last page.

Rev. date: 04/29/2019

To order additional copies of this book, contact:
Xlibris
1-888-795-4274
www.Xlibris.com
Orders@Xlibris.com
791458

CONTENTS

Introduction to Essential Guide to Metals and Manufacturing........vii
Disclaimer..xi

Chapter 1	Making of Iron and Steel	1
Chapter 2	Making of Cast Iron	15
Chapter 3	General Classification of Steels	28
Chapter 4	Material Properties and Testing	45
Chapter 5	Nonferrous and Precious (Noble) Metals	55
Chapter 6	Heat Treatment of Steel	63
Chapter 7	Ferrous and Nonferrous Metal Casting and Powder Metallurgy	71
Chapter 8	Metal Cutting Processes for Metal Fabrication	79
Chapter 9	Thread Systems	93
Chapter 10	Shaping of Materials	102
Chapter 11	Welding Methods	132
Chapter 12	Machining and Related Processes	157
Chapter 13	Machinery Components and Electrical Systems	211
Chapter 14	Fluid Power Systems	229
Chapter 15	Lubrication of the Equipment	258
Chapter 16	Plastics	272
Chapter 17	Quality Control in Manufacturing	290
Chapter 18	Engineering Drawings	301

References 313
Index—Essential Guide to Metals and Manufacturing..................325

INTRODUCTION TO ESSENTIAL GUIDE TO METALS AND MANUFACTURING

DURING MY FORTY year career, I was fortunate to work for five Chicago area leading manufacturing companies. These companies are leaders in the field of CNC machine tools, consumer electric appliances, diesel electric locomotives, and systems for concrete bridges, dams, and buildings and are manufacturers of power press coil handling equipment.

The topics covered in this book are based on my actual experience and mechanical engineering education. The following key areas are covered in this book:

1. Materials—ferrous and nonferrous—for castings, heat treatment, and testing
2. Welding, forging, metal fabrication processes, and quality control guidelines
3. CNC and other machinery
4. Hydraulics and lubrication systems
5. Mechanical and electrical components
6. Blueprint reading

The book introduces you to several metals, processes, and technologies. This book is for people who want to know processes but do not want to spend too much time reading dedicated texts. It is my hope that a new design or manufacturing engineer, purchasing manager, or any person just starting with a metal processing company may benefit from the various chapters in this book. This book gives a glimpse of major current suppliers (as of 2018) in their respective fields.

It took nearly twenty years to gather the topics discussed in this book. I have tried to give credit to every author possible. Some acknowledgments are included in the chapter, and some are listed in the separate reference list.

I have reviewed hundreds of websites for this book. Based on them, I have listed brief profiles of steel companies, machine builders, forging and casting companies, and quality and welding equipment suppliers. The websites listed and the companies can be a source of information for your business.

All chapters in this book are independent of each other. You can read any chapter in any order. This book is written in plain English with simple words. All sketches were drawn based on present prevailing concepts. These sketches are for explanation only and not to be used to design product and process.

I thank my wife, Suman, for her support and my sixth grader grandson, Yash Gupta, who kept me on track by asking, "Nana, when are you are going to finish your book?" Thank you, Yash.

Also, I like to thank my parents, Murari Lal and Lakshmi Devi; brothers, Bishamber Lal, Rajinder, Surinder, and Sushil; and sister, Sanjogta Talwar, for their support throughout my engineering college studies. Also, I am thankful to my daughter, Rewa; son, Navin; son-in-law, Sachin; grandson, Amar; and granddaughter, Arya, for their continued encouragement for this book.

Also, I am thankful to Shri GS Institute of Technology and Science, Indore, India, for providing me an opportunity to finish my mechanical engineering degree. Also, I am thankful to IIT Chicago, College of Dupage and Joliet Jr. College in Illinois for introducing me to new technologies.

I am thankful to FJ Little Machine Co., Sunbeam Appliances, Electro-Motive Diesel (previously part of General Motors and now a division of Caterpillar), Toyoda Machinery (Japanese owned), and DYWIDAG-Systems International (German owned) for giving me an opportunity to work at their plants.

Also, I am thankful to the hundreds of contract manufacturers involved with machine shops, plastic injection molders, plastics fabricators, sheet metal, forgings, castings, heavy steel plate fabricators, and digital printing companies in Illinois, Wisconsin, and Michigan that allowed me to visit their facilities in the last seven years.

I am thankful to the publisher for their support.

My sincere hope is that the subjects discussed here and listed websites may help the readers to develop a greater understanding of metals and manufacturing methods. And I hope this brief guide will help readers in contributing and improving the enterprise they choose.

Thank you!

Krishan Katyal
January 24, 2019
Lisle IL 60532

DISCLAIMER

THIS BOOK WAS written by the author' with nearly forty-year experience in manufacturing and engineering with leading technology companies in Chicago. This book is a summary of specialties in metals and manufacturing.

Websites of companies listed in this book were not paid. The companies listed may or may not suitable for your business. Please use your own judgment for sourcing their equipment or services.

The information in this book is based on nearly twenty years of studying hundreds of articles in over two dozens trade journals, websites, and several textbooks. In some cases, there is possibility that the information may be outdated due to advancement in technology.

All technologies described in the book are for your information only. Please seek the advice of professional in her and his field to design and manufacture your product.

It takes years to master the topics discussed in this book. There is no quick way of learning, which I described in less than three hundred pages here. Before using information of metals and processes, please verify with other professionals and other reliable sources. Keeping in view the above situations, the reader of this book will not hold the author and the publisher responsible for anything caused directly or indirectly by using this book.

Thank you!

Krishan K. Katyal
Author: Essential Guide to Metals and Manufacturing
January 31, 2019

CHAPTER 1

Making of Iron and Steel

Topics covered are steel production capabilities of major countries, making of pig iron, iron ores, making of steel, type of steel melting furnaces, suppliers of furnaces, stainless steel, and glimpse of major US plant.

IN NATURE, THERE are about 120 elements. These elements exist in earth with combined form. These groups are further divided into organic and inorganic elements. Any group that has carbon and hydrogen is called organic element. Petroleum is an example of an organic compound. Item such as steel, copper, gold, and aluminum are called inorganic.

The study of composition of elements starts with a smallest particle called an atom. The atom consists of charged nucleus with positively charged particles called proton and negatively charged electrons. The combination of two atoms is called a molecule. The following are some of the chemical symbols for a few elements:

Hydrogen—H, Carbon—C, Aluminum—Al, Silicon—Si, Sulfur—S,

Titanium—Ti, Vanadium—V, Molybdenum—Mo, Copper—Cu, Iron—Fe

Steel is key metal in growth of any nation. In this chapter, we will discuss the making of iron and steel.

Steel is an alloy of carbon and iron. Steel contains maximum 2% carbon. In addition, steel contains manganese, silicon, phosphorus, and sulfur. Steel is used extensively for industry, transportation, buildings, and bridges. Steel is used in various forms and strengths. Steel could be recycled after its use in cars, trucks, and ships. In the presence of water and oxygen, steel rusts. For usage outside, steel is galvanized and painted to protect it from rusting.

According to www.worldsteel.org, the worldwide output of crude steel in 2016 was 1,630 million metric tons. For sixty-four countries, the output of steel for the month of November 2017 alone was 136 million metric tons. And production for the month of May 2018 was 154 million tons. Per Worldsteel.org, there are 3,500 grades of steel.

Based on World Steel 2017 report, the following are 2016 crude steel production numbers from the major countries in millions of metric tons:

China	808
United States	78.5
Russia	70.8
India	95.9
Germany	42
Japan	104.8
South Korea	68.6

The following are some of the major steel producing companies (from World Steel Association) with their 2016 crude steel production:

ArcelorMittal	95.45
China Baowu Group	63.81
Tata Steel	24.44
Thyssenkrupp	17.40

China Steel Corp.	15.52
Gerdau	15.95
SAIL	14.38
Kobe Steel	7.26
U.S. Steel	14.22
SSAB	7.99
Hyundai Steel	20.09

Stainless steel is produced by adding nickel and chromium to steel. Per the World Steel website for the first nine months of 2017, the worldwide production of stainless steel was thirty-six million tons.

Making of Pig Iron

Steel is manufactured from pig iron. The pig iron is manufactured in a blast furnace. The blast furnaces are usually about 7 to 12 meters diameter and 30 to 60 meters high with daily output of 350 to 12,000 metric tons.

Based on AIST—2011 (Association for Iron & Steel Technology—www.aist.org) web information, there are over twenty-eight operating blast furnaces in US. Beside smaller blast furnaces, there are two large blast furnaces in the world. One is located in Germany. It is part of thyssenkrupp Company (joint venture Tata Steel and thyssenkrupp). This furnace has an output of 12,000 metric tons (info from Youtube) per day.

At the same time, based on February 20, 2016, report of www.nwi.com (*Northwest Indiana Times*), number 7 furnace owned by ArcelorMittal at East Chicago, Indiana (Indiana Harbor) can produce 11,500 tons of pig iron every day.

The raw material for charging the blast furnace usually consist of iron ore, coke (coal), and limestone.

The iron-rich ore from the mines is ground to size and magnetically separated and washed to remove impurities. The actual iron ore may have concentration of 20% to 30% iron content and is further turned into small pellets. The following are names of certain iron ores:

Hematite	Fe_2O_3
Magnetite	Fe_3O_4
Pyrite	FeS
Taconite	

The blast furnace is fabricated with steel. It is lined with refractory bricks. Using special carriage and weighing systems, the blast furnace is loaded from the top in layers with iron ore, coke, and limestone. The furnace is furnished with blast of hot air through tuyeres, which are water cooled and located near the base. The ore has oxides, and the process of removing oxygen is called smelting.

The heating of the raw material is done by hot gases. These hot gases are produced separately in stoves, which are lined with bricks to retain heat. The hot gases are pushed through the mixed material in the blast furnace. The rising heat and gases are recirculated back to stoves.

The combined iron ore, coke, and limestone takes about six to eight hours to melt. Once the blast furnace starts, it runs continuously for few years with a few maintenance stops. The temperature at the molten iron stage could reach to 1,450°C, while the top reaches to 250°C or more.

Heavy molten metal sinks to the bottom of the furnace. Limestone chemically binds with the impurities to form slag. Slag floats on top of the molten metal and is extracted. Slag is used for making concrete bricks. The molten pig iron is removed from the bottom of blast furnace every three to five hours

The molten pig iron is poured into special bottle cars, which take the material to steel making facility. Also, pig iron is solidified in long troughs. The molten pig iron is hard and brittle when solidified. The pig iron has 3.8% to 4.7% carbon content. The solidified pieces are sold to foundries to make gray iron.

Making of Steel

The pig iron has a lot of carbon, and it needs to be burned off by the decarburization process. The molten iron or cast ingots from the blast furnace are transferred to any one of following processes:

A. Open hearth furnace
B. Basic oxygen furnace (BOF)
C. Electric arc furnace
D. Induction furnace

Open Hearth Furnace

This is an older method of making steel, but it still being used by several plants. A large hearth measuring forty feet by eighty feet and can make five hundred to six hundred ton of steel in one heat. It uses air, liquid fuel, or natural gas to heat the molten metal from the blast furnace. It also uses blast of oxygen to speed up the production. A single heat can take eight to ten hours to melt. The molten steel is tapped from the bottom.

Basic Oxygen Furnace

This can make one hundred to three hundred tons of steel per hour. The furnace uses gaseous fuel to heat the molten pig iron. In addition, the process uses oxygen, which is pumped into the molten pig iron. The temperature in furnace can reach up to 3,000°F. For certain properties, additional elements are added to the molten metal. After the chemical reaction, the molten steel is poured into ingot molds using continuous caster.

Electric Arc Furnace

To produce clean steel, the electric arc furnace uses high-quality scrap Iron. It also uses pig iron. The furnace is lined with refractory bricks. The furnace uses three carbon electrodes (three-phase power supply) to melt the steel. The resistance to heavy current creates the heat and melts the charge. Ferroalloys are added to the furnace to make special alloy steels and stainless steels. No air is used in electric arc furnace. Depending on the load, it takes three to six hours to finish a heat. This process also creates slag, which is removed from the top. Due to the absence of oxygen and other gases, high-quality steel is produced with this process.

During the steelmaking cycle, three steps take place:

1. Oxidation—This step involves oxidation of iron ore (FeO) to Fe (solid).
2. Deoxidation—To improve the microstructure, steel is deoxidized to convert to the following:
   - Rimmed steel—It is used for sheet products.
   - Capped steel—It is similar to rimmed steel.
   - Semi killed steel (deoxidized with aluminum or silicon)—It is used for forgings and cold extrusion.
   - Killed steel—It is completely deoxidized. It is a tougher steel and used for pressure vessels.
3. Ladle refining—This is done to remove dissolved gases or sulfur on other inclusions.

Induction Furnaces

For making steel from scrap, induction furnaces are used. This furnace requires scrap with known composition. It uses non conducting crucible to hold scrap. The crucible is surrounded by water-cooled copper tubes.

Induction furnaces from Inductotherm are available from 350 kg to 100 mt capacity. For more information, visit the following websites:

- www.ajaxtocco.com
- www.inductotherm.com (This website [December 2018] claims to have built 36,500 melting and heating systems for metals.)

- www.inductiontech.com
- http://buyersguide.aist.org/pages/Steelmaking/Electric_arc_furnaces/index.html
- https://goempco.dudaone.com/
- https://en.wikipedia.org/wiki/Induction_furnace

Ingot Handling

Molten steel from the processes is also poured in ingot molds. The poured ingots could be in the shape of a rectangle or square. The ingots are removed from their molds. The ingots are carried to soaking pit. The temperature of these pits could be 2,200°F. The purpose of this treatment is to improve the chemistry of each ingot.

The ingots are then transferred to rolling mills to shape the material into angles, channels, or W-beams. Also, the steel slabs are put through a hot strip mill to form a flat milled coil. The coils are further processed by tempering cold rolling surface texture and applying tin.

Common Steel Alloys

Commercially you can buy steel bars with designation 86L20, 41L40, 4140 annealed, 41L5, and with other alloys.

Stainless Steel

Corrosion resistance to stainless steel is provided by an excess of chromium. Stainless steel contains carbon, manganese, silica, nickel, and about 10% to 18% chromium. The following are some of the common stainless steels:

1. Martensitic—Least common stainless steel. It contains 4%–12% chromium. Common designations are 403, 410, 470, 501, and 504. This category of steel is magnetic and could be hardened. Steel 403 has 70 ksi (70,000 pounds per square inch) tensile and 35 ksi yield strength.

2. Ferritic—This steel contains about 10% chromium. They are less ductile. They are non hardenable (magnetic). Type 409 is a low cost used for automotive exhaust system.
   A. No. 405 contains 11.5% chromium and has 60 ksi tensile and 25 ksi yield.
   B. No. 446 contains 23% chromium.
   C. Common grades are 430 and 434.
3. Austenitic (most common)—They can develop high strength. Common designations are 201, 205, 301, 303, etc. S.S. 201—95 ksi tensile strength and 45 ksi yield strength—highly ductile. Type 203 and 303 are free to machine. These are nonmagnetic stainless steels and provide highest corrosion resistance. Type 316 is more expensive than 304 because of higher nickel and molybdenum. Type 316 is higher corrosion resistant and strong.
4. Precipitation hardening grade—17-4 / type 630—It is high strength with corrosion resistance. Other common grades are PH 13-8, 15-5PH, and PH 15-7.
5. Duplex steel—They have a mixture of austenite and ferrite properties.

For more information on stainless steel, see chapter 3.

References: www.steel.org, www.asw-steel.com, www.worldsteel.org, www.aist.org, www.sassda.co.za, www.worldstainless.org, www.steelvaristy.org, www.slideshow.net/steelmaking, www.ikenstore.com, US steel Youtube video—start to finish, www.steeldynamics.com, Aiifa.org, www.wikipedia/wiki/pig-iron--/blast-furnace, www.marlinwire.com, www.steellinks.com, https://astm.org, and https://www.sae.org.

Steel Plants in the USA

According to the website of AIM market research of Pittsburgh, Pennsylvania, the following companies are major producers of steel:

- AK Steel
- Allegheny Technologies
- ArcelorMittal

- Carpenter Steel
- Charter Steel
- Commercial Metals Co.
- Ellwood Group
- EVRAZ North America
- Gerdau Special Steel
- Nucor Corp.
- US Steel

In addition, there are over thirty smaller steel producers.

A Glimpse of a few US Steel Plants

Information was based on September 2018 websites.

US Steel Works, Gary, Indiana (www.ussteel.com) has annual capability of 7.5 million tons hot-rolled and cold-rolled steel, four blast furnaces, three basic oxygen furnaces, and four continuous slab casters.

US Steel Granite City Works, Illinois, has annual raw steelmaking capability of 2.8 million tons, two blast furnaces, two blown basic oxygen process (BOP) vessels, and continuous slab casters.

ArcelorMittal Steel (https://usa.arcelormittal.com)

As per their website, this company is one of the largest steel making companies in the world. In 2017, their annual sales were $68.7 billion. Worldwide, they produced 93.1 million tons of crude steel. And they shipped 85.2 million tons of steel.

In the US, ArcelorMittal operates twenty facilities and produced 15 million tons of steel. ArcelorMittal has the following key steel making facilities in the US:

1. ArcelorMittal Burns Harbor, Indiana

This facility can produce 5 million ton of steel annually. The company has 2 blast furnaces, two coke plants, 3 basic oxygen furnaces, two continuous casters, and hot-dip galvanizing. Primarily, they make steel for the auto industry.

2. ArcelorMittal Indiana Harbor, East Chicago, Indiana

This facility has 3 blast furnaces and 6 basic oxygen furnaces. They have five continuous casters and two hot-dip galvanizing lines. The plant has an annual steel melting capability of 5 to 6 million tons and five continuous casters. They employ 3,800 to 4,000 people. They make flat hot and cold steel. They also make API pipe and motor laminations steel.

ArcelorMittal plant in Coatesville, Pennsylvania, produces annually 900,000 tons of steel by electric arc furnace.

AK Steel

Based on information on their website, produce the following products in their factories:

1. Carbon steel—hot rolled, cold rolled, electrogalvanized, hot-dipped galvanized, aluminized steel
2. Stainless steel—grade 409, 410S, 430, 439, 444, etc.
3. Electrical sheet for motors and transformers
4. Mechanical steel and stainless tubing—from 0.750" to 6.625"
5. Antimicrobial coating

Carpenter Steel

They produce corrosion resistant stainless steels (405, 430, 304, 316, 20Cb3) and wear resistant, high-strength, and heat-resistant alloys.

Nucor Corporation (www.nucor.com)

Per their October 3, 2018, website, they produced twenty-six million tons of steel in their two hundred operations. They produce steel plate, sheet, alloy bars, special bar quality, alloy steel bar, rebar, floor deck, roof deck, hex nuts, and structural bolts.

The company melts steel scrap in electric arc furnaces. They have extensive rebar making and fabricating capacity. In addition, they supply epoxy-coated, galvanized, stainless steel, and fiberglass rebars.

Wheatland Tube (https://wheatland.com [www.zekelman.com])

This US company makes structural tubing, electrical conduit, and mechanical tubing.

More information on US Steel producers is available in *2018 Directory of Iron Steel Plants* published by the Association for Iron and Steel Technology. You may visit their website at www.aist.org.

Steel Tariffs

Steel manufacturing is the most competitive business in the world. Due to low wages and low construction costs, the steel is cheaper to produce in countries such as Mexico, China, India, Russia, and east European countries.

To support the US Steel industry, in March 2018, US President Donald Trump imposed 10% to 25% duty on all aluminum and steel imports. In March 2019, the negotiations are still going on between the US Commerce Department and rest of the world governments on roll back the tariffs. The additional tariffs on incoming imports do increase the cost of the products, which are made from imported steel and aluminum.

Country of Origin

In the US, several large federally funded construction projects, including Federal Highway Administration, specify that all steel used must be melted and processed in the USA. As a project engineer or an administrator, you can request for material certificates, which may specify the origin of melting country.

US Customs and Border Protection, a federal law enforcement agency specifies every item of foreign origin shall be marked with the country of origin. The reader of this book should be aware of the local rules and the requirements of the project owner.

Steel Recycling

According to https://steelsustainabilit.org (Steel Recyling Institute), steel is the most recycled material in the world. Steel can be recycled again and again.

Recycled steel mostly consists of automobiles, steel packaging, construction and demolition sites and scrap products at the mills. According to Recycling Institute 98% of the Automobiles, 88% of appliances and 70% of steel cans are recycled. It is estimated by the Institute 15 million tons of steel scrap is generated by 11.5 million vehicles annually.

Key steel distributors: www.emjmetals.com, www.rsac.com, Reliance steel, www.ryerson.com, www.chicagotube.com, www.servicesteel.com and https://www.dywidag-systems.com/

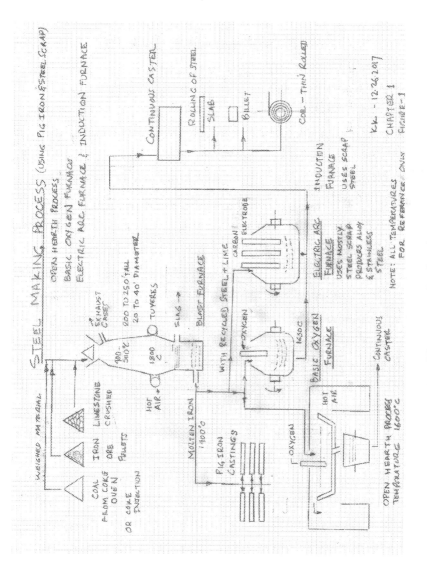

Figure 1—Steelmaking

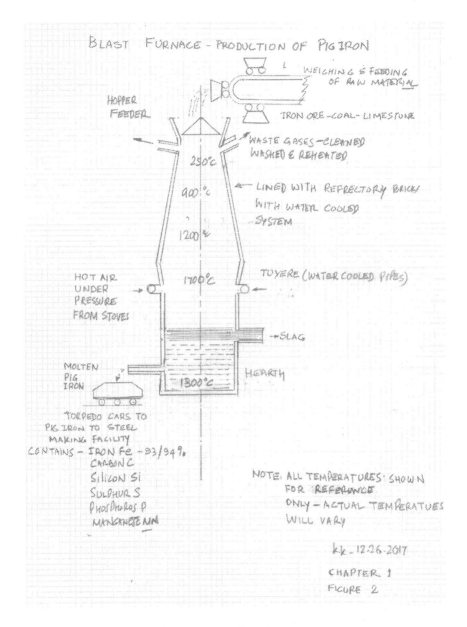

Figure 2—Blast furnace

CHAPTER 2

Making of Cast Iron

Topics covered are types of sand molding methods, iron melting methods, types of cast irons and steel castings, foundry magazines and societies, glimpse of major US casting manufacturers, and ancient steel casting and tool manufacturers in India.

CAST IRONS ARE a mixture of pig iron, carbon, and silicon. Cast irons are manufactured as gray iron, white iron, malleable iron, ductile iron, graphite iron, and alloy iron.

In a casting process, melted iron is poured into a mold or cavity and allowed to solidify. The resulting solid part is then removed from the mold by taking apart the two halves.

The most common cast item on the street is a sewer manhole cover. Historically, machinery bases, railroad, and bridge parts were made of cast iron.

The two major casting methods are green sand and dry sand methods.

Green Sand Molding

The green sand molds are built in two halves. The upper part of the mold is called the cope while the lower portion is called drag. For solid parts, a wooden or metal pattern is used to form the cavity. A gating system is provided in the sand mold to pour and distribute the molten metal. If the part to be cast has a hollow area, then a core made from sand is located inside the mold cavity.

Cast iron mold uses mixture of sand with chemically bonded clay. This sand mixture is designed to withstand heat of molten metal. To achieve the strength of the mold, sand is pushed against the wooden or metal pattern.

This method is used to make cast housings, small and large machine frames, diesel engine blocks, sewer covers, automobile engine blocks, brake drums, railroad parts, and large pump-turbine. Castings are used to dampen vibrations on large locomotives, ship engines, large milling machines, manual or CNC lathes, and power presses for stampings. Castings are designed with generous radii to improve stress concentration factor.

Dry Sand Molding

For very heavy and large cast iron parts, the dry sand molding process is used. Here, the sand mold is completely dried before pouring the molten metal. The dry sand provides strength to withstand weight and force of the molten metal. This method is also used to cast very accurate parts. The drying of mold is done in an oven or small heaters.

No-Bake Process

For large castings, no-bake method is being used. The cores for castings are made by using a synthetic oil binder. With this method, the cores for casting box can be dried at room temperature.

Carbon Affect

The steel and cast iron are specified according to carbon content in the molten metal. If the carbon content is less than 2%, the metal is called steel. If the amount of carbon is more than 2%, then the resulting mixture is called cast iron. Beside carbon, the cast iron contains over 1% silicon. Excess carbon in cast iron precipitate out as graphite and cementite. This excess carbon results in reduced tensile strength and brittleness.

Castings made by malleable and ductile alloys are of higher quality. Gray cast iron has 2% to 4% carbon. It is very hard and brittle. However, it has high compressive strength. It has good vibration damping capability.

Melting of Iron

Cupolas, electric arc furnaces, and induction furnaces are used to melt the pig iron or scrap iron.

Cupola furnace consists of steel shell, which is lined with refractory bricks. It is usually five feet in diameter and fifteen to thirty feet high. Cupolas are charged from the top with pig iron, coke, iron scrap, and limestone. The cupolas are usually loaded with coke first. Cupolas, once started, run continuously. The molten metal is tapped at bottom. The reaction inside the cupola is not easy to control. Due to creation of coal burning pollutants, cupolas have been phased out in the foundry industry. These are being replaced by electric arc furnaces and induction furnaces.

Electric arc furnace. This furnace uses carbon electrode to melt the material. It uses low voltage but high current to melt the material. This method melts the material rapidly. Electric arc melting helps in controlling sulfur.

Induction furnace. This furnace is also used to melt steel rapidly. It uses high- and low-frequency current to melt the scrap material. The magnetic field induced by the current creates natural stirring and provides uniform temperature for the melting of steel. This is useful for smaller heats. For more information on induction furnaces, visit www.ajaxtocco.com and www.inductothermo.com.

Types of Iron Castings

The following are major categories of cast irons:

1. White iron
2. Gray iron
3. Ductile iron
4. Austempered ductile iron
5. Malleable iron

White Iron

It contains 1.8% to 4% carbon and 0.5% to 3% silicon. It does not contain graphite. It has good machinability. This iron contains iron carbide. This iron lacks graphite and, as such, looks white. White cast iron is hard and brittle. This is made by rapid cooling. Due to its hardness, this metal is recommended for abrasive conditions. It is suitable for making brake shoes of railroad cars and grinding mills.

White iron is manufactured under ASTM A532. For corrosion resistant and elevated temperature application, white iron is made with high chromium and nickel chromium.

Gray Iron

Gray iron consists of 3% carbon and 2% silicon. Once molten iron is poured in the mold, the carbon inside turns into graphite. Due to dark microstructure (pearlite, ferrite, and martensite), this iron is called gray. Graphite works as a lubricant, and it provides extreme machinability and is wear resistant. This iron has good vibration damping quality, and as such, it is used for machinery bases, electric motor housings, and engine blocks. This iron is weak in tension (not ductile) but good in compression. The yield strength of gray iron can vary from 20,000 to 50,000 psi.

This iron is used to make internal combustion engine liners, engines blocks, and manifolds. Additionally, it is used to make gas burners, forming dies, and machine tool bases.

Following are some of the gray iron classes and standard specifications:

Class 25 187 Brinell hardness—29.9 ksi (206Mpa)—Tensile strength—ASTM-A48

Class 30 207 Brinell hardness—33.7 ksi (232 Mpa)—Tensile strength

Class 40 235 Brinell hardness—41.9 ksi (235 Mpa)—Tensile strength

Some of the gray iron components are manufactured under ASTM A48, A74, A126, A159, A278, A319, etc.

Malleable Iron

This iron is ductile and has more strength than gray iron. This change is accomplished by heating white iron to 925°C and holding for longer hours. The castings are then allowed to cool slowly. This process changes the microstructure of white iron.

Ductile Iron

This is also called nodular iron. Casting applications requiring severe situation are good candidates for ductile iron quality. Here the graphite is found as spheroids rather than flakes. Components for oil Industry, road vehicles, valves, and construction are made by the ductile iron process. Some ductile iron can have yield strength of 30,000 psi and tensile strength of 60,000 psi.

Nodular iron is used for cylinder heads of cars and chuck bodies for machines. This iron has good toughness and can be surface-hardened by induction method or flame hardening.

The ductile properties are achieved by special heat treatment process. The following are the major ductile iron categories:

Austempered Ductile Iron (ADI)

Austempering is a special heat treatment process that provides superb strength, toughness, fatigue strength, and wear resistance to iron castings. It involves heating castings from 1,500 to 1,700°F and then suddenly cooling down to 450°F in a salt bath. The resulting parts are ductile and hard as forged steel.

Parts such as refrigerators crankshafts, brake shoes, axles, and shell projectiles are made by austempering process. An automotive company has replaced their forged ring and pinion gear forgings by austempered ductile iron castings.

This process can achieve 125 ksi (870Mpa) tensile strength and 10% to 15% elongation.

The other ductile iron process is called CGI. A few of CGI grades (ASTM A842—source 2011—www.metalcastingdesign.com) are shown under.

Grade 250—36 ksi (250 Mpa) tensile—25.3 ksi (0.2% yield strength)—179 BHN—3% elongation

Grade 450—65 ksi (450 Mpa) tensile—45.6 ksi yield strength—207-269BHN—1% elongation

For more information on austempering process, visit www.appliedprocess.com.

Malleable Iron

These iron castings have low strength but high ductility. These castings are made according to the following (from iron casting society brochure):

ASTM A47 (50,000 psi tensile—32,000 psi yield and 10% yield), .

ASTM A220 (60,000 psi tensile—40,000 yield and 10% yield), and

ASTM A338 use for pipe flanges, valve parts.

Some chain sprockets and drive train components are made with this process.

Steel Castings

Beside plain carbon steel, steel castings can be made with manganese, low and high alloy, and heat- corrosion-resistant alloys.

Steel alloys with more than 12% of chromium and nickel combined can provide corrosion resistance. Items such as vanadium (V) and tungsten (W) can improve resistance to temperature. Nickel improves toughness. Manganese steel can be hardened. At the same time, phosphorus and sulfur can reduce toughness and ductility. The following ASTM qualities of steels are for specific usage (source: www.asfinc.org):

For structures under fatigue, look into ASTM A27, A148, and A747.

For pressure vessels, look into ASTM A127 and A487.

For impact resistant, look into ASTM A352 and A743.

For wear resistant, look into ASTM A128, A351, and A532.

Based on class and heat treatment, you can source cast steel from 63 ksi tensile with 35 ksi yield strength to 205 tensile to 170 ksi yield strength.

Welding of Iron Castings

Typical, it is not safe to weld cast iron and expect the joint to hold the load. However, there are situations—a critical machine casting cracks—that have to be welded. The high carbon and phosphorus in iron are the cause of difficulties. If you are required to weld, heat the area to be welded from 400 to 500°C using oxyacetylene torch. The idea is to remove excess graphite from the surface to be welded. Following heating, the area should be cleaned by wire brush and then welded with a suitable filler electrode. You can consult your local welding distributor for a suitable welding filler rod. You can consider using an oxyacetylene, stick welding or gas metal arc welding method.

Continuous Casting

Several steel mills have equipment to continuously cast flat bars. Dura-Bar (subsidiary of Charter Manufacturing), a suburban Chicago company makes a continuous cast ductile iron bar. They manufacture bars with following the machining grades:
Tensile, yield strength and elongation
65 ksi 45 ksi 12%
80 ksi 55 ksi 12%
100 ksi 70 ksi 3%
Above cast bars can be used for machining gears, hydraulic manifolds, hydraulic cylinder caps, valve bodies, couplings, etc. For more information, visit www.dura-barms.com (Dura Bar Metal Services).

Inspection of Castings

The following are some of the techniques used for checking the quality of castings:

1. Ultrasonic testing
2. Magnetic particle testing
3. Dye penetrant liquid
4. Radiographic testing

Dimensional verification of castings are done by portable coordinate measuring machine and laser scanners.

For more information on metal casting industries, please review the additional following sources:

1. www.afsinc.org (American Foundry Society)
2. www.metalcastingdesign.com (Source for material specifications and classes), www.foundrymag.com

Casting manufacturers and industry groups:

1. www.farrarusa.com
2. www.meehanitemetal.com
3. www.eaglegroupmanufacturers.com
4. www.stiprecision.com
5. www.stmfoundry.com (gray iron)
6. www.willmanind.com (gray iron)
7. www.dotson.com
8. www.somersetfoundries.com, www.azom.com (material sciences), and www.en.wikipedia.org/wiki/cast_iron
9. https://www.metaltek.com/capabilities/processes/metal-casting/investment-casting

A Glimpse of a variety of Foundries & Equipment Builders Websites

The following information was taken from their websites (October 2018), and no persons at the facilities were contacted:

1. www.elyriafoundry.com-elyria (Ohio)—The company produces gray iron and ductile iron castings. They can produce parts ranging from 50 to 10,000 pounds
   They have following melting capability:
   - Four fifty tons channel furnaces
   - Two twenty tons channel furnaces
   - Two twelve tons coreless induction furnaces

- Three thirty tons channel induction furnaces in their Hodge foundry
2. www.oscoind.com (Osco Industries Inc.)—Gray iron foundry specializing in green sand and shell molding. They can cast parts from one-pound to forty-pound weight. They can cast G2500, G3000, and G3500 grades of iron. They have the following furnaces:
   - Two 66" water-cooled cupolas—18 tons per hour melting capacity
   - One inductotherm—40 tons 600 kW furnace

   Their New Boston, Ohio, branch has the following:
   - Three inductotherm—10 tons 8,000 kW vertical furnace
   - One inductotherm—50 ton 750 kW vertical furnace
3. https://williamind.com (Cedar Grove, Wisconsin)
   - Provides green sand, ductile iron, Meehanite, and no-bake castings
   - Provides nineteen grades of gray iron and twenty grades of ductile iron
   - Can make green sand castings up to 1,500 lbs.
   - Can make no-bake castings from 500 to 40,000 lbs.
   - Has three coreless melting furnaces—9 tons each
4. www.waupacafoundry.com—This company has a group of seven foundries with daily capacity to melt 10,000 metric tons per day. The company provides the following grades of castings: gray iron, ductile, austempered ductile iron, and compacted graphite iron.

   Waupaca Foundry provides refresher course in metal casting. They are a good source of alloy guide.
5. www.ecands.com (EC&S Furnace Co.)—The company can design and build the following:
   - Cupolas
   - Electric arc furnaces
   - Electric induction furnace including emission control and water cooling system

Ancient History of Iron Making in India

It appears that iron casting technology was very well-known to ancient Hindus of India. As a child, I made several visits to the premises of Qutub Minar at the outer fringes of Delhi, the capital of India. This thousand-year-old minaret is the highest in the world. This 240 feet stone tower is located in the midst the ruins of a Hindu temple with a remarkable non rusting iron pillar. According to Wikipedia, this rust-resistant iron tower is 23 feet high and weighs 13,000 pounds. It probably was installed at this location by one of the Gupta kings between third and fourth century. Based on my several visits to this tower, my estimate is that this iron tower has diameter of about two feet at the base.

In 2010, I visited the massive thirty-six Buddhist caves complex located at Ajanta, Maharashtra, in central India. According to legends, it took worshippers of Buddha about four hundred years to finish the caves. According to local guide, lots of excavation and carving iron tools were discovered near this two-thousand-year-old Buddhist caves. It appears that ancient people of India had good knowledge of iron-making tools. To produce excavating iron tools and tower castings, the local metalsmiths must have known the coal and iron ore fields of Orissa and Chhattisgarh states in Eastern India.

Another set of wonderfully carved caves with Hindu gods is known as Ellora. These are just about seventy miles away from Ajanta. In my opinion, these caves are just as remarkable as the pyramids of Egypt. For more information on these caves, look for Ajanta and Ellora caves on the web. Both sets of caves are located near Aurangabad, Maharashtra, which is about an hour flight from Mumbai, India.

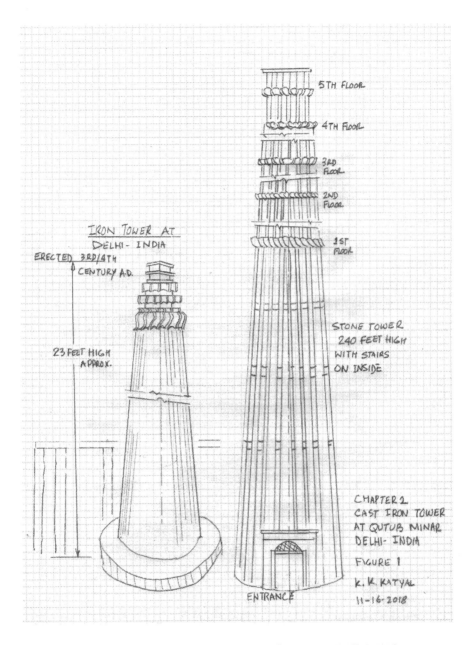

Figure 1—Cast iron tower at Qutab Minar, Delhi, India

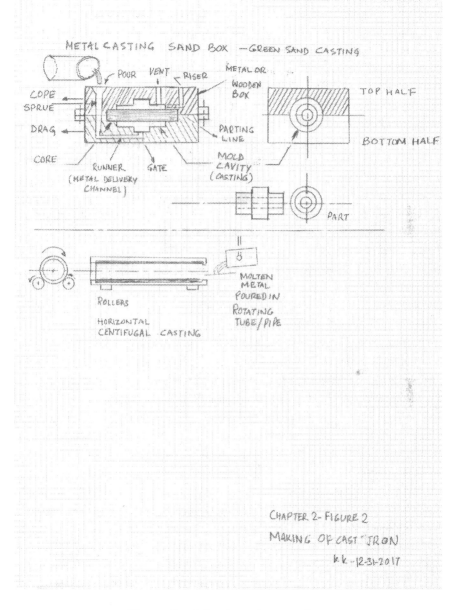

Figure 2—Metal casting sandbox

CHAPTER 3

General Classification of Steels

Topics covered are types of steels, steel alloying elements, steel specifying authorities, steel applications, types of stainless steels, ASTM specs., steel terms, international standards, tool steel, and US steel producers and distributors.

CARBON STEELS ARE specified according to four-digit numbers set by the American Iron and Steel Institute and the Society of Automotive Engineers. The last two digits of these numbers indicate the amount of carbon in the steel. For example, AISI 1010 steel contains carbon from 0.08% to 0.13%. The first two numbers indicate if the steel is resulfurized or none sulfurized. More information is provided later about these categories.

There are three major categories of plain steels:

1. Plain-carbon steels—These steels contain carbon from 0.06% to 0.29% carbon. These are easy to shape or form. They are used for making stampings, rolled rings, angles, channels, and simple extrusion. The other shapes of steel are round, hex, flat bar, strip, and steel plates. Low-carbon steels are very easy to weld. In terms of carbon content, these steels lie between AISI 1005 and 1026. These steels cost less as compared to high-carbon and alloy steels.

These steels are ductile. They can be used to make low-strength fasteners. They can be easily bent, punched, drawn, and cold-formed. The tensile strength of these steels can vary from 43 to 64 ksi (64,000 pounds per square inch). These steels are low in wear resistance. To increase the wear resistance of finished parts, the steels with carbon content from 0.15 to 0.20 (AISI1015 and AISI 1020) are heated in a carburized atmosphere. In heated state, the carbon powder or gas diffuses on to the outer surface of finished product. The extra carbon on the surface provides wear resistance.

In the US, the most common structural material is ASTM-A36. A36 has the following properties:

- Carbon 0.26 max, phosphorus 0.04 max, sulfur 0.05 max
- Mechanical properties—minimum yield strength of 36000 psi (250 Mpa)
- Tensile strength—58,000 to 80,000 psi (440–550 Mpa)
- Percentage elongation—20% min.
- Weldability—very easy to weld

2. Medium-carbon steels—These steels contain carbon between 0.30% and 0.59% (AISI 1030 to AISI 1059). These steels have tensile strength from 68 to 90 ksi. And can be heat-treated to further enhance the properties. AISI 1045 material is used for making forgings of construction bolts and automotive crankshafts. Material with 0.50% carbon is used for making gears and axles.
3. High-carbon steels—These steels have carbon from 0.6% to 1% (AISI 1055 to 1095). These steels have tensile strength from 94 to 120 ksi. They are used to make wear-resistant parts and springs.

Common Alloying Elements in Steel

The following are common alloying elements:

1. Aluminum (Al)—About 1% inclusion in steel helps in providing hard case by nitriding.
2. Bismuth (Bi)—It helps in improving machining.
3. Calcium (Ca)—It helps in improving strength and ductility.
4. Carbon (C)—It is the main alloy for steel to improve tensile strength.
5. Chromium (Cr)—It helps in preventing corrosion and improving strength and wear.
6. Cobalt (Co)—It improves strength and hardness.
7. Lead (Pb)—It improves machining. Due to possible harm to environment, some businesses avoid using it in any form.
8. Manganese (Mn)—It helps in carburizing low-carbon steel.
9. Molybdenum (Mo)—It increases hardness and strength of steel.
10. Nickel (Ni)—It helps in making stainless steel. It improves hardness and strength.
11. Silicon (Si)—It helps in improving hardness and strength.
12. Sulfur (S)—It improves machinability of steel.
13. Titanium (Ti)—It helps in making stainless steel.
14. Tungsten (W)—It provides high strength to steel at elevated temperature.
15. Vanadium (V)—It provides shock resistance and high strength to steel.

Steel Identification

The following specifying authorities are responsible for steel specifications:

AISI—American Iron and Steel Institute
SAE—Society of Automotive Engineers
ANSI—American National Standards Institute, Inc.
ASME—American Society of Mechanical Engineers
ASTM—American Society for Testing and Materials
AISI—American Iron and Steel Institute
API—American Petroleum Institute

US Federal—General Services Administration

US Military—Naval publications—Philadelphia

UNS (Unified Numbering System)—It has developed by ASTM and SAE, which devised five-digit number preceded by letters

UNS number Axxxxx—It is for aluminum and its alloys.

Society of Automotive Engineers (SAE) and American Iron and Steel Institute (AISI)—They have devised a four-digit numbering system for steel identification.

XXXX—The last two digits represent the percentage of carbon in steel. The four digits are used if the carbon content is less than 1%. If the steel has more than 1% carbon, then the numbering adds fifth number to the description. For the four-digit system, the first number signifies the type of steel.

10XX—It signifies plain carbon. It can have up to 1% carbon and 1% manganese. The number 10 indicates that steel is non-resulfurized.

1012—10 series is carbon steel with 0.12% carbon.

1040—It has carbon content of 0.40%.

1018/1020—These are available in hot-rolled and cold-finished steel.

Machining grades—Steel starting with 11 and 12 provide good machining quality.

11XX—Resulfurized steel with grades 1112, 1115, 1108, and 1151 provide good machinability.

12XX—Resulfurized and rephosphorized steel 1215/1244 screw machine stock provide good chip control.

13XX—Manganese steel

23XX—Nickel steel (nickel up to 3.5%)

25XX—Nickel steel (nickel up to 5%)

31XX—Nickel chrome steel (nickel 1.25%, chrome 0.65%)

32XX—Nickel chrome (nickel 1.75%, chrome 1.07%)
40XX—Molybdenum steel (Mo 0.20% to 0.25%)
50XX—Chromium steel
61XX—Chrome vanadium steel

Alloy steel examples:

4320—Nickel 1.65%-2%, chromium 0.40% to 0.60%, molybdenum 0.20% to 0.30%
8615—Ni 0.40% to 0.70%, Cr 0.40% to 0.60%, Mo 0.15% to 0.25%

Selection of Steel for Application

Steels are specified as per finish, such as cold-rolled or hot-rolled, any ASTM number, tensile and yield strength, dimensional size, bar, plate, any cut-to-size length, any specific chemical content.

Suggested metals:

For sheet metal parts, use 1010 AISI steel
Machined parts—1020, 1244, etc.
Induction or flame hardened—1040
Heat-treated, high-strength parts—4340 and 4140
Structural shapes—A36 steel

Steel Fabrication Capability

- 1010 steel—It contains 0.08% to 0.13% carbon and 0.050% sulfur. This steel is very ductile. This can be easily welded and brazed. Due to low sulfur content, it is not easy to machine.
- 1110 resulfurized—This steel has carbon from 0.08% to 0.13% and sulfur of 0.08% to 0.3%. It is good for machining but not for welding. It is less ductile.
- 4340 alloy steel—It contains carbon from 0.38% to 0.43%. Additionally, it contains silicon, nickel, chromium, and

molybdenum. This steel is easy to harden. Welding is not recommended for this steel due to high carbon.

Types of Stainless Steel

There are three kinds of stainless steels:

A. Austenitic—This steel is nonmagnetic and have high corrosion resistance. The most common grades are 304, 316, and 317. They can become magnetic by cold-working. Common 18-8 SS has 18% chromium and 8% nickel and 0.08% carbon. Typical 304 SS has tensile strength of 75 ksi (515 Mpa) and BHN of 201. The quarter hard grade of 304 SS has tensile strength of 115 to 35ksi.
B. Ferritic stainless—Its composition has less nickel. It is magnetic and has 430, 434, and 442 grades. These grade costs less than 304 grades.
C. Martensitic stainless—Its common grades are 410, 416, and 420. These steels are magnetic. These stainless steels have high hardness.

Series 200—Cr-Ni-Mn-Nonmagnetic steel

Series 304 has 8% to 10.5% nickel and 18% to 20% chromium with 2% manganese. The series 304 and 304L are used for restaurant equipment. Series 304H is a high-strength steel with carbon from 0.04% to -0.10%. Series 303, 304, 316, 410, and 416 SS are easy to machine. Also, series 301, 302, 304, 316, and 321 SS are easy to weld.

Series 316 has 10% to 14% nickel and 16% to 18% chromium and 2% to 3% molybdenum.

Series 316 are more expensive than 304 but has higher tensile strength. It is more resistant to chemicals.

Series 304L and 316L denote low-carbon stainless steels. The L grades have less 0.03% carbon. The 304 and 316 grades contain carbon up to 0.08%.

Series 316 and 316L grades are used for marine application. These grades cannot be hardened.

Series 321 has 9% to 12% nickel and 17% to 19% chromium. This SS can be used for high-temperature application.

Series 330 SS is used for high-temperature application. It has 35% nickel and 35% chromium.

Stainless steels are available in mill, no. 2B mill, no. 3 and no. 4 satin and no. 8 mirrors like finish.

Steel for Forgings

1005—C-0.06, Man 0.35 Max
1045—C-0.43–0.50, Mn 0.60 to 0.90—Gears, shafts, axles, etc.

Steel Castings

Steel castings are used where they are subjected to shock and very high loading. For such application of cast iron, malleable and wrought iron should be avoided. Following are some of the steel castings composition:

1. Low-carbon steel casting contains less than 0.2% carbon.
2. Medium-carbon steel contains carbon from 0.20% to 0.50%.
3. High-carbon steel contains carbon more than 0.50%.
4. Alloy steel castings are made with higher content of manganese, molybdenum, vanadium, chromium, and nickel. The additional materials provide strength, corrosion resistance, and toughness to steel castings. These castings are further heat-treated to enhance their properties.

Steel for structures, plate, and strip—1010—C 0.08 to 0.13

ASTM Specifications

The following are some of the ASTM specifications:

A36 (carbon 0.25% to 0.29%) has minimum yield of 36 KSI, tensile of 50 to 80 KSI, and yield of 21%. This steel could be welded and bolted.

Other common steel 1018—hot rolled and cold finished—has yield strength of about 54,000 psi and ultimate tensile of 64,000 psi. Following are common steel tube qualties:

ASTM A 519—cold-drawn seamless 1026 material tubing produced to OD/ID

ASTM A 513—drawn on mandrel (welded) carbon 1020/ 1026 tubing

ASTM A 513—butt-welded tubing 1020/ 1026

Shapes of Commercially Available Steels

1. Hot-rolled bars—round, square, rectangular, and hexagon
2. Cold-finished steel bars—cold drawn through die and could be turned or polished
3. Steel wire—carbon steel (low, medium, or high carbon) or alloy steel
4. Tubular steel—electric resistance–welded or seamless tube
5. Structural shapes assigned by AISI (American Iron and Steel Institution)—W (beams), S, M, C (channels), and MC

Steel Processing Terms and Mill Finishes

The most common are the following:

1. Hot rolling (HR)—The steel slabs at the rolling mill facility is heated and repeatedly pass through a set of roughing stands to squeeze the hot steel. The process reduces thickness from the slab to coiled steel, sheets, and bars. Hot-rolled bars and plates have a brownish color, and they are stocked as they come from the mill. They may have small amount of scale. Being

in annealed condition, hot-rolled bar and plate can be welded easily.

Flat hot-rolled steel is sold for thickness from 0.020" to 0.50" in coil form. This steel is used for making truck wheels, stampings, construction, and agriculture equipment.

2. Cold-rolled (CR) and cold-drawn steel—The process involves pickling hot-rolled bars to remove scale and then drawing through a die. This is done to reduce thickness and improve surface finish. The cold-drawing improves tensile strength, increase yield strength, toughness, and weldability but decreases ductility. This process is done at a room temperature.

Cold-rolled bars are used for components that are machined on multiple spindle and high-productive screw machines.

Flat cold-rolled steel is used for making car and truck bodies, sheet metal ducts, steel furniture, and tubing.

For high finish, cold-drawn bars are turned and ground (TG). And some bars are turned ground and polished (TGP). Ground and polished bars have high accuracy and straightness and used for instruments and electronic parts.

3. Cold-drawn seamless (CDS) tube
4. Electric resistance–welded (ERW) tube
5. High-strength low alloy (HSLA)

For a glimpse of a manufacturer of cold-rolled and hot-rolled steels, visit the following websites:

https://worthingtonindustries.com/Products/Flat-Rolled-Steel/Cold-Rolled-Steel

https://www.clarkdietrich.com/about-us/about-clarkdietrich (for house construction) https://www.wheatland.com/products/mechanical-tube (round and structural tubing)

Material Certificates

End users, such as military, building owners, bridge builders, and aircraft builders, want to make sure their product is manufactured to certain specifications. To meet customer's guidelines, the contractor should buy the material according to physical and chemical properties specified in the contract. The machining or fabrication facility must keep track of material certificates (heat numbers, etc.) received from their supplier and provide the same data to their customer with the finished product.

Machinability of Steels

Steels are rated according to ease of machining. The following are some of the steels about their rating to machine:

Steel	Rating	Alloy Steel	Rating
Grade 1212 carbon steel	100%	8620	66%
Grade 1040 carbon steel	64%	4620	100%
Grade 1018 carbon steel	78%	4130 annealed	72%
Leaded steel	193%	304 stainless steel	45%
Grade 1117 carbon steel	91%	416 stainless steel	110%

Above is just a sample of various steels. It is important to know the machinability rating of steels.

International Standards for Steels

Finished steel is exported from major producers to different countries. Steel made in France could be exported to Italy, and the finished parts could be sent to USA. There is no common worldwide system to classify steel. In the US, the common standard for steel is

ASTM (American Society for Testing Materials). Other US systems are ASME/AISI and SAE. Steel and nonferrous products are marketed by the mechanical properties and chemical composition. The following are some of the standard organizations for steels:

1. United States of America—ASTM/AISI/SAE
2. United Kingdom—BS/ BSI
3. Germany—DIN
4. Japan—JISC (Japanese Industrial Standards Committee)
5. France—AFNOR
6. CEN—European committee for standardization has set up EN10027-1–2 steel standards
7. China—GB and YB
8. India—IS
9. Russia—GOST (For more info visit, https://schmidt-export.com/gost-declaration.)
10. Brazil—NBR and Italy
11. Italy—RINA

For more information, see *Handbook of Comparative World Steel Standards (ASTM DS67B)* by John Bringas.

Tool Steels

These steels are used for making gauges, saw blades, drills, steel punches, stamping, and plastic dies. These steels have high carbon and alloy content. After heat treatment, they provide high wear resistance.

They are used for making dies for stampings, forming, plastic injection molding, forging, steel rolling, and extrusion dies. These steels are designated by the manufacturers name, AISI and unified numbering systems (UNS). In the US, most tool steels are designated by letters A, D, F, H, L, M, O, P, T and W:

Water-hardening tool steels (W)—W2 steels (UNS No. T72302) contain 0.60% to 1.40% carbon and 0.25% vanadium, W2 (contains vanadium) and W5 contain 1.1% carbon and 0.05% chrome. These steels are quenched rapidly in water or sodium chloride brine. To prevent cracking, these steels are tempered. After heat treatment, these steels develop hard surface and soft core.

These steels are also called as drill rods. They have the hardness of 241 BHN. They can be heat-treated to Rockwell C60.

Cold-work steels fall under group A, O, and D.

Group O tool steel—These are oil-hardening steels. Common steels are O1, O2, O6, and O7. These can be used for stamps, draw dies, and shear blades. These steels can be heat-treated to Rockwell C63 to C65. O7 steels have UNS number of T31507 (1.2% C, 0.75% Cr, and 1.75% W).

Group A (air-hardening)—The most common are A2, A5, and A10 tool steels. A2 steels have better wear resistance than O1 steel. These are good for heat-treating thin parts (A2-T30102—1% C, 5% Cr, and 1% Mo).

D tool steels—These have good wear resistance. These are high-carbon and high-chrome tool steels. These are used for thread rolling dies and other steel rolls (D2-T30402—1.5% C, 12% Cr, 1% V, and 1% Mo). The most common steel is D2; however, other qualities are called D3, D4, and D7.

Shock-resistant steels—These steels have low carbon (from 0.4% to 0.6%C). Steel S1 and S7 contains medium carbon, tungsten, chromium, and molybdenum (S1-T41901—0.5% C, 3.25% Cr, and 2.5% W). Common application is where the tool is exposed to repeated shocks.

Group M (high speed)—Among the molybdenum steels, the most common is M2 type. Common steels in this category are M1, 2, 3, 4, 6, 7, 10, 30, 33, 34, 36, 41, 42, 43, 44, 46, and 47. M2 steel has UNS designation of T11302 and has composition of 0.85-1% C, 4% Cr, 2% V, 6% W, and 8% Mo). Some M steels have molybdenum with cobalt to make end mills, broaches, chasers, and taps.

Tungsten-based steels—These steels are from T1 to T15 (T1-T12001—0.75% C, 4% Cr, 1% V, and 18% W).

Mold Steels (P)—This steels contain low carbon, chromium, and nickel. The most common steels are P2, 3, 4, 5, 6, 20, and 21. Steel P20 has UNS no. T51620 and contains 0.35% C, 1.70% Cr, and 0.4% Mo.

Hot-Work Tool Steels

A. Chromium type (H10 to H19)
B. Tungsten type (H21 to H26)
C. Molybdenum type (42) (H10-T20810-0.4% C, 3.24% Cr, 0.4% V, and 2.5% Mo)

Glimpse from tool steel manufacturer's website (December 2018) of Crucible Industries (www.crucible.com). This US company makes the following tool steels: A2, A6, A9, D2, M2, 01, 06, S5, and S7.

These steels are used for making molds for plastics, hot-forming tools, cutting tools, and dies.

Major US steel producers are www.ussteel.com, www.aksteel.com, www.arcelormittal.com, and www.cartech.com. For more information on steel, see chapter 1.

Major US and international steel plants (Consult *2018 Directory of Iron and Steel Plants* published by American Iron and Steel Technology or visit www.AIST.org.)

Key US steel distributors are www.emjmetals.com, www.rsac.com (reliance steel), www.ryerson.com, www.chicagotube.com, and www.servicesteel.com.

US tool steel distributors are www.fordtoolsteels.com, www.cintool.com, and www.steelforge.com.

Glimpse from the website of special steel components supplier for heavy concrete construction (www.dywidag-systems.com):

The company products, such as bars, steel strands, castings, and forgings, are used for concrete bridges, water dams, high-rise buildings, high-rise car parking lots, wind power tower foundation, liquefied natural gas tanks, and slope stabilization along mountain roads and tunnels.

DSI is key supplier for fully threaded hot-rolled and cold-rolled, low- and high-strength bars. Their bars have large trapezoidal thread pitch and immune to construction dirt.

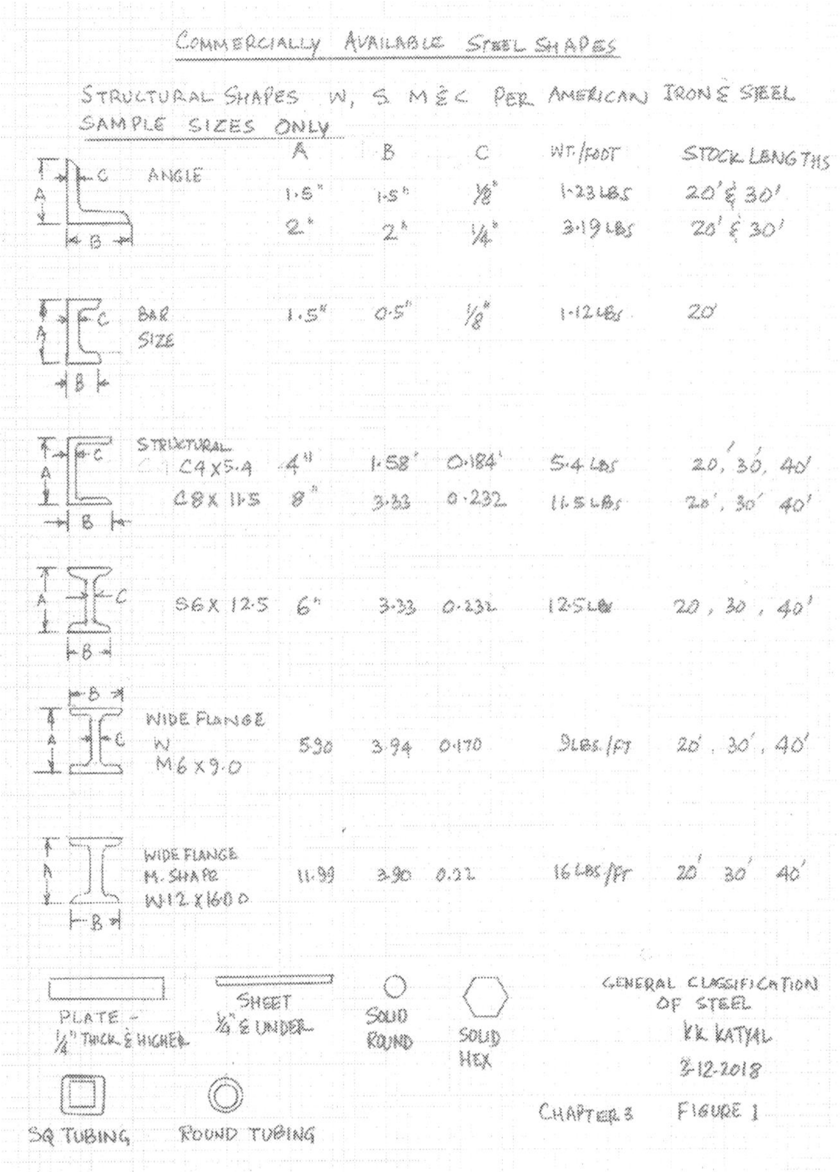

Commercially Available Steel Shapes

Structural Shapes W, S, M & C per American Iron & Steel
Sample Sizes Only

Shape		A	B	C	WT./FOOT	STOCK LENGTHS
ANGLE		1.5"	1.5"	1/8"	1.23 LBS	20' & 30'
		2"	2"	1/4"	3.19 LBS	20' & 30'
BAR SIZE		1.5"	0.5"	1/8"	1.12 LBS	20'
STRUCTURAL	C4 X 5.4	4"	1.58"	0.184"	5.4 LBS	20', 30', 40'
	C8 X 11.5	8"	3.33	0.232	11.5 LBS	20', 30', 40'
	S6 X 12.5	6"	3.33	0.232	12.5 LB	20', 30', 40'
WIDE FLANGE W	M6 X 9.0	5.90	3.94	0.170	9 LBS/FT	20', 30', 40'
WIDE FLANGE M. SHAPE	W12 X 160	11.99	3.90	0.22	16 LBS/FT	20', 30', 40'

PLATE — 1/4" THICK & HIGHER
SHEET 1/4" & UNDER
SOLID ROUND
SOLID HEX
SQ TUBING
ROUND TUBING

GENERAL CLASSIFICATION OF STEEL
K.K. KATYAL
3-12-2018

CHAPTER 3   FIGURE 1

Fig. 1—commercial shapes

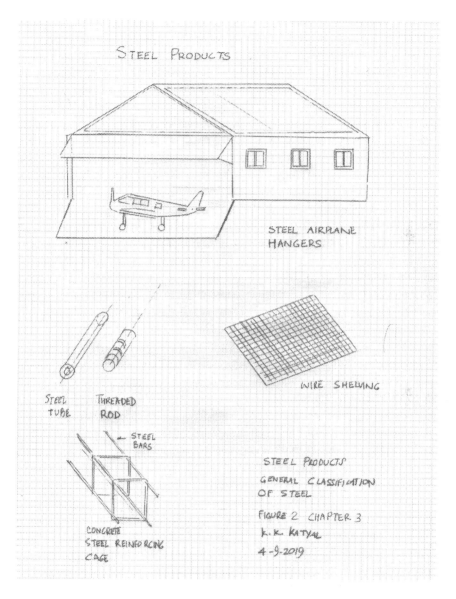

Fig. 2—steel building

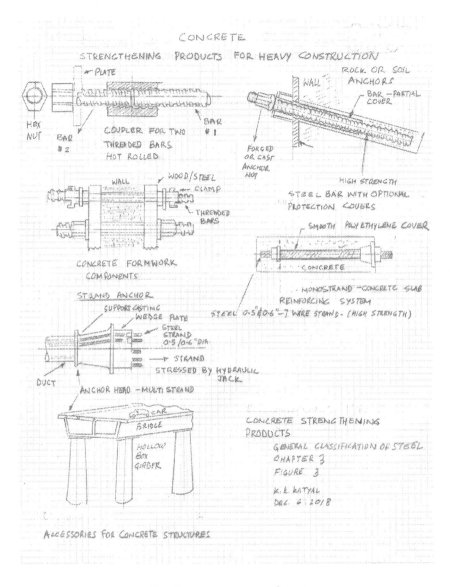

Fig. 3—concrete products

CHAPTER 4

Material Properties and Testing

Topics covered are material-testing for ultimate and yield strength, stress-strain curves, tensile test equipment, and types of hardness test systems.

IN NATURE, THERE are about 125 elements. These elements are found in combined form with another material. The elements are divided further into organic and inorganic. Any group that has carbon and hydrogen is called organic (e.g., petroleum, etc.). The other group that does not have carbon and hydrogen is called inorganic (e.g., copper, gold, aluminum, etc.)

For any application, the selection of material is critical. The combination of two or more elements is called a molecule. The molecules can be gaseous, liquid, or in solid form. Metals consisting mostly of iron (Fe) are called ferrous. Metals such as aluminum, copper, silver, and nickel are called nonferrous.

All the elements usually follow the periodic table, which lists them according to atomic number. The atomic numbers consist of number of protons in the nucleus. All the elements are assigned a symbol. The following are some of the symbols of elements: hydrogen (H), carbon (C), aluminum (Al), silicon (Si), sulfur (S), titanium (Ti), vanadium (V), copper (Cu), magnesium (Mg), iron (Fe), and nickel (Ni).

Metallurgists are interested in metal microstructure, crystal structure, and mechanical properties of the metals.

All metals obey certain laws of strength. Semi-finished and rolled material suppliers for steel, alloy steel, aluminum, and its alloys, copper, and stainless steel do provide data to their customers about each mechanical strength and other properties. The material specifications or data list includes properties such as ultimate tensile strength, yield strength, and hardness.

Beside these properties, it is important to know if the material is resistant to wear, certain chemicals, and good current carrying conductivity. Also, it is important to know if the material can be easily welded, stamped in a metal press, machined, not crack in extreme low temperatures, elongate at warm temperatures, and can be heat-treated to increase its strength.

The ductility and brittleness of a material at certain temperature are critical for engineers who design bridges, aircraft components, and high-speed machines with cyclic fatigue loads.

Whenever a steel round or flat bar is pulled by a force, then we are subjecting the bar to tensile forces.

The tensile stress is calculated by dividing the force by it cross section area:

Stress = force (load) / cross section area

Example 1: Force applied 10,000 lbs—cross section area of bar—2 sq. inch

Stress= 10,000/2 = 5000 psi (pounds per sq. inch)

Example 2: Stress in ¼" square metal bar subjected to 1,000 lbs. load

1000/ 0.25" x 0.25" = 1000/0.0625 =16000 pounds / square inch

During the pulling operation, if the bar elongates, then the amount of elongation divided by original length is called strain.

Strain = (total length of part after applying load—original length) / original length

Example: original length of wire or bar—10"

Extended length after load application: 10.1"
Strain = (10.1-10) /10 =0.1 in /10in = 0.01 in/in

Stress-Strain Curve

Material-rolling and metal-casting facilities subject their first samples through tensile testing machines. The load is applied to a machined sample. The tensile test machines usually are fitted with attachment that provides graph of the test sequence before the sample fractures. This graph is called stress-strain curve.

During the process of load application to the metal specimen, the sample continues to elongate slightly. There is a critical point at which if the load is removed, then the material may return to its original shape and length. In the graph, the region is called elastic state.

However, if you continue to add more force to the specimen, the material does not return to its original shape and goes beyond elastic region. This point of no return is called *yield point* (proportional limit) of the material. Also, beyond this point, the test sample elongates with small amount of extra force.

Usually, mechanical and civil engineers design their equipment and structures around the yield point of the material and ultimate tensile strength.

If you continue to apply force or load beyond yield point, the sample breaks. This force is called ultimate tensile strength or breaking strength of the material.

Before selecting certain materials for critical products, engineering companies usually take the help independent test laboratories and conduct the following mechanical tests:

Tensile Test

This test is conducted to find the mechanical properties of the material. The specimen for testing is machined to fit the testing machine and pulled apart from both ends. The mechanical properties we are seeking are yield strength, elastic limit, and breaking strength.

This test is conducted on a universal testing machine with an extensometer.

The test specimen could be of a half-inch diameter in the center. The diameters of specimen at both ends are larger. This is done so that the sample breaks in the middle and not at the ends.

For more information on equipment, visit www.instron.com, www.ametektest.com, and www.sunteccorp.com. These companies build systems to find following material properties:

- Compressive strength—This test is the ability of material to stand compressive forces. This test is done in a universal testing machine. The specimen for compression is usually small.
- Shear strength—Here, the forces are applied from both sides to shear the sample.
- Torsional strength—It is the ability of material to withstand the twisting force while being held at one end.
- Fatigue strength—Here, the sample is subjected to several thousand load cycles. And the sample usually fails due to tension and compression cycles.
- Impact strength—Charpy and Izod are two impact tests. Both utilize a sample that has a notch. It utilizes a pendulum to break the sample.

Hardness

The study of hardness provides us information about resistance to deformation from the applied loads. Hardness is critical for the performance of ferrous and nonferrous materials. Measurement of hardness provides information about metals ductility, strength and brittleness.

Measurement of hardness involves the use of hard penetrating tools. The hardness is calculated by measuring the size of penetration. If the material is hard then the size of penetration is small.

The following are some of major hardness-testing methods:

1. Brinell
2. Vickers

3. Knoop
4. Rockwell
5. Shore scleroscope.

In the metal industry, it is very common for engineers to use Brinell (HB) and Rockwell (RH) hardness with *A* to *V* scales to indicate the hardness for their parts.

Brinell Hardness Test (HB)

This is a popular method for checking hardness of castings, forgings, and machine components. The method uses a small table testing machine with a 5 or 10 mm diameter penetrating ball. A flat smooth surface sample to be tested is put on an anvil. A force of 500 to 3,000 kg is applied to the sample using suitable ball. Hardness of the sample is determined by measuring the size of indentation with a portable microscope.

BHN = Force / surface area in sq. mm.

The Brinell test method is good for softer steels and provides BHN or HB numbers. The value of hardness for typical cold rolled steel is 150 BHN.

Vickers Hardness Test (HV)

The Brinell test is good for thicker samples of material. Vickers test system is used for thin sheet metal, thin foils, case hardness, glass, and ceramics.

As compared to Brinell, Vickers hardness tester uses less force and a square diamond penetrator and 50 kg of force. In this test, the length of diamond diagonal impression is measured by a microscope. The Vickers equipment is similar to Brinell; however, it uses much less force.

Knoop Hardness Test (HK)

This method uses 25 grams to 4 kg load with a 136 degrees diamond cross section penetrator to test the hardness. The indentation is measured by the microscope and checked with a chart to determine the hardness of the product. This method does not damage the sample, and a very small surface area is affected.

Rockwell Hardness Test (HR)

The symbol for this test is called HR. This method is similar to Brinell; however, it does the testing with three different penetrators and three different loads.

There are two kinds of Rockwell test systems:

1. The first system starts with a minor load of 10 kg load. The second step involves use 60, 100, or 150 kgf load.
2. The second Rockwell test is called superficial and uses first a 3 kgf followed by 15, 30, 25, and 45 kgf loads. This method is used for thin and case-hardened samples.

The final step utilizes a diamond penetrator for both systems.

There are thirty different scales in Rockwell test system. Majority of these scales are covered by *C* and *B* tests. Final hardness values are read directly on the testing machine.

The following are the hardness scales or categories used in the Rockwell test equipment:

1. Rockwell A—This method is used to check hardness of thin-steel, case-hardened, and cemented-carbide tools
2. Rockwell C—It is used to check hardened alloys such as M2.
3. Rockwell B—It is used for checking hardness of aluminum, copper, and softer steels.
4. Rockwell H—It is used to check softer materials.

For specific information on Rockwell tester, visit www.starrett.com and look for model 3816B for digital bench type Rockwell hardness tester.

For more information, visit www.sunteccorp.com, www.starrett.com, www.instron.us.en, and https://www.buehler.com/hardness-testing.php. Buehler site lists Wilson hardness tester model 574, which uses hardness scales A, B, C, D, E, F, G, H, K, L, M, P, R, S, and V.

Shore Scleroscope Hardness

This method of hardness testing uses a ball, which weighs three grams. This ball is allowed to fall on a specimen. The height of the bounce is recorded. The test assumes that if the sample is hard, then the ball will bounce higher. Zero shore value is assigned to material in which the ball does not bounce. Set of shore numbers are assigned to different bounce heights.

The hardness of material has direct relationship with yield strength of the material. The higher value (Rockwell C) of hardness is very critical for cutting tools, ball, and roller bearings. High hardness can be achieved by heat-treating components made from D2 and M2 steels.

In addition to destructive tests, companies can use the following nondestructive tests: eddy current, liquid penetrant, magnetic particle, radiographic, and ultrasonic to find the soundness of finished parts. These testing methods are covered in chapters 11 and 17 under welding and quality control.

More information about test equipment is available on Tinius Olsen and other websites listed under:

A. www.tiniusolsen.com for the following equipment:

1. Tensile and compression testers
2. Indentation testers—Rockwell, Brinell, Vickers, and Knoop
3. Pendulum impact testers for conducting Charpy and Izod tests

B. www.sunteccorp.com for Rockwell type testers, tension/compression/Vickers/Knoop, and Brinell testers.
C. www.instron.com for universal testing, dynamic and fatigue load, impact drop tower, and torsion testing equipment.

For torque, durometer, and force testing, visit https://hoto-instruments.com and https://imada.com.

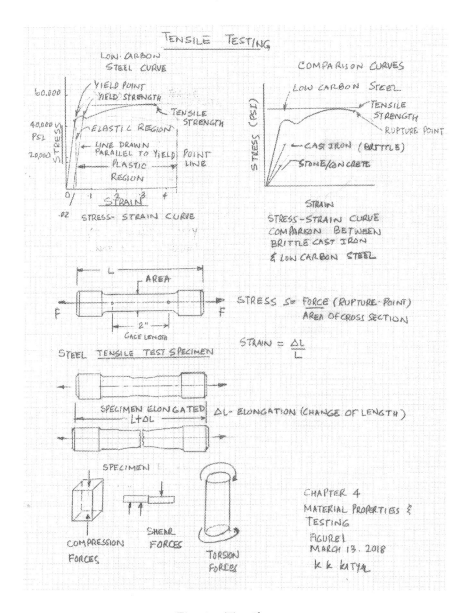

Fig. 1—Tensile test

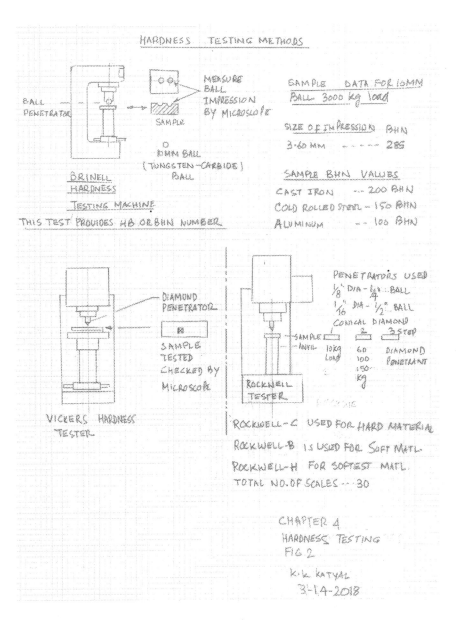

Fig. 2—Hardness test

CHAPTER 5

Nonferrous and Precious (Noble) Metals

Topics covered are aluminum—source of ore, types, major US producers, and glimpse of Alcoa Co.; copper types; brass; bronze; zinc; nickel; cobalt; tin; chromium; titanium; price of metals; and gold, silver, and platinum.

THE MOST COMMON nonferrous metals are aluminum, copper, zinc, magnesium, nickel, cobalt, chromium, tin, and titanium.

Aluminum Bauxite Ore (Al)

It is abundant in nature and exists in about 6% to 8% on earth's crust. There are extensive deposits of aluminum in Brazil, Australia, and Africa. The bauxite ore is electrically processed to form pure aluminum.

Per Alcoa Corp.'s website, after China and Russia, Canada is third largest producer of aluminum in the world. Alcoa itself is the world's eighth largest aluminum producer.

Pure aluminum is made in the form of bars, plates, wire, sheet, and coil. It weighs one third the weight of steel. It is resistant to corrosion and chemicals. Beside copper, it is good for commercial transmission of electrical energy. Aluminum is easy to machine, stamp, bend, and weld. Due to its ductility, aluminum is used for airplanes and automobiles.

Series 1100 of aluminum has a tensile strength from 14,000 to 24,000 psi. The aluminum alloy with magnesium, manganese, and chromium has tensile strength range from 40,000 to 50,000 psi.

Aluminum is white gray in color. It is a ductile material. It is used for kitchen utensils, cars, trucks, buses, passenger trains, aircrafts, and many Apple computer's components. Due to low cost of aluminum, it is also being used for making automotive radiators. Also, it is used in building trade for making roofing, flashing, window, and door frames. Aluminum die-cast parts are used in automobile engine blocks. Aluminum door and window frames are anodized for corrosion protection. It weighs 168.5 lbs/cubic ft. (0.0972 lbs/cubic inch). Please note that steel weighs 487 lbs. /cubic ft.

Classification of Aluminum and Its Alloys

The extruded Aluminum is produced in series 1000, 3000, 5000, 6000, and 7000. Each is heat-treated to achieve different strengths.

> **1000 series**—It has low strength. And this series is good conductor of electricity. 1100 series is 99% pure aluminum and can be welded. It is non-heat treatable. It is an electrical grade alloy. This material is easy to form. Soft-annealed sheet has hardness of 23 BHN and yield of 5,000 psi. Nonhardened bar has 32 BHN and 1,7000 psi yield. It can be used for heat-exchanger fins. It could be welded and brazed.
>
> **2000 series**—Alloy 2024 is used for aircraft skin. It is alloyed with copper. It is heat treatable. It has tensile strength of 68 ksi and yield of 47 ksi. It has good strength and machinability.
>
> **4000 series**—It contains silicone and is used as filler metal for welding.

5000 series (with magnesium)—It is used to make plates and structures. Group 5054 is used for truck bodies and 5152 is used for automobile hoods. Group 5052 has 38 ksi tensile and 31 ksi yield strength. Alloy 5052 is corrosion resistant against salt water. Rectangular bars have Brinell hardness of 60 and yield strength of 28,000 psi.

6000 series—It can be extruded. Window frames are made from 6063 series. Aluminum canoes are made from 6010 series. Alloy 6061 has yield strength of 35,000 psi and hardness of 95 BHN.

7000 series—It is alloyed with zinc. 7075 series has a tensile strength of 83 and yield of 73 ksi. This series is used for aircraft parts.

Aluminum is extruded in the Industry from 7" to 12" billets. Based on extruder size, the extrusions are cut to length from 18" to 40". The aluminum billets are heated from 850°F to 950°F. The heated material is pushed through a die opening. The shape of the part is determined by the die.

For window and door frames, aluminum is anodized. Anodizing provides an electrochemical film on top of existing natural oxide film. The thickness of anodizing varies from 0.0002" to 0.001". Aluminum can also be powder-coated and painted.

Aluminum is highly resistant to corrosion. Also, it is resistant to acids, alkalis, and sea water. The average melting point of aluminum is 1,218°F (659°C)

For more information on major producers of aluminum, visit www.hydro.com, https://www.alcoa.com/global/en/home.asp, and http://www.riotinto.com/aluminium/aluminium-in-depth-4765.aspx.

Aluminum Castings

Aluminum castings are used extensively for automobiles, medical equipment, robots, railroads, and aircrafts. Aluminum products are cast in sand as well as by die-casting.

For your reference, please visit the following:

> www.thoni-alutec.com—a Poland-based aluminum sand-casting company. They can cast parts up to 90 kg.
> www.curto.com—a Chicago-area aluminum and magnesium sand-casting company.

Glimpse from www.alcoa.com website:

1. Alcoa has active four bauxite mines including second largest in the world at Huntly, Australia.
2. Alcoa has annual capacity to produce 17 million metric tons of alumina (aluminum oxide).
3. Alcoa produces aluminum billets, foundry ingots, slab, rod, and powder.
4. Apple computer is a major user of aluminum for their computers. In 2018, Alcoa Corp. developed the first carbon-free smelting technology on the coaxing of major customer Apple. Apple computer put together Rio Tinto, Alcoa, and Canada to build a smelter, which produces oxygen rather than carbon dioxide as by-product. This new experimental smelter will reduce annually several million tons of greenhouse gases from their operation.

Copper (Cu)

Pure copper has high thermal and electrical conductivity. More than 50% of copper produced in the world is used for making electrical wires. The major usage of copper is for making copper tubing for homes, electric motor windings, radiators for trucks, cars, smart phones, computers, and electronics. It is also used in making brass and bronze alloys.

According to www.riotinto.com website, the major producer of copper, the world uses 19 million tons of copper annually. Rio Tinto owns copper mines in Mongolia, Indonesia, Chile, and US.

Additional copper mines are located in Central Africa and Russia. Melting point of copper is 1,981°F (1,083°C). Copper and its alloys are identified by five-digit unified number system. The following are some of copper alloy classifications:

C1xxxx—C10200 with 99% copper

C2xxxx—C22000 commercial bronze with 90% copper and 10% zinc

C3xxx—C33500 low-leaded brass with 66% copper, 34.5% zinc, and 0.5% lead

C7xxxx—C73500 with 72% copper, 10% zinc, and 18% nickel

Note: Above compositions are based on *Metals Handbook* published in 1985.

Brass

Brass is used for making utensils, household hardware, radiator parts, and musical instruments. This metal could be easily brazed and soldered. It is an alloy of zinc and copper. If we add lead, the brass could be easily machined. Certain marine hardware is made of naval brass, which has 39% copper and 39% zinc. Average melting point of brass is from 1,616 to 1,700 degrees. Brass weighs around 512 lbs. per cubic ft.

Bronze

It is an alloy of copper and tin. The amount of tin could be up to 25%. The two common bronzes are the phosphorus bronze and aluminum bronze for making bearings.

Tin helps in improving strength of copper. Other alloys include zinc, lead, and aluminum. Bronze alloys are easier to cast than copper. Average melting point of bronze is 1,675°F (913°C).

Other non-ferrous metals:

1. Magnesium (Mg)—It is a lighter material and corrosion resistant. It is used in die-casting machines to make medical equipment housings, video camera housings, wheels for racing cars, computer cases, and other automotive components. It is made from ore by electrolytic refining. It weighs 108.6 lbs / cu. ft. Its designation starts with letter *M* and has a five-digit number. Average melting point of magnesium (wrought) is 1204°F (651°C).
2. Cobalt (Co)—It is used to make cutting tools and components of aircrafts.
3. Lead (Pb)—It is being used to make automotive batteries and radiation protection sheets for x-ray equipment. It is also used as flashing on the roof to cover plumbing pipes. The average melting point of lead is 621°F (327°C).
4. Nickel (Ni)—It is used as an alloy with other materials. As an alloy, it is resistant to corrosion. In addition, it is used for aerospace components as well as food equipment. Per Belmont Metal website, about one million ton of nickel is produced every year. Average melting point nickel is 2646°F (1452°C). Nickel 200 (UNS N02200), and nickel copper alloys are called monel alloys. It's melting point is 2646°F. Its weight is 549 lbs. /cu. ft.
5. Zinc (Zn)—It is made from zinc sulfide. It is used to make die-cast parts. The die-cast parts are usually made with alloys of aluminum and magnesium, which provide extra strength. Being corrosion resistant, it is used as a coating for steel parts. Hot-dip galvanizing is used for steel bars and structures. Average melting point of zinc is 787°F.

For more information on commercially available alloys, visit www.belmontmetals.com, www.neymetals.com, and www.atimetals.com (for nickel, titanium, zirconium, stainless, and powder-based alloys).

The following zinc alloys are recommended by www.dynacast.com for die-casting:

> Zamak 2—This alloy has high strength.
> Zamak 3—This is used commonly by die casters.

The other alloys are Zamak 5 and 7 and ZA 8 and ZA 27.

6. Tin (Sn)—It is white in color. It is used for plating steel, brass, and bronze for food application. Tin is used to make solder. It is added to copper to make bronze. Its melting point is around 449°F and weighs 455 lbs. / cu. ft. Major producers of tin are located in Russia, China, Australia, Indonesia. and Thailand.

Tin is used for making tinplate and electroplating strip of steel coil. Tinplate is used to make cans for food industry. Tin is also used for making sleeve bearings.

7. Titanium (Ti)—It weighs half as steel. It is silver gray in color. It is used for aircraft jet engines. It has high tensile strength.
8. Chromium (Cr)—It is used for electroplating, decorating, and corrosion protection of bicycle and automotive parts.

Nonferrous Material Prices

The following price information is based on December 23, 2016. Report is published by www.infomine.com.

Aluminum	0.79 USD/lb.
Copper	2.49 USD/lb.
Lead	0.95 USD/lb.
Nickel	4.79 USD/lb.

Tin	9.64 USD/lb.
Zinc	1.17 USD/lb.
Cobalt	680 USD/ton

Noble (Precious Metals)

The following are the most common precious metals in use:

- Gold (Au)—Melting point is 1,945°F and weighs 1,204 lbs. / cu. ft.
- Silver (Ag)—Melting point is 1,761°F and weighs 654 lbs. / cu. ft.
- Platinum (Pt)—Melting point is 3,224°F and weighs—1,335 lbs. /cu. ft.
- Iridium (Ir)—Melting point is 2,443°C and weighs 22.65 grams/cc. It is the densest material.

The other precious metals are palladium (Pd), rhodium (Rh), ruthenium (Ru), and osmium (Os).

Palladium and rhodium are used for electroplating. Platinum, palladium, and ruthenium are used as a catalyst for vehicle's exhaust system.

These metals are expensive to mine. South Africa is the largest producer of platinum. Gold and silver have high thermal conductivity and used for electroplating. Most precious metals are resistant to corrosion as well as to hydrochloric, nitric, and sulfuric acids.

For further information, consult *Metals Handbook—Desk Edition* published by American Society for Metals (https://www.asminternational.org).

CHAPTER 6

Heat Treatment of Steel

Topics covered are hardening of medium- and high-carbon steel; hardening surface by gas, nitriding, and electric induction technologies, annealing, stress relieving, normalizing, tempering, quenching furnace manufacturers, vacuum heat-treating, cryogenic treatment, laser-heat treatment, shot peening, and glimpse of US heat-treating companies.

TO ACHIEVE CERTAIN properties in steel parts, a set of controlled heating and cooling steps are taken with the help of suitable equipment. These steps change the microstructure of the steel. Heat treatment can harden, soften, and toughen steel parts. The controlled heating can harden the material to the core.

Heat treatment is done below the melting point of steel. The transformation in microstructure takes place at certain temperature.

Standard parts, which are used for machinery, construction, automotive, and aerospace, need heat treatment. Also, heat treatment is required for press brake dies, stamping dies, steel rolling mill rolls, injection mold dies, aluminum and plastic extrusion dies.

Medium- and high-carbon steel parts are hardened to improve wear life and strength for machines, oil exploration equipment, bridges, dams, and ships. The low-carbon steel is ferrite in microstructure at room temperature, while it changes to austenite above 1660°F.

Heat treatment specifications are written by design engineers and a staff of metallurgist who supervises the treatment of steel. The steps follow an iron equilibrium diagram about the transformation of microstructure at different temperature. In the diagram, steel with less than 0.5% carbon is called hypo eutectoid, while steel with carbon content from 0.5% to 2% is called hypereutectoid steel. The steel becomes ferrite at room temperature, while it becomes austenitic from 1,666 to 2,600°F. The steel turns to liquid at about 2,600°F.

The final properties of the part subjected to heat treatment depend on:

a. on the temperature exposed to and how long the part was held at that level,
b. on how fast the part was cooled as sudden low-level cooling creates martensite microstructure, which is magnetic and hard (It has a hardness of 53 to 67 HRC.),
c. on a slower cooling results in pearlite microstructure, which is softer as compared to martensite,
d. on a very slow cooling rate (The resulting material is complete pearlite, which has a hardness of 15 HRC.), and
e. on alloy steel that can attain uniform properties (tempering) by heating to 400°F and holding it for two hours.

Tempering reduces hardness and tensile strength.

Hardenability

The ability of materials to harden depends on its carbon content and the method used to affect change.

The following are common heat treatment processes:

1. Surface hardening (case hardening)—This process is mostly used for low-carbon steel products. The process involves packing carbon powder around the heated part. The outer surface of parts hardens due to diffusion of carbon. This method is used to improve wear resistance of the surface of parts. Surface hardness provides martensitic layer on the part. The case depths vary

from 0.25 to 1.0 mm. The parts after case hardening are still soft on the inside. They are still tough and not brittle.
2. The most common methods of case hardening are nitriding, gas carburizing, carbonitriding, and cyaniding.
   A. Gas carburizing uses an environment that is rich in carbon. The idea is that the process causes the absorption of carbon into the surface of parts. Natural gas (methane) is a common gas used for this process. This process is carried around 1700°F.
   B. Carbonitriding—This process uses ammonia gas with other heating gas. The nitrogen from ammonia gas penetrates into the metal to provide good hard case to the steel surface.
   C. Nitriding—This process uses gas as well as molten salt bath to improve the case. Nitrided case is much stronger than carburize case.
   D. Flame hardening—This process uses handheld torch supplied with oxy-acetylene flame.
   E. Induction hardening—Heating is done to the surface only by electromagnetic induction.
   F. Cyaniding—It is a liquid carburizing process. It uses sodium cyanide and sodium carbonate in a molten bath.
3. Annealing is done to soften the material so that the parts could be machined or cold-worked. This process reduces hardness and brittleness. This process involves heating the metal above transformation (critical) temperature and is followed with slow cooling inside the furnace.
4. Stress relieving—The process is used to stress relieve highly worked material, which has gone through processes, such as heavy welding, heavy machining, rolling, and casting. This heating of parts takes place below the transformation temperature.
5. Normalizing—This is done to improve structure of grain of hot worked and forged items. The process involves heating above transformation range followed by rapid cooling in air.

This method improves machinability and reduces internal stresses.

6. Tempering—This is done to already heat-treated or quenched material. This process is done to improve impact resistance (develop toughness and ductility) and reduce hardness. This process relieves oil- or water-quenching stresses. The process is carried below the transformation temperature. To improve machining of hardened parts, tempering must be done at high temperature (900 to 1,200°F). Tempering affects the following mechanical properties of steel:
   A. Reduces tensile strength
   B. Reduces yield point
   C. Improves ductility, decreases hardness, and increases toughness

Laser hardening is another way of hardening the surface of steel castings and machined parts.

Quenching of Steel

It is a method to harden the heated metals by sudden cooling. The process involves dipping of parts in water or oil after the steel parts are heated above the transformation temperature. The sudden rate of cooling or quenching is faster for water than oil. This sudden cooling changes the microstructure from austenite to martensite. The final properties are achieved based on how fast the part loses heat.

The quench media could be air or water and consists of salt, caustic soda, or polymer. The oil media delays the quench affect.

For small heat treatment furnace, visit www.paragonweb.com (Mesquite, Texas) and www.luciferfurnaces.com.

Heat Treatment Guide

If you are hardening, tempering, and annealing alloy steel materials such as A2, A6, D2, 01, W1, S7, H13, M2, T2, 1040, 4130, and 4140, visit Lucifer furnace website or your material supplier for suggested temperatures.

Furnace Environment

For conventional heat treatment, the atmosphere is air inside the furnace. The air consists of 79% nitrogen and 20% oxygen. For normal medium-carbon steel parts, we find a fine scale develops by oxidation during the heat treatment operation. This scaling is the loss of carbon on the surface. For certain parts, this scaling is acceptable because the part will be machined later. For certain parts, the scale is not acceptable. There are furnaces made for different atmospheres including vacuum.

Vacuum Furnace

Some critical components need superior finish, practically no distortion, and uniform heat treatment. Vacuum furnace does meet some of these requirements. The parts are heated by radiation. Due to absence of oxygen, there is no oxidation of parts.

Cryogenic Treatment of Tools

The life and performance of cutting tools could be improved by cryogenic treatment. The process uses very low subzero temperature down to -300°F to change the microstructure of heat-treated metals. The process helps in removing heat treatment–related stresses. The process also improves physical and mechanical properties of expensive metal components.

Cryogenically treated tools, such as steel rolls, knives, high-speed steel drills, and reamers, can take high abrasive wear and are less prone to cracking. This process is carried out after the heat treatment of tools. The process realigns the molecular structure of the metal. It provides additional

1. wear resistance and dimensional stability to the heat-treated parts,

2. help in transforming softer austenite microstructure to harder martensite carbide, and
3. tensile strength of parts.

Cryogenic treatment can increase the life of items such as firearms, golf clubs, stamping tools, punch and die sets, large taps, saw blades, shaving razors, thread rolling rolls, milling cutters, transmission shafts, etc.

According to 300 Below, Inc., cryogenic treatment can also be used to remove stresses of aluminum castings. Cryogenically treated machined aluminum castings will be stable after the machining operation.

The cryogenic processer usually puts the parts in a special chamber, which cools the parts to -110 to -300°F. The parts are slowly cooled for about twenty hours and slowly brought to room temperature.

I have personally had large taps, thread rolling dies treated by cryogenic process. I did notice increase in the life of these tools.

To summarize, the cryogenic process provides the following benefits:

1. Relieves stresses due to machining and welding
2. Improves grain structure of metal
3. Increases resistance to wear
4. Increases life of cutting tools

For more information, please consult *Cryogenics* by William E. Bryson published by Hanser Gardner.

Laser Heat-Treating

This method of heat treatment is excellent if you wish to harden only the surface of the steel part such as only the cylinder surface of a diesel engine blocks and not the whole part.

US Laser Corp. uses a ND:YAG laser with 1.6 micro meter wavelength to harden the surface of metal. Laser has the benefit of localizing the heat treatment by changing the microstructure of the metal. The process does not distort the part.

For more information, visit www.precoinc.com and www.uslasercorp.com.

Shot Peening

This process is used to strengthen highly stressed parts. The process is similar to forging. In forging, we use large hammers to squeeze the grain structure for better properties.

In shot peening, the part to be treated is put inside a closed chamber. In the closed chamber, millions of steel balls are impinged on the desired part area. The balls make microscopic indentation on the part. The process creates compressive stresses on the metal surface.

I have personally used the process to prolong the life of 6" diameter shaft on a rolling mill, which failed sometime.

This process is being used by manufacturers of earth-moving equipment and jet engines.

Glimpse of a Few Heat-Treating Companies

The information is based on their websites.

1. https://www.aberfoyle-mt.com (Toronto, Canada)—Company that specializes in stress relieving, normalizing, annealing, quenching and tempering with 100-ton crane. It has five furnaces of car-bottom type. One furnace has capacity to hold 400-ton material and generates up to 2,000°F, with 40,000 gallon water quench tank.
2. https://www.paulo.com (several locations in the US)—The company provides the following services:
   - Vacuum heat-treating—It can hold 60" diameter pieces 72" long with quench gases.
   - Case hardening—The process diffuses carbon and nitrogen on to the surface of steel parts.

Other services include induction heat treatment, austempering, and cryogenic treatment of cutting tools.

3. https://www.solaratm.com (four location in the US)—It has sixty vacuum heat-treating furnaces that can hold 48-feet-long piece with capacity to hold 150,000 pounds.

For additional information, visit the following websites:

> www.bodycote.com (heat-treating, cryogenic treatment, and HIP processing)
> www.century-sun.com
> www.inductionheating.com
> wwww.heattreat.net
> www.nitrofreeze.com
> www.ihtcorp.com
> www.300below.com
> https://www.industrialheating.com (directory of heat treaters)

CHAPTER 7

Ferrous and Nonferrous Metal Casting and Powder Metallurgy

> Topics covered are investment castings, hot isostatic pressing, permanent mold casting, die-casting, centrifugal casting, powder metallurgy, metal injection molding, and related websites.

THERE ARE SEVERAL methods to make ferrous and nonferrous components. The following are some of the methods of making castings and powder metal parts.

1. Investment casting
2. Steel-mold casting
3. Die-casting
4. Centrifugal casting
5. Powder metallurgy
6. Metal-injection molding

Investment Casting

This method is used for both ferrous and nonferrous metals. This is also called as lost wax-casting process. The process is used for jewelry, stainless steel, and alloys products, which require thin walls, high tolerances, and fine outer finish. The finished part may not require any machining. Due to high-surface finish, parts for aircrafts, armaments, pumps, valves, medical- and defense-related industries are commonly made by this process.

The process involves making a die for the part to be molded. A wax pattern of the part is molded in the die. Then the wax pattern is dipped into the slurry of refractory material. The pattern is then allowed to harden, and wax is removed by heating. The molten metal of the alloy is poured into the slurry-based hollow mold.

After cooling, the resulting casting is removed by breaking the ceramic mold. The parts are taken apart by cutting off by hand and grinding. The parts are inspected before shipping or further machining.

American Machinist magazine covered Thompson Investment Casting Co. in their July 2008 issue. The following is a glimpse of information based (November 2018) on their website: www.thompsoninvestmentcastings.com.

The company provides investment castings for ferrous, nonferrous, and alloy metals. Per their website, they describe the investment castings process as follows:

1. Multi-cavity wax injection mold using aluminum is built.
2. Multi-cavity wax patterns with gates are produced.
3. Wax pattern is dipped in ceramic slurry.
4. Ceramic shell is dried. The waxed is removed by heating.
5. Molten metal is poured into ceramic molds.
6. On cooling, castings are removed.
7. Parts are cut and ground from the casting tree.

Also, you may check www.avalon-castings.com for their services. This company was covered in the August 10, 2006, issue of www.machinedesign.com. Following is a link to Metaltek Casting Company, which provides investment, sand, and centrifugal castings.

https://www.metaltek.com/capabilities/processes/metal-casting/investment-casting

Additionally, the following societies may be of interest to you:

1. Investment casting institute (www.investmentcasting.org)
2. American Foundry Society (www.afsinc.com)

Hot Isostatic Pressing

There are concerns that investment castings may not be fully dense. Some heat-treating companies provide hot isostatic pressing (HIP) service. This process applies 20,000 to 30,000 psi of argon gas pressure on parts in an enclosed heated-pressure vessel.

Example of investment casting companies are www.epcast.com (Engineered Precision Casting Co.), www.acracast.com, www.aerometals.com, www.wisconsinprecision.com, www.shellcasting.com, and www.spokaneindustries.com.

Permanent Steel Mold Casting

In the sand-molding process, the two-part mold is broken to remove the part.

In the permanent steel-mold casting, the molten metal is poured into a preheated clamped mold. As soon as the molten material solidifies, the finished part is removed. Aluminum, copper, and magnesium are cast in permanent steel molds. The following companies are involved in permanent metal casting: www.batesvilleproducts.com and www.cifmetal.com.

Die-Casting

In this process, the molten metal is forced into hollow metal die cavity. The parts produced in this process have very smooth surface. The most common materials used in die-casting are zinc and zinc alloys. Zinc melts around 750°F. The other two materials that can be used in die-castings are copper and aluminum. Aluminum melts at 1,200°F.

As compared to sand casting, die-casting is a much faster process. This process is suitable for high-volume requirement. According to Deco Products Co. website, www.decoprod.com, the following are the advantages of zinc die-casting over aluminum:

1. Due to high melting temperature, aluminum parts die life is tenth of zinc die.

2. Dies for zinc casting can last for million pieces.
3. Zinc can provide thin walls and tighter tolerance than aluminum and plastics.

Per https://diecasting.org website, US die-casting (Aluminum Association) industry shipped 3.4 billion pounds of products in 2016, while total aluminum castings shipped were 5.19 billion pounds.

Several items for automobiles and window frames are die-casted. The most common items made by die-casting process are locks, doorknobs, automobile door handles, and motorcycle hand control levers. Die cast dies are made from alloy steel. There are two kinds of die-casting machines: hot chamber and cold chamber.

Some die-casting machines use pressure up to 10,000 psi to force the molten metal into the die cavities. It is a high-speed process. Hot chamber is used for zinc castings, while cold chamber is used for aluminum, copper, and magnesium. Die-casting process provides high tolerance and excellent outer finish. The following companies provide die-casting services: www.decoprod.com, www.tcdcinc.com, www.productioncastings.com, and www.crecocast.com.

Glimpse from www.decpprod.com: The company has 86 die-casting machines with locking force from 14 tons to 500 tons.

For more information, visit https://diecasting.org (North American Die-Casting Association).

For equipment, visit www.yizumi.com for cold chamber die-casting machines.

Centrifugal Castings

This is an alternate method to cast cylindrical shapes, rings, and tubes. The process involves pouring molten metal inside spinning preheated mold. The rotating cylindrical mold exerts very high centrifugal forces to the molten metal. The clean material clings to the outside of the mold, and the impurities are forced on the inside. The impurities are removed by machining.

This process produces less waste, involves less machining, and provides a product with no porosity. Material such as aluminum, bronze, and copper alloys can easily be casted by this method. For more information, visit the following websites:

> www.deltacentrifugal.com
> www.johnsoncentrifugal.com
> www.metaltek.com
> www.dwclark.com

Powder Metallurgy (PM)

This is a chipless method of making metal parts. The process can make both ferrous and nonferrous parts. The process involves mixing metal alloy powders with a binder. The mixture is compacted in a die (mold), which has a shape of the final part.

The compacted part is heated or sintered to bond the powder particles together. The process can produce complex shapes from a few ounces to four pounds weight. The most common parts made by this process are cams, gears, chain sprockets, and pulleys. Automotive, business machines, appliances, and agriculture equipment manufacturers use powder metal parts. According to European Powder Metal Association, PM parts are made in two densities: 6.46 to 6.9 grams per cubic centimeter and 7 to 7.4 grams/cm3.

This process provides the following advantages:

1. Its cost does not sacrifice the strength.
2. It eliminates machining scrap.
3. It provides flexibility of using high-strength alloy powders.
4. Parts have excellent surface finish.
5. Its resulting parts can be welded.
6. The process can control porosity.

Manufacturing steps:

1. Mixing the alloy powders with lubricants or other additives.
2. Compacting the powder in a precise die. The pressing of powder can be done by hot method, warm or cold compaction. The compaction pressure could be from 10 to 50 ton per square inch of surface.
3. Sintering—The compacted parts are put through a furnace where they are heated below metals melting temperature to achieve the right hardness. The parts stay in furnace from one to three hours. Depending on requirement, parts could be further heat-treated or electroplated.

The following critical areas are evaluated for these parts:

1. Assurance that the density of powder metal parts are from 75% to 80% of the forged parts. If not, the density could be increased by HIP (high-pressure system) process.
2. Porosity
3. Permeability—This is ability to allow oil or gas to pass through the parts.

Strength of Powder Metal Parts

1. Ductility—Due to pores between particles, the parts are not as ductile as rolled steel bars.
2. Mechanical strength—The yield strength of powder parts are 60 to 80% of steel-rolled parts.

Related websites are https://mpif.org (Metal Powder Industries Federation), www.pickpm.com, www.psmbrown.com, www.metalpowderpro.com, www.netshapetech.com, www.pim-international.com (magazine), www.metal-am.com (3-D printing magazine), *Powder Metallurgy Review*, www.psmindustries.com, and www.keystonepm.com.

Metal Injection Molding (MIM)

This process is a combination of injection molding and powder metallurgy. This process is an alternate to powder metallurgy, die-casting, and investment casting. It is believed that Apple's iPad and series 5, 6, 8, and 10 iPhone's charging jacks are made by MIM process.

The process provides very high dense and high-strength parts. It is being used to make parts for firearm-, aerospace-, surgical-, dental-, electronic-, and sports-related industries. The process is used for parts that weigh from a fraction of gram to one pound. The most common parts weigh from 30 grams to 50 grams. The process can make intricate shape. Parts made by this process have high impact and fatigue strength and excellent finish.

As described in article written by Barbara Donohue during an interview with David Smith of Advanced Forming Technology of Colorado, the process uses very fine metal powder (20 micron that is about 0.0008"). The powder is mixed with a plastic or wax binder. The combined mixture could be 60% powder and 40% binder. As per FloMet website, the molded part could be 20% bigger than required.

The molded parts are first put through debinding process, which removes the binder from the molded parts. Debinding process involves heating the parts and chemically treating them to remove the binder.

After debinding, the parts are sintered in a vacuum or a furnace with a gaseous atmosphere. As per FloMet website, the part could be heated to almost 85% of parent-material melting temperature.

The finished parts are 95% to 98% dense with smooth surface. If 100% dense parts are required, then a hot isostatic pressing process is used. It may be necessary to machine the part after sintering.

Molds for MIM process are very precise and expensive and usually recommend for high-volume usage parts.

For more information, visit the following websites:

www.aftmim.com (Advance Forming Technology)
www.advancedpowderproducts.com

www.phillipsmedisize.com
www.pmdatabase.com (Global Powder Metallurgy Property Database)
www.epma.com (European Powder Metallurgy Association)
www.flomet.com

CHAPTER 8

Metal Cutting Processes for Metal Fabrication

Topics covered are laser cutting system and glimpse of equipment suppliers, oxy-fuel cutting and glimpse of equipment suppliers, plasma cutting and glimpse of equipment suppliers, and water-jet cutting and glimpse of equipment suppliers.

IN THE METAL manufacturing environment, materials such as carbon steel, aluminum, stainless steel plates, and thin sheets are needed to be cut for further processing. The physical size of the material to be cut could be 8"×12" to 6"×6" in various thicknesses. In the industry, there is frequently a need to cut metal bars and tubes. The saw cutting of bars and tubes is covered in another chapter.

Selection of Optimum Method of Cutting

The most common methods of cutting flat metal sheets and plates are CNC laser, water-jet, plasma, and oxy-fuel.

The selection of the right cutting equipment for the manufacturing depends on the specialty of the business. The owners of business must consider the following parameters before choosing the right cutting equipment:

1. Type of material to be cut are carbon steel, stainless steel, aluminum, copper, brass, etc.
2. Thickness of material

3. Cost of equipment
4. Cutting equipment operation cost
5. Quality of the material cut-edge squareness
6. Production speed
7. Size of heat-affected zone (HAZ) at the edge

The following are additional considerations for selecting plate and sheet metal cutting methods:

1. Material cutting abilities—Waterjet can cut practically all materials except ceramic and some glass. Plasma and EDM cutting are limited to conductive metals such as steel, aluminum, and stainless steel. Laser is limited to metals, plastics, and fibers. Oxy-fuel process is limited to ferrous (iron-based) materials from ¼" to 12" thick.
2. Material thickness—Plasma cutting is good for cutting metals only up to 2" thickness. Laser is good up to ¾" thick steel. Oxy-fuel can cut steel up to 12" and higher thick steel plates. Waterjet can cut up to 24" (www.flowjwateret.com). EDM can also cut up to 12" thick steel
3. Cost of equipment—Laser is more expensive than plasma and oxy-fuel equipment. The cost of plasma equipment ranges from $50,000 to $150,000. Depending on the number of cutting torches, oxy-fuel equipment could be cheaper than plasma.
4. Operation cost—The cost of operation for water-jet cutting is more than plasma and laser. Plasma is cheaper to run than laser cutting equipment.
5. Quality—The best quality cut is achieved using water-jet process. It provides clean square edge. Water-jet cutting does not leave any dross on the bottom. Laser cutting does leave dross while cutting thicker steel. Laser cutting provides high accuracy. Plasma cutting leaves some bevel edge and large kerf at the edge. Oxy-fuel consisting provides large fluctuation in cutting tolerance.
6. Production speed

The following are some estimated speeds of different cutting operations:

A. Plasma process is limited to conductive materials and can cut from 60" to 200" per minute.
B. Water-jet cutting may cut from 6" to 12" per minute for ¾" aluminum using 60,000 psi pump system.
C. Laser system can cut from 15" to 70" per minute. The speed depends on thickness, material, and type of laser.
D. Oxy-fuel cutting (also called flame cutting system) can cut the steel and alloy plates from 3/8" to 12" thick. Specially equipped machines can cut up to 30" thick plate. The cutting speed can vary from 5" to 16" per minute.

Laser Cutting

Carbon dioxide (CO_2) laser has been very common for cutting sheet steel until 2014. The newer cutting system uses a fiber laser system. Most of the laser cutting systems are designed to cut flat carbon steel, aluminum, and stainless steel materials. The newer machines are provided with a cutting torch, which could change the angle. Also, available are pipe-contouring (visit www.ghdiv.com for tube cutting) machines. A 2,000-watt laser cutting machine can cut ¼" to ½" thick steel.

Laser cutting provides cleaner and burr-free edges. It provides the least heat-affected zone (HAZ) at the cutting edge. Laser cutting uses less consumable as compared to plasma, water-jet, and oxy-fuel cutting. The new fiber lasers need very little maintenance. But I understand from a representative of major builders that CO_2 cut edge is superior to fiber laser.

Laser cutting machines have higher capital cost as compared to water-jet, plasma, and oxy-fuel cutting systems. CO_2 and fiber lasers are very common with sheet steel and nonferrous metal fabricators.

Fiber lasers are being substituted for CO2 Laser cutting systems. The cost of operation of fiber laser is much lower than CO2 laser. In addition it has the following benefits:

1. The size of footprint of fiber laser is smaller
2. Laser source and chillers are smaller
3. No mirrors to align and lens to change
4. Fiber lasers use solid-state diodes
5. Can cut aluminum, copper, brass and titanium which are difficult to process by CO2 Laser

Laser cutting and other machine manufacturers:

www.amada.com/america (punch press, laser cutting, press brakes)
www.amada miyachi.com (laser marking, cutting, laser welding)
www.bystronic.com (laser cutting, waterjet, press brakes)
www.e-ci.com (Cincinnati Inc., fiber laser, press brakes, powder metal press)
www.control laser.com (laser marking)
https://fslaser.com (full-spectrum laser)
www.mcmachinery.com
www.bosslaser.com
www.lvdgroup.com
www.salvagnini.com (for laser cutting, press brake, and punching)
www.kernlasers.com- (low power CO2 laser from 50, 100, 250, and 400 watts for engraving and cutting)
www.epiloglaser.com (for marking, etching metals, and permanently marking plastics)
www.lasermarktech.com (for marking)
www.suite.orlaser (for welding)
www.farleylaserlab.com

For cutting contour on pipes and tubes, the following companies build special laser cutting systems: www.trumpf.com, www.blmgroup.com, www.lvdgroup.com, and www.mazakoptonics.com.

Oxy-Fuel Cutting

This process is also called flame cutting. The process uses special torch and tips with natural gas, propane or acetylene (C2H2), and oxygen (O2) to cut the steel. The combination of fuel gas and oxygen creates up to 5,800°F in temperature to cut the steel. This method is used for cutting thick steel where high tolerances are not desired. The cutting surface is heated by flame. And as soon as the surface is fully hot, high-pressure oxygen is injected to start the cutting process.

During the oxy-fuel cutting process, a spot on the surface is heated to red hot to about 1,600°F. This step is called preheating. At this stage, high-pressure pure oxygen is aimed at the heated spot through the cutting nozzle. This causes the oxidation of steel. This rapid process cuts the material from the steel plate or structure. Materials which cannot oxidize with oxygen gas cannot be cut by this method.

Be the force of oxygen, the removed area from the material is called kerf; it varies from 1/8" to ¼". The operator use certain speed for cutting to achieve clean-cut surface. Depending on the material thickness, this speed can vary from 5" to 15" per minute for oxy-fuel cutting.

A steel worker in the field uses hand cutting torch to pierce holes, bevel plates and pipes for further welding.

The oxy-fuel cutting process leaves bead on top and oxidized slag underneath the cut parts. This slag is easily removable and should be cleaned before using the part for further welding or machining. The heat of oxy-fuel cutting also causes the cut edge to harden for carbon steel. At times, it is necessary to normalize (heat treatment for softening) the flame cut part before machining. This process is not used for cutting aluminum and stainless steel because they cannot be oxidized.

Acetylene, propane, and oxygen gases are delivered in special cylinders by welding supply houses to customers. Like another manufacturing process, there are hazards in the use of oxy-acetylene equipment. It is important to learn the handling of equipment before using it.

Following are some of the safety guidelines:

1. Floor and wall around cutting area must be fire proof.
2. Gas cylinders must be chained for storage.
3. Wearing of safety shields, glasses, safety shoes, sleeves, and safety hat is a must.
4. Equipment must have proper gas hoses, pressure gauges, gas regulators, and flashback arrestors.

Oxy-fuel cutting employs manual hand cutting torches as well as CNC cutting machines with several cutting torches. The machines are provided with a plate-cutting table with a traveling beam, which holds two to eight cutting torches. This method is economical in case the part needs to be machined after cutting.

For five years, I was involved with oxy-fuel cutting process as a tool engineer with Electro Motive Diesel Co. (maker of locomotives, initially owned by General Motors in Chicago and now part of Caterpillar Co.). Due to tremendous heat of gases, there is always adjustment required in the program to cut a perfect piece with this process.

Prior to the advent of CNC flame cutting machines, the older machines were fitted with an electric eye (photo electric), which follows the edge of template to cut the shape of steel. The newer "computer numerical controlled" machines can be programmed to cut any shape.

This cutting process creates a heat-affected zone along the cut edges. This heat zone becomes very hard on cooling and is detrimental to milling and drilling tools. To improve machining, certain parts cut by oxy-fuel process must be sent for normalizing to soften the steel.

The following are some of the equipment builders for oxy-fuel process:

www.esabna.com—Victor torches for hand cutting and CNC cutting systems
www.messer-cs.com/us—CNC cutting systems
www.zinser.de—hand-held cutting torches
www.gullco.com—beveling machines
www.bugo.com—beveling machines and welding automation

Plasma Cutting Systems

This is a low-cost, low-tolerance cutting method for steel, stainless steel, and nonferrous metals. Compared to oxy-fuel cutting, the process provides less distortion to cut material. The temperature of plasma can reach from 50,000 to 60,000°F. While in oxy-fuel process, the temperature can reach up to 6,300°F.

The process involves passing electrically charged gas arc through an orifice. The process heats the gas. Heated gas becomes electrically conductive plasma. Depending on the thickness of the material to cut, the process can cut the material almost 200 inches a minute.

As per Thermal Dynamics website, depending on ferrous and nonferrous materials, their plasma cutting process uses oxygen, nitrogen, and air as plasma gas. And it also uses air, oxygen, water, and nitrogen as a shielding gas. Water shielding traps any smoke and helps in preventing the top-rounded cutting edge. Thermal Dynamics Auto-Cut 200 XT system cuts nonferrous metals with nitrogen plasma gas with water mist. Air plasma with air shield is also an economical way to get good cut. Beside steel, plasma with nitrogen gas can also cut stainless steel, aluminum, and titanium.

Thermal Dynamics build systems, which CNC-plate cutting machine builder can incorporate in their machines. CNC-plate cutting table machine may have one or two torches. Some plasma cutting machine builders sell equipment with a drilling head attachment with 8-pocket tool changer. These machines can cut and drill ¼" to 1" thick steel.

Plasma is faster than oxy-fuel cutting system. Plasma cutting causes large heat-affected area at the cut edge and it forms slight dross underneath the edges. Solidification of excess material at the edges needs to be cleaned before using the parts.

Manufacturers for plasma cutting systems are www.thermal-dynamics.com, www.ajanusa.com, www.akscutting.com, www.burny.com, www.koike.com, www.rhinocutting.com, www.plasmacam.com, www.torchmate.com (or www.lincolnelectric.com), and www.thermacut.us.

Glimpse of plasma / oxy-fuel and laser cutting equipment manufacturer—https://www.messer-ca.com/us/na (Messer Cutting Systems Inc., Menomonee Falls, Wisconsin)

1. Metal Master 2.0 plasma / oxy-fuel cutting machine—cuts width 5' & 10' long pieces; can cut with plasma up to 1" thick mild steel, stainless steel, and aluminum.
2. Fiber laser / plasma combination—fiber laser 2kw to 8kw, material cut from 0.75" to 2". Mild steel cut up to ¾", stainless steel up to 0.50" and aluminum up to 3/8" thickness.

Glimpse of a plasma cutting system builder (www.thermal-dynamics.com):

1. Auto-cut 200 and 300 XT systems can cut from 1 to 25 mm thick ferrous and nonferrous materials.
2. Systems cuts stainless steel using air as plasma and air as shield.
3. Systems can cut nonferrous metals using nitrogen and water.

Thermal Dynamics Ultra-Cut 200 XT—iCNC system has the following features:

1. Design for low-cost CNC machine builders
2. Support two plasma or four oxy-fuel torches
3. Built-in torch height control
4. Laser pointer for torch position on plate
5. Built-in Wi-Fi for easy service

Water-Jet Cutting

This is a method of cutting metals, plastics, running-shoe inserts, and stones using a very high-pressure stream of water. For cutting hard metals, the waterjet is assisted with a stream of abrasive material. A CNC water-jet cutting machine for metals does not create any fumes. There are no blades to sharpen, and complex shapes are cut easily.

As compared to laser, oxy-fuel and plasma, water-jet cutting is slower; however, it provides the best cut edge. In addition to clean edge, this method provides high accuracy and very thin kerf width. Plasma and laser cutting methods leave heat-affected zone near the cut edge. For machined parts, materials cut by Plasma and Laser processes may need extra material for further milling. The water-jet cut edge does not require extra stock for milling. This process can boast of providing cut dimensions within +/- 0.003" for 3" thick steel (source: Omax website).

The system consists of a cutting table, water filter, cutting head (for water only and abrasive), controller, hydraulic pump to boost low-pressure water, and the intensifier pump to create pressure from 60,000 to 90,000 psi. The high-pressure water is delivered to water-jet cutting head. The cutting head has an orifice diameter, which varies from 0.006 to 0.018".

For cutting hard metals, abrasive material such as fine hard rock or special sand is supplied to the cutting head. These machines are controlled by CNC programming.

Following are major manufacturers' websites for water-jet cutting systems:

> www.hypertherm.com
> www.kmtwaterjet.com,
> https://www.flowwaterjet.com/Machines/Mach-700
> www.omax.com
> https://jetedge.com
> www.cmsna.com
> www.waterjetusa.com/www.waterjetcorp.com

A glimpse of equipment from www.waterjetusa.com (information from their brochure).

With KMT streamline Pro3—125 HP—6,200 bar—90,000 psi pressure

Water consumption 5.5lt/min (1.37 gal/min) with 0.35mm–0.014" orifice can hold 1 to 4 cutting heads with following options with numerical control:

1. Touch probe sensor with anticollision, laser pointer, and vacuum assist
2. Tapering control
3. Edge 5 axis +/- 55 degree interpolation
4. Tube cutting lathe
5. Semiautomatic sludge removal
6. Automatic sludge removal

Other sheet metal (up to 3/8" thickness) cutting equipment offered by many machine builders:

1. Guillotine CNC shear provided with:
   a. touch screen,
   b. adjustable stroke length,
   c. back gauge,
   d. ball material transfer system, and
   e. four cutting edge of blades.
2. Punch press (CNC controlled)—These are single-head punching or cutting machines, which can also bend and form. They also have twenty to thirty tool of indexable attachment. They could have force of 20 tons and provide several hits per minute. These machines are mostly being replaced by laser cutting machines.

Glimpse of Machine Builder's Websites for Laser, Plasma, Water-Jet, and Shear Operations

- Cincinnati Inc. (www.e-ci.com)—Company that makes laser cutting, plasma and sheet metal shearing, and bending machines.

A. Fiber laser cutting system CL-900—available in power source of 4kW, 6kW, and 8kW-with table sizes of 5" x 10", 8" x 10" and 2Mx4M
B. CO2 laser cutting system CL400 dual pallet—available in 4,000 watts and CO2 resonator with table sizes of 5"x10" and 2Mx4M. Also, it provides air-assist cutting instead of nitrogen.
C. Plasma CPX 300—300 amp power source with 5'x10' cutting table with following specifications:

½" thick material—cut at 155" per minute with 0.185" kerf
1" thick material—cut at 75" per minute with 0.223" kerf
2-1/2" material—cut at 14" per minute with 0.270" kerf

D. Hydraulic shear—HS series ¼ to ¾" capacity up to 14 feet long model 375 Hx10 that can cut 3/8" thick material up to 122" long with force of 14.9 tons.

- Bystronic (www.bystronic.com)—Company that manufactures fiber and CO2 laser metal cutting system.

	Fiber	Fiber	Fiber
	3,000 W	4,000 W	10,000 W
Material thickness—steel	20mm	20mm	25mm
Material thickness—copper	6mm	8mm	13mm
Power consumption	19kw	21kw	35kw
Cutting area	3100×1350×100	4105×2100×100mm	

- Omax (www.omax.com)—This is a water-jet equipment cutting company.

Sample machines and pumps:

Omax 2626—X-2"-5"—Y-2"-2"--- Z-8" travel
Omax 55100 --X-8"-4" x Y 4" 7"
Enduromax Pump 100 HP-60,000 psi-3.5 gallons/per minute orifice size 0.022"-2.25 gpm
30 HP-60,000 psi orifice 0.012"/0.63 gpm

- Flow International Corp. (www.flowwaterjet.com)—company provides systems to cut stone, carbon fiber and metals.

  Model Mach 200 has machine base from 2M × 3M to 4M
  Pump options with pressure from 60 ksi to 87 ksi
  Can cut 2D or multi-axis.

- Koike Aronson Ransome (www.koike.com)—Information here is based on their general product catalog 01/18 KENG available at September 2018 IMTS show.
  - CNC plasma / oxy-fuel cutting machine models 2000, 2500, and 3100
  - cutting width of 10 feet
  - Oxy-fuel and plasma cutting capabilities
  - Up to 4 oxy-fuel stations available (automatic ignition and height control)
  - Koike Ultra high-pressure water-jet cutting systems models 44, 48, 510, 610, and 612
  - 4'×4' to 6'×12' tables and Z-axis travel of 6 in with 60,000 psi Intensifier system
  - Wide span CO_2 laser cutting machine (cutting capacity of 3 mm to 25 mm thick steel)
  - Available in 4kW and 6kW power capacity

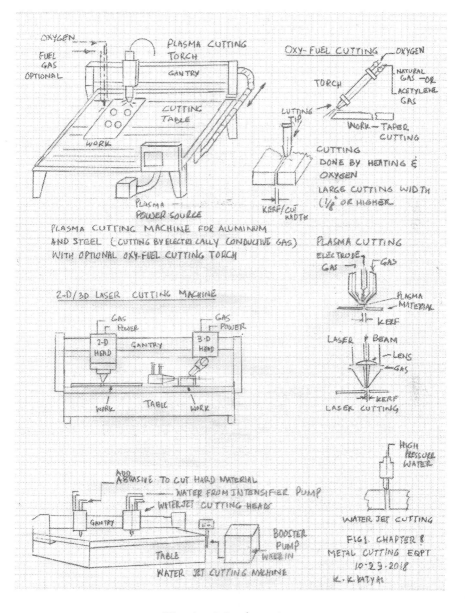

Fig. 1—Metal cutting

Prestige Metal Laser Pic. 1 (courtesy of Dave Kerr of Prestige Metal, Bristol, Wisconsin)

CHAPTER 9

Thread Systems

Topics covered are UNC/UNRE and UNF thread systems, class of threads—unified and ISO, pipe threads and pipe fittings, square, ACME, and buttress threads, screw thread terms, threads for hydraulic fittings, and British screw threads.

MACHINED AND ROLLED threads are used for screws, bolts, threaded bars, assembling pipes, and tubes. Threads are used for transmitting power. Inch and metric threads are used for fasteners and tubular connections. Standards for threads are laid down by American National Standards Institute (ANSI) and ISO system.

Screws are specified according to diameter and pitch. In Inch system the screws are defined by nominal diameter and number of threads per inch. Usually, smaller diameter screws may have more threads per inch than larger diameter.

In the US, the most common threads are American National standard Unified National threads. These threads are produced as coarse, fine, and extra fine.

1. **UNC/UNRC (unified national coarse threads)**: They are used for easy assembly and disassembly of components. These threads are used for low strength application. For example, ¼" UNC screw has 20 threads per inch. UNC and UNRC threads are identical except their root diameter. UNRC system is used for the external threads only. These are rolled threads with

rounded root diameter to prevent stress concentration. The rounded root provides extra fatigue strength to the screws. The rolling of threads is done on a special thread rolling machine.

2. **UNF/UNRF (unified national fine threads):** These threads are used for high-strength applications and tubes with thin wall. Also, UNF threads are specified when the part is subjected to vibration. UNRF threads have rounded root to improve fatigue in the screws or bolts. For example, ¼" UNF screw has 28 threads per inch as compared to 20 TPI for UNC threads.

3. **UNEF/UNREF (unified national extra fine threads):** These threads are used where the mating parts have thin wall. For example, for UNEF 0.2160" (no.12), diameter screw has 32 threads per inch.

4. **UNM (unified national miniature threads)**

The threads are described as below:

½-13 UNC-3A-LH means the thread has ½" nominal diameter, 13 threads per inch-left hand.

Class of Threads

For fitting reason, the designer of the equipment specifies the class of threads. Class of threads is based on the tolerance allowed. The external threads are specified by 1A, 2A, and 3A, while internal threads are specified by 1B, 2B, and 3B.

Unified Threads

Class Fit	External (screw or bolt)	Internal (nut)
Class 1—loose	1A	1B
Class 2—standard	2A	2B
Class 3—Close fit	3A	3B

For assembly purpose, the most common threads are specified with class 2A and 2B fit.

The other two threads are UNS (unified national special) and UNJ, where the minor diameter of threads is large.

International Standard Organization

In the ISO system, the threads are described by nominal diameter in mm, pitch, and class fit. Example:

M12 × 1.75 6g × 75

Here *M* stands for metric, 12 is nominal diameter in mm, 1.75 is pitch in mm, 6g is a class of fit, and 75 mm is length of the part

Metric

Fit	External (screw)	Internal (nut)
Loose	8g	7h
Standard	6g	6h
Close	4g	5h

Pipe Thread

The thread standard for coupling pipes is called American National Standard Taper Pipe or commonly called NPT. There is 60 degree angle between the two threads and a taper of ¾ inch per foot. The typical pipe threads are 1/16, 1/8, ¼, 3/8, ½, ¾, 1, 1-1/4" and higher size. Typical ¼" size has 18 threads per inch while ½" has 14 threads per inch.

In the NPT category, we also have NPTF (fine) threads. BSPT is common thread in Europe. This is used for pipe and pneumatic fittings. BSPT stands for British standard pipe taper. While NPT (US) system has 60 degree, the BSPT system has 55 degree angle between the thread crests. BSPT and NPT threads have different pitches. The British system also has parallel pipe system called BSPP. In this system, the threads are not tapered.

The following are additional straight threads systems for joining pipes:

National hose / national standard thread	NH/NST
American National Standard Taper Pipe threads for railing joints	NPTR
Garden hose thread	GHT
National pipe straight or parallel threads coupling (pressure tight joint)	NPSC
National pipe straight hose	NPSH (loose free fitting)
National pipe straight mechanical	NPSM (free fitting mechanical joint)
National electric lamp socket thread	

Pipe Size Measuring Tools

The size of threaded pipe components can only be checked by gauges and published tables in the machinery handbooks. For maintenance purpose, major manufacturing companies stock the pipe fittings such as: couplings, 90- and 45-degree elbows, tees, crosses, square head plugs, and threaded pipe nipples in various sizes. It is essential to keep quick tools to check the pipe size of threads. The following are commercially available tools to check the size of fittings.

Thread Pitch and Pipe Size Measuring Kit

Please note for a typical pipe size of 1/8", the actual outside diameter of pipe is 0.405" and for 1" pipe the pipe outside diameter is 1.315". This could be source of confusion for anybody. As such, these kits could be great help for maintenance crew of any major manufacturing facility.

Pipe fittings are made from steel forgings, castings, bar stock, stainless steel, and brass. Fittings are made for low- and high-pressure applications. They are available from 1/8" to 4" pipe sizes.

Power transmission threads are additional threads for transmitting load and allow rotation.

Square thread is difficult to manufacture; however, it can couple two parts and transmit load.

Acme thread is a common thread for machines and used as lead screws on manual lathes with a half nut. These threads have 29 degree angle on each face.

Buttress threads have one side slanted and other side square. These threads are very strong in one direction. There is a 45 degree angle between the vertical and slant sides.

Screw Thread Terms

The following terms are used for thread forms:

1. Major diameter—It is the outside diameter of threads of external threads and the internal major diameter.
2. Minor diameter—It is common for both the external bolt and internal nut.
3. Pitch diameter—It is the diameter where the space and width of threads are same.
4. Pitch—It is the space between crest of two threads.
5. Lead—When turning, screw advances one complete pitch on a single-threaded screw. The pitch and lead of single-threaded screw are the same. On a double-threaded screw, the screw advances twice with one turn.
6. Thread depth—It is distance between the crest and root of thread.
7. Angle of thread—It is the angle between two sides.
8. Helix angle—It is the angle between a vertical line, the thread at pitch diameter.

Screw Pitch Gauge

This a commercially available gauge used to check sizes of bolts and nuts. It consists of set of blades that have notches to suit different standard pitches of threads. This is a very helpful tool to check the sizes of nuts and bolts on any machinery. They are available both in inch and metric system.

The following are some of the categories of threads for the **hydraulic fittings**:

1. UN/UNF—Unified
2. NPT/NPTF—American Tapered Pipe Thread
3. BSPP—British Standard Pipe Parallel
4. BSPT—BSP tapered-Metric Parallel and Metric Tapered

The Japanese Industrial standard threads for parallel and tapered parts are similar to British Standard

British Screw Threads

The following are main categories:

1. BSW-British Standard Whitworth—Thread angle is 55 Degrees. The UN and UNF threads have 60 degree angle
2. BSF---British standard fine thread
3. BSP –British standard pipe thread (Parallel)
4. BSPT-British standard pipe Thread (Tapered)
5. BA-British Association—Miniature thread

A. For example ¼" BSW threads has 20 threads per inch, while ¼" BSF threads have 26 threads per inch
B. B. For example ¼" BSP (parallel) threads are 19 threads per 1" while ¼" BSPT (tapered) and have 19 threads per inch.

Attachments:

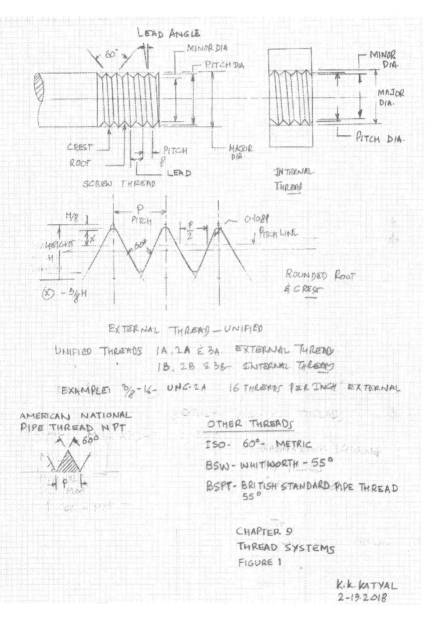

Fig. 1—Unified ext threads

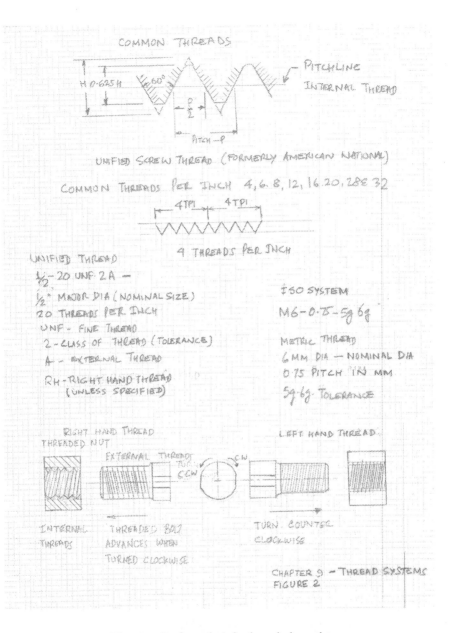

Fig. 2—Left and right hand threads

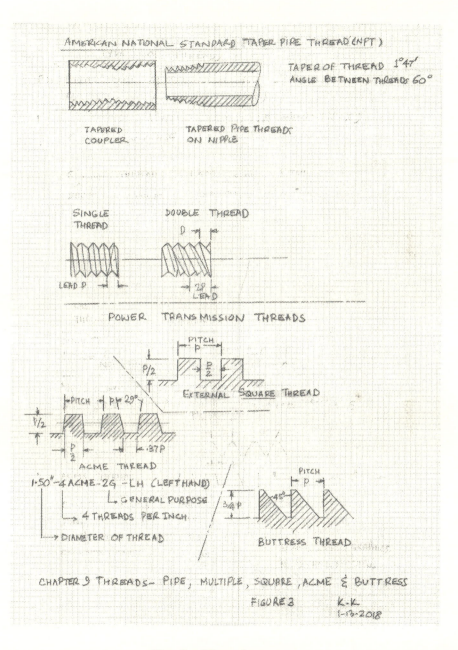

Fig. 3—Thread systems

CHAPTER 10

Shaping of Materials

Topics covered are hot forgings, cold forming, sheet metal terminology, stampings and presses, small presses, press dies, press operation, materials for stampings, press and coil processing equipment, CNC turret punching machines, thread rolling, plate rolling-2, 3, and 4 roll machines, press brakes, roll forming, hydroforming, hot isostatic pressing (HIP), and metal spinning.

STEEL IS COMMERCIALLY sold in the form of plate, sheet, tube, pipe, rounds, hex bars, wire, and structural shapes.

Steel plates are further cut by various processes. They are bent and rolled to make machine tools, ships, locomotives, windmills, etc. According to an article written by Steven Weber in *Assembly* magazine in August 2018, GE Locomotives may contain up to 80,000 pounds of fabricated steel. Steel bars are further threaded or rolled to make the foundation of street lamp posts, windmills and to strengthen bridge slabs.

The design engineer takes the help of various manufacturing methods used to shape the material for its usage. The following are some of the methods to shape the raw materials:

1. Hot forgings
2. Cold forming, drawing, extrusion, and upsetting
3. Stamping
4. Rolling of threads

5. Rolling of plates and bending of angles, channels, tube, and pipes
6. Fabrication of sheet steel
7. Hydroforming
8. Hot isostatic pressing
9. Cold isostatic pressing
10. Metal spinning

Nearly all shapes of material will experience tension, compression, and shear during its lifetime. The product engineer uses the materials' ultimate tensile strength, yield strength, and ductility to design the metal parts.

The design engineer takes the help of various manufacturing methods to shape the material for its usage. The following are some of the methods to shape the raw materials:

Hot Forging

According to www.forging.org, the most common forged items are wrenches and hammers. A Boeing 747 has close to 18,000 forged items. Automobiles, agriculture equipment, and mining equipment have number of forged items.

Forging is the process of heating the material to plastic state. This reshaping of raw steel and other metals is done by heating and using forging equipment with a set of dies. Forged parts are stronger than machined parts. In forged items, the material grain flows along the outline of the part, while in machined items, the grain is broken. Forging improves strength and toughness of the final piece. For a forging made from 1020 steel, the blank material is heated to about 2,200 to 2,400°F before forming in the press.

The following are three major kinds of forging processes:

A. Open-die forging—The heated material is forced between flat or shaped Dies. The flow of squeezed material is not restricted. Most common parts made by this process are Discs, Rings,

Shafting, Bars and Blocks. In this process, for some time reheating of the part may be required

B. Closed-die or impression-die forging—In this process the plastic deformation of heated steel stays inside the 2- part die. A small amount of flash does take place around the two halves of the dies. Most of the commercially produced parts do use the closed die forging process.

C. Rolled-ring forging process—The process consists of upsetting piece of round heated stock. The rounded –mushroom type piece is pierced with a punch. The punch piece is then rolled with ID and OD Rollers to make a rolled ring.

The other forgings processes are upsetting, bending, swaging, and weld forging.

The following are types of the forging equipments:

1. Hammer with high energy could go up to 50,000 lbs. force
2. Mechanical presses with stroke adjustment
3. Hydraulic presses with the limit of pressure
4. Screw Presses
5. Induction heaters

Forging related websites:

www.forgingmagazine.com, www.trentforge.com, www.bharat forge.com, www.clifford-jacob.com, www.cantonforge.com (closed die forging), www.commercialforgedproducts.com, www.mcinnesrolle drings.com, www.atimetals.com, www.pccforgedproducts.com, www.patriotforge.com, and https://www.butechbliss.com/our-products/extrusion-forging-equipment.

Key Forging Companies websites:

1. www.standardsteel.com—This company has been in business since 1791. They are the leading manufacturer of forged steel wheels and axles for freight cars, locomotives, and passenger

railcars. This company is based in Burnham, Pennsylvania. It is owned by Nippon Steel and Sumitomo Metal Corporation.
2. www.whemco.com—This company is based in Pittsburg, Pennsylvania. It provides the following services:
   - Melting and casting—The company can melt and pour 130 tons of steel and can make casting up to 90 tons.
   - Forging—This company can forge part up to 165 tons using 10,000 ton hydraulic press. It can provide steel mill rolls, marine shafts, and mill liners. Additionally, this company can provide heat treatment and machining.
3. www.andersonshumaker.com—Chicago-based company that provides open-die forging.

Equipment:
   2,500 ton hydraulic forging press
   Three steam-driven hammers (4,000, 3,500, and 6,000)
   Two ring rollers
4. www.kroppforge.com—Chicago-area company that does closed-die and open-die forging.

Equipment:
   Steam-driven hammers from 6,000 to 50,000 lbs.
   Hydraulic forging presses from 750, 1,000, 1,500 to 2,500 tons
5. www.scotforge.com—The company does open- and semi-closed die forging. It has the following equipment:
   Large press 16,500 tons with four post with 2,000 ton upset
   Pneumatic hammers, ring mill, and bar rolling

6. www.viking-fiorge.com—The company has the following major equipment:
   400 kW to 2,000 kw induction heaters
   1,300 to 4,000 ton forging presses
   125 to 400 ton trim presses

Materials for Forging

Forgings are made both from ferrous and nonferrous materials. The most forged items use carbon steel, stainless steel, aluminum alloys, titanium, brass, copper, and alloy steels.

The following are other similar processes:

1. Drawing of bar, wire, and tube—This is a cold-drawing process, where the material is pulled through a set of dies to reduce its diameter. This process is carried out at a room temperature; however, the material could be hot or warm to improve its ductility. The final shape of material could be round, flat, or hex shape.

The drawing of steel tube requires an internal mandrel. The wires are drawn usually held on payoff tray and then pulled through a set of dies. The dies are usually conical with bell-shaped mouth on the entry size.

The dies are made from tool steels, such as AISI type M2, D2, or tungsten carbide.

2. Hot extrusions—This process involves the use of very high hydraulic force to push heated billet of copper, aluminum, brass, or steel through a shaped die. The extruded sections could be thin, thick, or hollow. The ultimate extruded shape has uniform properties and good surface finish. Aluminum is a good material to extrude architectural shapes and tubes. Magnesium and its alloys are extruded for aircraft parts. Zinc and copper alloys are also extruded.
3. Cold and warm extrusion—This process provides net shape to the part, and as such, there is no material loss. Some steel and nonferrous metals are extruded. The process uses mechanical and hydraulic presses. Mechanical presses are used for high production. They have lower tonnage capacity.

Hydraulic presses have higher tonnage, lower speed, and long stroke. Both kind of presses use dies and punches made from M2 and M4 tool steel. These tools have hardness of 62 to 64 Rockwell C.

For aluminum extrusion, the material is heated above 800°F before processed by horizontal hydraulic press. The extruded shape could be hollow (tube) or solid.

4. Upsetting (See more information under cold forming)—This process is used for parts that have T-shape. Cold upsetting machines are used to make heads of nails, bolts, screws, and rivets. Upsetting increase the strength of the material. This is an economical way of increasing the shape of material without increasing the main diameter of blank. The process uses special die and punch to create the head at fast speed. Upsetting is done both cold and hot. For machinery information, visit www.ajax-ceco.com.
5. Swaging—This process is used to reduce the outside diameter of tubular part. The process could involve tapering, outer forming, or squeezing the material. The process is used for tubular heaters and attaching a round hollow part to a rebar. The method involves quick blows or pulling of the material through a die.

Cold Forming

The process is a combination of upsetting, forging, and extrusion. The related process is called cold heading. Machines used for this process are called headers. Similar to upsetting, this process is used for making nails, screws, bolts, nuts, electrical contacts, rivets, pen parts, and electronic parts.

The process cuts the coiled metal wire or bar to length. The cut slug or wire piece is passed through several tools and die stations to forge or extrude to final shape at room temperature. The slug is hammered or hit several times while being moved from one station to next. This automatic process makes metal parts without machining. It is a chip-less forming operation. The following are the benefits of cold forming:

1. Reduces total manufacturing cost
2. Provides good surface quality
3. Reduces material cost
4. Finished parts are stronger than machined parts

This is a high-speed process, which creates no scrap and provides hundreds of parts per hour using wire from 0.010 to 1" diameter metal wire and rod.

The tool and die alter the material to final shape. The material in these stations is worked just beyond yield point and not beyond tensile strength.

The tooling is made from tool steel and carbide.

Warm Forming

This process is used for making aerospace hot-formed parts from titanium, stainless steel, alloy steel, and inconel. The process uses header machine with induction heater for the blank or slug.

Cold-forming machine builders are www.nedschroef.com, www.sacmagroup.com, and www.nationalmachine.com.

Magazines related to cold forming: www.fastenertech.com, www.wireformingtech.com, and www.linkmagazine.com.

The following companies provide cold-forming services:

    www.stsintelli.com
    www.bdcoldneadedproducts.com
    www.akkofastener.com
    www.reedandprince.com
    www.flaig-hummel.de

Sheet Metal Terminology

Steel, stainless steel, aluminum, copper, and brass are used in the form of sheet and coil for stampings. In addition, flat sheets are cut by laser and bent on press brakes and welded.

Sheet metal thickness is specified as gauge number. The following are two standards for gauges:

1. US standard gauge system is used to specify sheet steel or its alloys.
2. American standard wire gauge or brown and sharpe gauge are used for nonferrous metals such as stainless steel, aluminum, copper, etc.

The design engineer selects the sheet metal based on tensile strength, yield point, and factors such as ductility and brittleness.

Commercially, steels are available as hot rolled; cold rolled; hot-dip, galvanized; electrolytic, zinc-coated with ASTM number and certain finish.

Stamping and Presses (For Sheet Metal)

Stamping is a high-speed process where thin sheet metal parts are formed by feeding suitable-size steel or metal to a set of dies held in a power press. The force for stamping is transmitted by moving slide or ram. The die consists of two halves. One part of the die is held to upper slide, while other part is bolted to bolster or bed of the press. The material is subjected to shearing, deep drawing, stretching, bending, and coining. The automotive industry is the biggest user of stampings.

Stamping Terms

Material thickness used for stamping could vary from 0.005" to 3/8". The stampings use the following multiple steps: shearing, blanking, punching, lancing, trimming, slitting, bending, deep drawing, embossing, coining, etc.

1. Shearing—It is cutting the material by sharp blades. One of the common machines in a sheet metal shop is a plain shear, which cuts thin sheet plate. However, the same process is used for cutting of scrap on the power presses.
2. Blanking—The flat sheet material cut by punch and die and is further used as a workable piece is called a blank. For high production, punch and die are an economical way of making blanks. However, for small requirements, laser cutting is an ideal method of making blanks.
3. Punching—It is the opposite of blanking. Usually, the punched material (or slug) is discarded while the rest of piece is used.
4. Lancing—It is the process for making louvers in sheet metal. These louvers are used on outside covers of commercial and residential air conditioning units. This process cuts the material without removing a scrap.
5. Trimming—It is a process of removing excess material after deep drawing or other forming operation.
6. Slitting—This process is used for roll of thin sheet metal. It uses a set of slitting wheels or cutters. Companies that make galvanized ducts for air conditioning buy slit coiled material.
7. Bending—It is a process of bending sheet metal with a certain radius or angle with a die set.
8. Deep drawing—The method is used to make deep or shallow cup shapes in sheet metal. It is done on a blank whose outer periphery is held tight on a shaped die while using formed punch.
9. Embossing—This is a process for forming shallow indentation, letter, or ribs on a sheet metal.
10. Coining—This is used to imprint certain design in a closed die. This process is used for making coins.

Sheet Metal Presses

The old press frames were made of cast iron. New presses are made from steel fabrications. The new steel press provides safety factor when overloaded. The press could be partly made by steel fabricated and partly made of cast iron. The press includes frame, ram, suitable electric motor, and controls.

Presses are rated by tonnage. The following are major categories of presses:

1. Mechanical presses—These presses use flywheel and crankshaft. Most common are C- frame or gap-frame presses (open back inclinable and straight). C-frame presses are available in 30- to 60-ton range. The other mechanical presses are available in straight-side and round-column press design. Mechanical presses are good for faster output. Large straight-side mechanical presses are rated between 30 to 600 tons and run from 10 to 20 strokes per minute.
2. Hydraulic presses—They are provided with complete hydraulic package. Hydraulic uses a pump and set of valves to provide optimum pressure to complete deep-drawing process. They are protected by relief valves. Their tonnage and stroke could be adjusted. They usually use large electric motors than mechanical presses. Beside sheet metal, these presses are used for sheet molding compound (see www.enprotech.com and www.beckwoodpresses.com). For hydraulic presses, visit www.multipress.com
3. Manual presses—They are hand and foot operated and used for light duty work.
4. Servo-driven presses—These are designed for high torque and low speed. These presses provide good accuracy. According to "Servo Advantages," an article written by Louis A. Kern of *Metal Forming* magazine in January 2018, servomotor on the press is able to control velocity changes of ram. The customer is able to program velocity for forming operation. Servo system

can especially control deep-drawing steps and spring back of high-strength material.
5. Pneumatic presses—They are low-cost units and used for light-duty purpose.

Selection of Press

This depends on the size, thickness, and the metal of the parts to be stamped. The press should have sufficient force and speed to make the parts. The press bed should have sufficient area for the die set.

Small Presses

Bench-type presses are available for small manufacturing operation. They can be used for watch-making, sign-making, electronic assembly, and riveting. These presses are available for low-volume and high-volume production. The following are some of the smaller presses:

A. Arbor press—This is a hand-operated press. The force is applied by a lever. These presses do not need external power and used for low-volume parts requirement.
B. Air/oil press—This press does not need external hydraulic power unit. To create hydraulic force, the air is used over oil. These presses can have a stroke of an inch and can be fitted two-hand control and safety light curtain.
C. Hydraulic Press—This press is full hydraulic and can be provided all safety controls.

The following are small press manufacturers websites: www.beckwoodpresses.com, www.emgpresses.com, www.durable-tech.com, www.carverpress.com, www.plastgrommet.com, www.schmidtpresses.com, www.janome-ie.com (for swaging, riveting, and coining), and www.stipmpson.com

Press Technologies

According to Victor Cassidy of *Fabrication News*, the following are some of the new technologies in the press room:

1. Remote press diagnostics for trouble shooting
2. Circle grid analysis as an Analytical tool
3. Software to simulate forming process
4. Die try out using Zinc
5. Pick and place robot
6. Press design by FEA technology
7. Feed system and parts transfer using servos
8. Controls for material coil handling system
9. Hydraulic straightener for material

Press Anti-Vibration Upgrades

Vibrations are present on running presses, CNC mills, thread rolling machines, trucks, cars, compressors, etc. Somehow there are more vibrations on high-speed presses and power brakes. Excessive vibration can reduce the life of the equipment.

To reduce shocks and vibrations, a proper vibration damping mounts are necessary in the foundation of the machinery. Vibration dampers can reduce the foundation thickness for the presses.

For more information, visit www.Qontroldevicesinc.com and www.efdyn.com.

Press Operations

Most of the stamped components in automobiles, kitchen appliances, cloth washers, and dryers are made by mechanical and hydraulic presses. To improve the efficiency of stamping operation, a continuous coil-fed feeding system is installed with the power presses. The material is usually purchased in the form coil and which could be 1" to 48" wide. The system consists of an uncoiler, roller straightener, feeder, and scrap processor. (For coil feeding system, see www.Littell.com.) This system flattens the curved material in the coils. For some application, the material is fed through a stretching operation.

Press Dies

Dies are made according to the component drawings. Some dies combine several stages of the forming operation and are called progressive dies. These dies include an ejection mechanism for the finished stamped parts.

The special die set mounted in the power press gap helps in making the stamping. The force of the press forms the final part. The following are the advantages of stamping process:

1. Low cost
2. Good strength
3. Can produce complex shapes with ease
4. Clean finish as long the Die sets is highly polished
5. Die helps in making high-volume parts.

For more info on die sets, visit www.diesetsinc.com.

Materials for Stamping

Stampings are usually made from steel, alloy steel, and nonferrous thin metal strips. The material should be ductile enough to accept drawing tools without cracking. The steel is usually low carbon (0.05% to 0.20%). The steel could be cold rolled (CRS) or hot rolled (HRS) depending on strength and finished required. Nonferrous materials may include aluminum, stainless steel, copper, etc.

Note: Presses are also used to punch blank material from a coil of steel. For high-volume blank requirements, the presses are being replaced by coil-fed fiber laser. This method eliminates mechanical dies and burrs and provides good edge quality. For more information, visit www.blankingwithoutdies.com.

The following are some of the related websites that can provide latest information about equipment and technology: www.metalforming magazine.com and www.thefabricator.com.

The following are press and coil processing equipment manufacturers: www.eaglepress.com, www.seyi.com, www.jier-na.com, www.cpec.com, www.komatsupress.com, wwwpentaflex.com, www.schulergroup.com, www.aptgroup.com, www.greenerd.com, www.dallasindustries.com, www.neffpress.com, www.aida-global.com, www.bihler.de (slide NC and servo stamping and forming machines), www.kalamazoometalmuncher.com (for punch, shear, coper, and notcher), www.stamtec.com, www.littell.com, and www.coltauto.com.

Glimpse of press manufacture www.seyi.com (type of equipment manufactured):

1. Straight-side mechanical press
2. Servo press
3. C-frame mechanical press
4. Tandem presses for automation for automobile industry

Glimpse of hydraulic press manufacturer (www.multipress.com):

1. Bench-type press 1–20 ton
2. C-frame-floor type 20–200 ton
3. Four-column press from 20 to 1000 ton

Glimpse of www.komatsupress.com (equipment range):

1. Straight side press 200 metric ton to 4800 m.ton
2. Mechanical Gap frames from 35 m. ton t 200 m.ton
3. Servo straight side press

Glimpse of www.aptgroup.com (automation press and tooling) make servo-driven hydraulic presses for deep drawing and embossing.

For stampings suppliers, visit www.ssprod.com, www.quasar.com (hydroforming), and www.truexinc.com (hose fittings).

CNC Turret Punching Machine

Prior to the introduction of the CO_2 laser metal cutting machine, the most popular method of cutting sheet metal was CNC turret punch machine. Some of US shops still have this equipment though they are used very sparingly. These machines are built with 20- to 30-ton force hydraulic punches. These machines are much slower than CO_2 laser cutting machine.

These machines are provided with set of grippers to hold the steel sheet. The CNC system provides cutting, punching, bending, and tapping of sheet. For more information, visit www.lvdgroup.com for Strippit PX and VX models.

Thread Rolling

This is a cold-forming method of making threads. Thread Rolling machines are used for rolling threads, worm gears, serrations, ball screws, and knurling on the outside diameter of bars. This method of rolling provides high-surface hardness and high-tensile strength to the part. This method of threading was patented in Germany in 1877.

Generally, most machined parts threads are cut on manual or CNC lathes. The machining or removing of material makes the cross section weaker for critical application. Thread rolling improves the tensile strength, shear, and fatigue strength in a metal bar.

For solid bars, the process requires two-roll machine. The rolls are designed with the required thread form. The material should be ductile enough to flow into the grooves of the thread rolls during the compressive rolling process.

Thread rolls are special machines, which are provided with one to two hydraulic cylinders. The blank round material to roll should have the pitch diameter of the threads you are trying to make.

The two common methods of rolling are In - Feed and Through-Feed. The in-feed method is used for smaller individual parts. The through-feed method is used for longer bars, which need continuous threads.

The following are the advantages of thread rolling:

1. The rolled thread form follows the grain structure of the metal.
2. The process increases tensile strength, fatigue, and hardness of the rolled surface.
3. This provides good surface finish.

Materials for thread rolling:

1. Low-carbon and medium-carbon steels (1005, 1095, 12L14, 1111 and 1144) are easy to roll with low pressure of rolls.
2. Hardened high-speed steel and stainless steel (304 and 316) need very high pressures and rounded grooves.

Personally, I was involved with through-feed rolling for fifteen years in which bars for reinforcing concrete for bridges and windmill foundations were made.

For thread rolling machines, check www.ortitalia.com, www.tesker.com, www.pee.de.com, www.kinefac.com, and www.reed-machinery.com.

Thread rolling contract manufacturers are www.rolledthreads.com and www.rayindustries.com.

Related show: www.fastenershows.com—International Fastener Expo (Las Vegas, October 30, 2018)

Plate Rolling

Plate bending rollers are used for making round cylindrical shape from 1/16" thick to 3" thick steel. This equipment is used to make windmill cone sections, large electric generator housings, pressure vessels, road and railroad tank cars, and large vertical storage tanks.

Plate bending rolls assist in rolling eight to ten feet long tank shells, which are subsequently welded at the seam. Usually a flat plate material is fed to three or four roll Machine. The operator pre bends the both ends of the plate, which is then rolled. The machines for bending are available for different strength of materials, roll lengths, and roll diameters.

Different Kinds of Plate Rolls

Two-Roll Bending Machines

Two-roll machines consist of lower adjustable urethane roll and an upper role with the inside diameter of the required piece part. The top roll is a die for the final piece part. These machines are used for rolling material 0.010" thick to 0.180" mild steel.

Three-Roll Bending Machines

These machines are used to roll mild steel from 3/16" to 4" thick material. In this machine, flat material is inserted between top and bottom and pinched.

By turning the roll, the leading edge is pre bent with the help of third roll. The pre bent sheet is taken out, and the other end is inserted to make pre bend on the second side. The final piece is rolled at second insertion.

Four-Roll Bending Machine

With this machine, we are able to pre bend both ends of the steel plate in one insertion. These machines have a CNC control and are used for making windmill tower cones, rocket housings, and other high-precision tank.

Several large fabrication shops have three- to four-roll plate rolling machines. The following are some of the known manufacturers and distributors of rolls:

Bertsch Roll—www.megafab.com
Swebend angle and plate roll—www.trilogymachinery.com
www.comeq.com
www.davi.com
www.faccin.com
www.rocciasrl.con

For bending of angles, channels, plates, and pipes, all of the above companies provide special equipment. To contact manufacturers of rolled tanks, visit www.cmrp.com (Chicago Metal Rolled Products) and www.aasteelfab.com for contract manufacturing information. For Tube bending, visit www.hydrotube.com. Outside US, visit www.tecknoweld.com.

For wire bending, visit www.generalchain.com, and for machine, visit www.4slide-nc.com.

Bending of Sheet Steel

Sheet steel is purchased flat for bending. They could be purchased such as 1/16" × 48" × 96". Beside shears, most good fabricating shops have a laser cutting machine. With the use of suitable software, the pieces are cut flat according to the final desired shape and then bent on the press brakes.

Press Brakes

These are used to form different angles on sheet metal. Typical parts made by press brakes are metal cabinets, electrical control cabinets, and telecommunication equipment housings.

Press brakes are classified as mechanical or hydraulic. Usually, hydraulic brakes have higher tonnage. The bed of press brake is designed to hold dies, while ram holds the punch. Press brakes are available from 4- to 25-foot lengths.

Power Squaring Shears

Beside laser power cutting, mechanical shearing equipment is an essential part of fabrication shop. Shears are used to cut the sheet metal before other operations are performed.

Power shears are classified according to the following:

1. Material thickness it can cut
2. Type of material it can shear (carbon steel, aluminum, stainless steel sheet, etc.)

3. Length of part to be cut
4. Mechanical or hydraulic
5. Maximum tonnage

Manufacturers of press brakes and shears are www.e-ci.com (Cincinnati Inc.), www.trumpf.com, www.lvdgroup.com, www.bystronicusa.com, www.betenbender.com (for hydraulic shear), www.trilogymachinery.com, www.amada.com/america.com, and www.butechbliss.com for heavy duty shear.

Sheet metal manufacturers are www.modeindustries.com, www.laystrom.com, www.marcolighting.com, and www.mjcelco.com.

Related show for sheet metal equipment is www.fabtechexpo.com.

Roll Forming

This process uses a coiled sheet strip to mass produce metal shapes at a high speed. The roll-formed shapes are used for angles, channels, seamed tubes, sign posts, automotive trims, store fixtures, aerospace, office furniture, solar, conveyors, rain water gutters, and truck components.

The machine consists of contour-shaped set of rolls through which steel or metal strip is pulled through at a high speed. This process is used to make thousands of parts in a year.

Materials such as cold-rolled steel, hot-rolled steel, stainless steel, aluminum, and brass are used to roll form shapes. The cost of roll formed depends on the cost of tooling, material, direct labor, and overhead cost.

For more information, visit www.voestalpine.com, www.rollerdie.com, www.cardinalmfg.com, and www.superiorrollforming.com.

Hydroforming

This process is used for deep drawing thin ductile metal parts. It uses the force of high-hydraulic pressure with a rubber pad.

A hydroform press may use a ½" or more thick rubber pad. The blank material to be formed is held between upper rubber pad and a lower-shaped punch. The hydraulic pressure is applied from top and bottom and on all sides of the blank material.

The rubber with a blank metal takes the shape of the lower punch and returns to original shape when hydraulic pressure is retracted. In this method, the thinning of the material is eliminated.

Some of the components for oil pipe line and tubular frame components for trucks and cars are being made by this process. The process uses the ductile material for pipe or tube. This hollow piece is kept between two halves of the final desired shape of die. Hydraulic pressure is applied to the tube. The pressure of oil forms the shape.

Verson Allsteel Press of Chicago is one of the builders of hydroform presses in 1960s through early 80s. Chicago-area original manufacturers' Verson and Danly presses are being made by a Japanese Co. (www.enprotech.com). This information is based on their website.

For more information, visit www.americanhydroformers.com, www.overtyonind.com (tube forming), and http://www.nikko-bulgeform.co.jp/e/company/company.html.

Hot Isostatic Pressing (HIP)

Engineers are always concerned about the porosity or density of critical parts for jet engines and defense-related parts. Also, it is difficult to assure 100% density of investment casting, forged, and cast alloy components.

To assure soundness, parts are subjected to hot isostatic pressing. The process consists of loading critical parts in a pressure vessel. The parts are then pressurized with argon gas from 20,000 to 30,000 psi. The vessel is further heated to very high temperature. The heat and high pressure of gas makes the parts dense.

The following are some of the companies involved with hot isostatic pressing:

www.atimetals.com
www.aiphip.com (American Isostatic Pressing)
www.pressuretechnology.com
www.isostatictollservices.com
www.quintustechnologies.com.

Another process called cold isostatic process (CIP) uses no heat to form metal or ceramic powders inside an elastomer/rubber mold. The rubber mold is compressed with high-pressure water (from 30 to 60 ksi). For more information, visit www.epsi.com, www.nikkiso.com, and www.dorst.de for equipment.

Metal Spinning

This is a low-cost method of making hollow sheet metal parts, which are circular and symmetrical around the central axis. It is used to make low-volume kitchen utensils, lighting domes, cones, and lids.

For high-volume parts, deep drawing on a press will be economical. As compared to deep drawing, the cost of tooling and lead time for spinning are very low.

The process consists of using predetermined size of thin sheet metal disc or deep-drawn preform. The machine used for the purpose is similar to a manual or CNC lathe. The chuck holds the mandrel, which has the inside shape of the part. The blank is held between specially designed rotating mandrel and the tail stock.

To form the shape, a rotating roll is pressed against the rotating disc. Multiple passes are required to finally shape the part against the mandrel. Some machines have more than two rolls to finish the shape. This is a cold-forming process which increases the strength of the material.

Due to size and thickness, before spinning, certain blanks may require the heating of blanks by gas or induction heater.

Metal Flow Forming

This process is used for high-strength tubular or hollow parts using preformed or deep-drawn parts. This process may need internal and external set of rolls to shape the part.

For more information, please visit the following website:

https://www.thefabricator.com/article/stamping/metal-spinning-versus-flow-forming

Some of the companies involved in metal spinning are www.owlandergren.com, www.cmspinning.com, www.krytonmetals.com, www.amsind.com, and www.ohiometalfab.com.

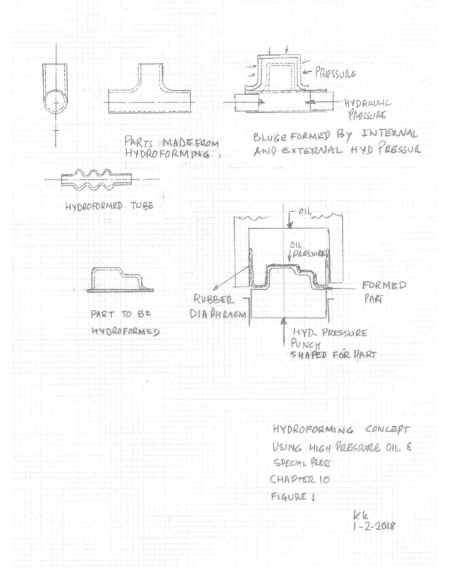

Fig.1—Hydroforming

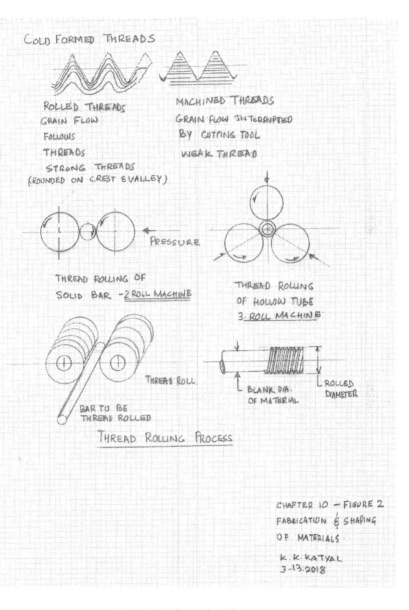

Fig. 2—Thread rolling

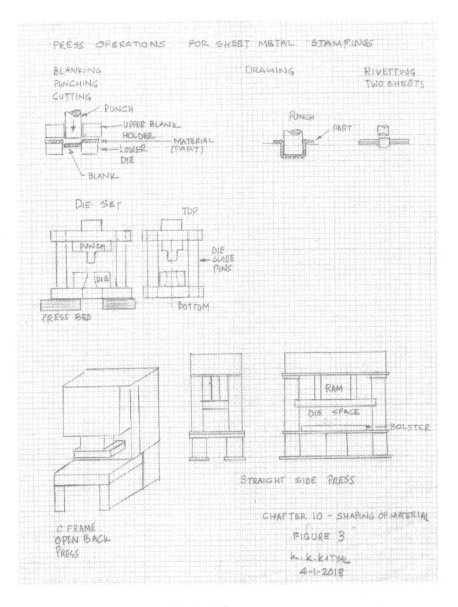

Fig.3—Shape press

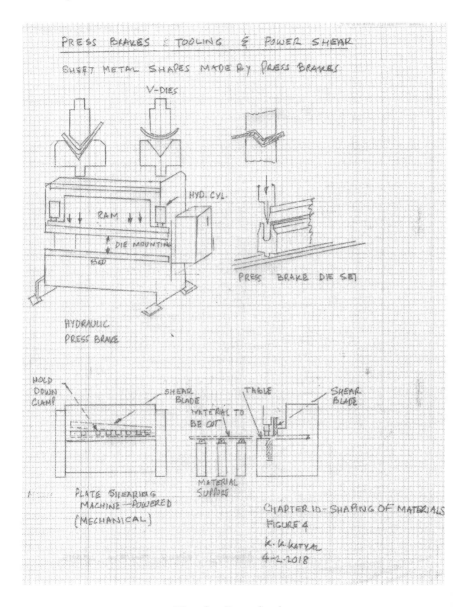

Fig. 4—Press brake

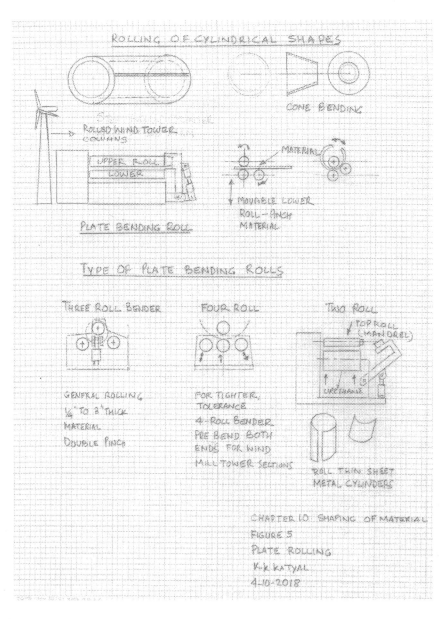

Fig. 5—Plate rolling

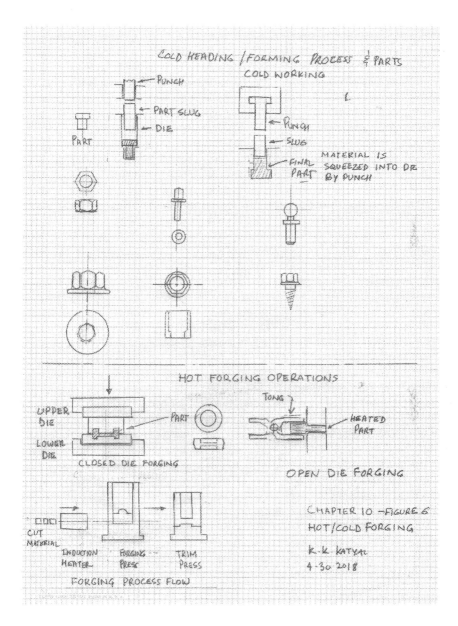

Fig. 6—Hot-cold forge

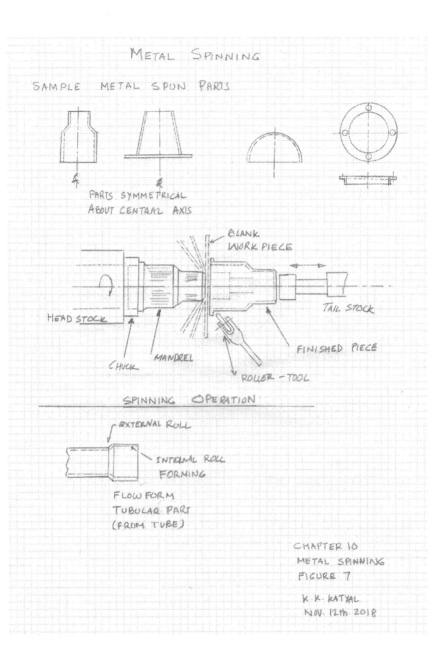

Fig. 7—Metal spinning

Prestige metal press brake operation

CHAPTER 11

Welding Methods

Topics covered are gas metal arc welding (GMAW-MIG), flux-cored arc welding (FCAW), gas tungsten arc welding (GTAW-TIG), shielded metal arc welding (SMAW-Stick), submerged-arc welding, electro slag welding, selection of welding electrodes, solid wire selection, commercially available steel for welding, weld preparation, friction welding, resistance welding, glimpse of welding equipment manufacturers websites, gas welding, electron-beam welding, laser welding, gouging, brazing, welding cost, heat treatment of welded assemblies, and quality check for welds.

THE PURPOSE OF welding is to join metals together with heat and filler metals. Experienced welders are employed by steel fabricators, ship builders, railroad coach builders, and steel bridge fabricators. Also, welders actively support the maintenance of large and small power and chemical plants.

The welding process adheres to American Welding Society codes. The codes are also issued by American Society of Mechanical Engineers and American Petroleum Institute.

I had the opportunity to work with one of the world's largest welding shops, which made diesel electric locomotives. The shop had hundreds of welding machines using stick, MIG, flux-cored, submerged-arc, and electroslag welding equipment.

The electroslag process is an uncommon method, which consist of welding two large thick plates with gaps from 1" to 4". The most common weld joints are fillet welds and groove welds. Fillet weld joints are of *T*-shape while the groove weld could be beveled or *U*-shape.

Arc welding methods are used both for production and maintenance. In the welding process, the arc is created between the work to be welded and the electrode. The heat of arc melts the electrode and the work piece. The molten metal solidifies to make strong joint.

The design, welding, or manufacturing engineer has to select the best filler material electrode, welding method and fixturing to hold the parts together. Material to be welded can be low or high-carbon steel, alloys, and nonferrous metals. Widely used steel is low carbon. It is also called mild steel. This steel is ductile and easy to weld. The common designations for these steels are 1020 and 1025. The following are carbon contents of some of the steels.

> Low carbon—0.1% to 0.3%
> Medium carbon—0.3% to 0.45%
> High carbon—0.45% to 0.65%
> Very high-carbon steel—0.65% to 1.5%

The following are most common methods of welding:

> Gas metal-arc welding MIG (GMAW)—The process uses solid metal wire electrode.
> Flux-cored welding (FCAW)—The process uses hollow-core wire as electrode.
> Gas tungsten welding TIG (GTAW)—This process may or not use filler electrodes.
> Shielded metal-arc welding (SMAW) stick—This uses flux-covered electrode rod.
> Submerged-arc welding (SAW)—This uses bare metal wire electrode with flux powder.
> Electro-slag welding (for large gaps)—This uses bare metal wire electrode.

Friction welding (FRW)
Resistance welding (RW)
Oxy-fuel gas welding
Laser-beam welding and electron-beam welding

Major Welding Processes

Gas metal Arc Welding (GMAW)

It is also called MIG (metal inert gas welding). The process uses power source, wire feeding system, spool of solid filler wire, welding gun, and shielding gas. The solid filler wire may have the same or higher strength of the material to be welded. To protect the molten metal, a shielding gas is pumped to the molten metal through the welding gun. A mixture of 75% argon with 25% CO_2 gas is used for protecting the weld. The gas for welding is supplied from portable gas cylinders.

In this method, welding wire is continuously fed to maintain the arc. And there is no need to remove any slag. As compared to stick welding, this method is fast and can weld steel, aluminum, and stainless steel at any angle. Most common wire size for MIG welding is 0.035".

Advantages of MIG Welding

As compared to stick, submerged, and TIG, the following are some of the advantages:

1. Parts can be welded in any position.
2. There is no need to remove slag.
3. There is less distortion of steel.
4. The quality of weld is consistently good.

Flux-Cored Welding

This method is similar to MIG welding. The solid welding wire is replaced with hollow-core wire. The hollow wire is filled with flux powder. Flux is used to avoid using shielding gases. Some applications of flux-cored welding still uses shielding gases.

Flux-cored methods have the following advantages:

1. This method is good for welding thicker materials.
2. This provides deep penetration.
3. This provides enough metal deposition.
4. This can be used outside drafty areas.
5. It avoids the use of shielding gas cylinders.
6. It is more productive than stick welding (SMAW).

Gas Tungsten Welding (GTAW)

It is also called TIG (tungsten inert gas). In this method, we strike the arc between non consumable electrode (tungsten) and work using inert shielding gas. This method differs from MIG welding in that the electrode does not melt. TIG is excellent for welding ferrous and nonferrous metals. This method provides splatter proof very high-quality welds. The filler metal is used for thicker metals. For some thin meals, no filler metal is used.

The power supply for this welding could be AC or DC. Tungsten electrode is used due to its very high melting temperature (6170°F). The process can use three types of electrodes:

1. Pure tungsten (ball end used for aluminum and magnesium)
2. Thoriated tungsten (pointed shape)
3. Zirconiated tungsten (used for nonferrous metals)

Shielding Gases:

The most common gases used are argon and helium. These gases protect the weld from the atmosphere. For welding heavier sections, helium gas is used since it provides hotter arc.

As compared to MIG and flux-cored methods, TIG method is slow, however, provides better quality welds. This method is used for welding steel, aluminum, and stainless steel.

This process uses both water-cooled and air-cooled TIG torches. It requires power supply, TIG torch, and gas supply and tungsten electrode. In addition, filler metal rods are needed.

Some companies prefer to use TIG welding for stainless steel material, which is less than 1/8" thick.

General safety precautions for welding:

1. To avoid electrical shock, do not stand on surface that is wet. Also, the equipment should be set in clean dry place.
2. The welder's face must be protected from infrared and ultra violet rays originating from electric arc.
3. Use protective leather shoes, apron, and arm covers.
4. Use welder helmet with proper shade lens to protect eyes. You may use auto darkening lenses.
5. To protect lungs, install exhaust hoods to remove the toxic fumes. Have good ventilation system to exhaust fumes from the welding area.
6. Welding fumes may contain zinc oxide, lead, and other airborne contaminants. Use tight-fitting respirator.
7. As per www.airgas.com, the most common gases are acetylene, carbon dioxide, hydrogen, and argon. These gases are supplied in different size of cylinders. You need to have a proper inside or outside storage for each cylinder.
8. There are several safety steps you should look into regarding handling of different kind of gas cylinders. Empty- and full-gas cylinders must be stored separately. Gas cylinders must be kept upright. Check with the distributor of compressed gases regarding storage and handling of gas cylinders

For more information on different gases and storage, visit www.airgas.com and www.lindeus.com.

Shielded Metal-Arc Welding (SMAW) or Stick

This process is used for assemblies that require non continuous welds. The process uses flux-coated rod electrodes. The electrodes for welding are available for steel, alloys, cast iron, and nonferrous metals. Due to ease of use, this process is used extensively in rail industry. It is used to rebuild parts or repair broken parts.

The electrode is a filler metal, which is covered with flux. The function of flux is to burn and create a gaseous shield to protect the weld. The flux eventually becomes a coating and is called slag. Slag is chipped away after cooling. For welding metal less than 1/8" thick, use a 3/32" diameter electrode? For material over 1/8", use 1/8" round material electrode. Most common identification for these electrodes is E6010, E6011, E7018, E7024, and E6013. To avoid hydrogen absorption, once opened, the electrodes should be stored in a heated oven. The following is the explanation of E6010 electrode:

E—Electrode
60—Tensile strength in ksi (60,000 psi)
1—All positions
0—Content of flux

This process does create slag and splatter. The slag is to be removed after welding. The splatter is cleaned by hand grinder.

This method is good for outdoor welding as well as in areas that are hard to reach. This method is good for rusty steel.

As compared to flux-cored and MIG welding methods, stick welding process is slower. This method is not good for thin materials and aluminum.

Submerged-Arc Welding

This method of welding is used for high speed, high metal deposition, and high welding speed. In this process, the arc is struck between bare metal electrode and the work. The arc is covered with granular flux.

The metal electrode becomes the filler metal. The flux turns into slag and provides a protective layer for the weld area.

The equipment consists of welding power source, wire feeding system, welding gun, the flux hopper, flux removal system, and travel mechanism.

Electroslag Welding Method

This method of welding is used for thicker material with wide gap. The process uses bare metal electrodes guided through a tube with conductive flux. The pool of molten metal and flux are protected by copper side covers and bottom pad. Water is circulated through side covers and bottom covers.

Like submerged welding, the bare electrodes become filler metal for the gap. The molten flux protects the weld. We need power source, wire feeder, water circulating system, flux source, and a controller.

Stress reliving: All large-welded assemblies may need stress relieving in a furnace. This step is discussed under heat treatment of welded assemblies.

Constant Current / Constant Voltage Description

There are two manual welding processes:

1. SMAW—Shielded metal arc welding (stick)
2. GTAW—Gas tungsten arc welding (TIG)

In both processes, we control angle by hand, travel, and speed; as such, constant source of current is used in these processes.

In automatically fed wire systems such as GMAW (gas metal arc welding) and FCAW (flux-cored arc welding), we use constant voltage system.

Glimpse of Lincoln electric welding equipment from their website (www.lincolnelectric.com):

1. Hand-held plasma cutters
2. CNC plasma cutters
3. Stick welder—Model AC225-K1170—input power 230/1/60, single phase—40–225 Amps.—225 Amps for 3/32" dia. mild steel electrode.
4. Idealarc—R3R 400 stick welder, K-1285-16-3 phase
   Input power 230/460/3/60—use for stick and TIG
5. MIG welder—CV-400=MIG Welder K 1346-13-3 Phase 60 Cycle

Input power 230/460/3/60-output: CV-DC—use for MIG and flux-cored wires

Selection of Welding Electrodes

Electrodes for steel are made from low-carbon steel and deoxidizing metals such as manganese, aluminum, and titanium. Electrodes are selected based on the material to be welded. For mild steel electrodes such as E60XX or E70XX, letter *E* stands for electrode while 60 and 70 numbers stand for tensile strength in 1,000 psi. The third and fourth digit stands for the position of the weld. The following are some of welding electrode specifications methods: (for detailed information on electrodes consult your welding supplies distributor):

E XX YY 1 HZ-R
E—stands for electrode
XX—indicates tensile strength in ksi
YY—welding position
number stand for toughness and ductility

HZ—meets hydrogen diffusible test and R----Meets absorbed moisture

The following is another classification for carbon steel electrode used for gas-shielded arc welding:

ER-XX-S-X-HZ
ER—stands for electrode
XX—weld material strength in ksi
S—solid
X—wire composition and HZ stands for hydrogen diffusion

Solid Wire Selection

According to an article written by Jonathan Will of Hobart Brothers of Troy, Ohio, in June 2016 issue of Metal Forming magazine, solid wire is the most widely used filler metal for welding fabrication and maintenance.

According to Jonathan, most solid wires are plated with copper to prevent rusting. The wire must be selected based on chemical and mechanical properties. The commonly used wire is AWS ER70S-6. The letters AWS stand for American Welding Society, ER stands for electrode and rod, 70 describes the tensile strength, S stands for solid wire, and 6 indicates shielding gas requirement. The electrode description ending with S3 and S6 are used for gas-metal-arc-welding (GMAW), while ER70S-2 is used for gas-tungsten-arc-welding (GTAW). Jonathan recommends using solid wire AWS ER80S-D2 for low alloy steels.

Glimpse of welding sample consumables from www.lincolnelectric.com website:

Flux-cored wire—Inner shield NR 152—available in 0.045" and 0.062" diameter in 25 and 50 lbs. spools respectively

Stick electrodes—Excalibur 7018-ET 7018H4R—available in 3/32, 1/8, 5/32, 3/16, 7/32" diameter in 50 lbs. open case

MIG wire (Superarc L-50–55)—70 ksi yield strength-use mix shielding gas or 100% CO_2- available in 0.030, 035, 0.040, 0.048 and 0.052 diameter in 33 and 44 lbs. box

Good quality welds are achieved by using right filler electrode, current, welding speed, and angle.

Types of Commercially Available Steel for Welding

The following are some of the types of steels:

1. Mild and alloy steel plates available from 3/16" thick to above 8"
2. Round and hex bars—hot finished and cold finished
3. Round, square, and rectangular tubes with thin and heavy wall
4. Bars flat in rectangular form
5. Structural shapes such as angle iron, channel, I-beams, zee, piling, and rail
6. Sheet steel less than 3/16" thick

Preparation of Metal before Welding

Prior to welding material, the following processes are used:

1. Saw cutting of tubes, bars, and structural shapes
2. Laser cutting of flat steel, stainless steel, and aluminum
3. Thicker steel (over 3/4") plate cutting using oxy-fuel system
4. Using plasma cutting for stainless steel, aluminum, brass, and alloy steel

In terms of accuracy for material under half inch, laser cutting provides very precise dimensions followed by plasma and oxy-fuel cutting.

Friction Welding

This method is used for welding together two cylindrical parts (tube or solid) of different metals and sizes. The process involves holding one part in a stationary chuck, while the other part is rotating at high speed with a flywheel. Slowly the parts are brought together to create friction. The heat creates plastic state to fuse the pieces together.

I have been personally involved with welding a 3.5" round OD—1.75" ID with 2.75" OD with 1.25" ID parts with length from 6" to 8". The resulting joint is as strong as the parental material. For example, you can weld low-carbon 1018 steel and some stainless and alloy steels. This process is satisfactory for low-carbon steel parts. The resulting welds have no porosity.

Manufacturing Technology Inc. of Indiana is the specialist for this welding. For more information about friction welding, visit their website (www.mtiwelding.com) and also check with www.taylor-winfield.com.

Aerospace, automotive, construction, and pump manufactures take advantage of this technology.

Resistance Welding

This method is used for welding two or more metals together by applying heat and pressure. A heavy current is passed through the metals while the pressure is applied for a short period.

The process does not use any filler metal electrodes, gases, or fluxes. This method is used in sheet metal industry for welding thin gauge (less than 6 mm thick) steel. Resistance welding includes the processes called spot, seam, projection, and flash welding. Several welds in the automobile frame are made by resistance welding using robots. In addition, this process is used for welding wire fences, electronics, furniture, and appliances.

This process needs less skill. In some designed components, you can substitute nuts and bolts with resistance welding. This process is not good for heavy structural parts, where MIG and TIG welding methods are more appropriate.

In this process, high rate of heat is generated using a transformer, which creates very low voltage but high current. The main voltage input to transformer could vary from 208 to 600 volts, while the secondary voltage could be from 1 volt to 30 volts.

Formula for resistance welding is W (heat energy) = square of current × resistance in ohms.

This method is good for spot welding metals, which are less than 1/8" thick. The process uses copper electrode to apply the current and pressure.

For more information, visit https://tjsnow.com, www.lynnwelding.com, www.merrill-mfg.com www.taylor-winfield.com, www.romanmfg.com (for DC power supplies), and Resistance Welder Manufacturers' Association (RWMA).

Glimpse from Taylor Winfield's Website

Taylor Winfield builds the following equipment:

1. Arc-welding cells—MIG/TIG and plasma
2. Dual robotic MIG-welding cells
3. Robotic cells with vision orientation
4. Robotic laser cutting and welding
5. Friction welders
6. Metal coil joining
7. Resistance welders—press welders, flash-butt welders (for rod and tube), seam welders, and band saw welders.
8. Induction heating systems

Glimpse from https://tjsnow.com. The following are types of welders built by T. J. Snow:

1. Pedestal-type resistance welder
2. Seam welder, stud welder, micro welder, etc.

Gas Welding

This process uses acetylene gas and pure oxygen with a welding torch to create cone-shaped flame of about 6,000°F. The heat of flame is used to heat base metal and to melt filler metal consisting of rod of 1/16" to 3/32" diameter.

Besides acetylene, other gases such as propane and natural gases are also used as a fuel.

Gas welding can also be used for general metal repairs. For heavier structural application, MIG and stick (SMAW) welding methods will be more economical and provide superior joints.

Electron-Beam Welding

According to Electron Beam Welding LLC, Buena Park, California, the following are the advantages of their process:

1. Gives small amount of heat input
2. Reduces distortion of parts
3. Can weld metals from 0.002" to 4" thick
4. Can weld dissimilar metals

This process is mostly used for aerospace components. This process is carried out in vacuum. Most applications are for rockets, aircraft engines, satellite, sensors, medical devices, and nuclear power components.

Process uses high-velocity beam. The kinetic energy of the beam is converted to heat. The vacuum environment keeps the impurities out of the weld.

For information on electron-beam welding, visit www.ebeinc.com, www.ktiinc.com, and https://www.roarkfab.com/eb-welding/.

Laser Welding

Laser welding is a noncontact method using narrow intense beam. The process puts minimal heat input and causes no distortion. The following are the main advantages of laser welding:

1. No distortion of material

2. No contamination of joint to be welded
3. Has high-power density
4. High-speed seam welding
5. Single pass weld
6. No use of solvents
7. Heat-affected area is small

Desk-type laser welding systems are used to weld gold jewelry, eyeglass frames, stainless steel, and titanium for dental bridges.

Also, according to www.rofin-inc.com (Coherent-Rofin Company), laser is used in

electronic, glass, jewelry, watch, automotive, medical device, photovoltaic, and packaging industry.

For more information using CO_2 and Nd:YAG laser welding for stainless steel, mild carbon steel, titanium, and aluminum, visit www.industrial-lasers.com, https://precoinc.com, www.laserstar.net, www.or-laser.de, www.laserage.com, www.ktiinc.com, www.laserguideinc.com, and www.ebindustries.com.

Glimpse of www.laserstar.net--laser for medical devices, dental bridges, and jewelry.

> Iweld Bench top 40 joule 5.5kW, 35 watts-30 Hz to 125 joule, 10kW, 80 watt 30 Hz
> Iweld Professional 60 joule, 10kW, 60 watt-30 Z to 150 joule, 10 kW, 80 watt 30 Hz

Other Related Processes

Gouging

This method of gouging is used by heavy-plate welding shops. It is required to remove or melt excess material or remove old welds. Gouging is used to remove unwanted parts from the assembly due to engineering revisions or other quality problems. Depending on the size of material or assembly, the following are a few methods of gouging:

1. Milling, grinding, or chipping
2. Gouging by oxy-fuel—In this method, the area is heated by the hand-held torch. After heating, the excess material is removed by high-pressure oxygen.
3. Air carbon arc—In this process, the arc is created between carbon electrode and the work (metal). This process is assisted by high-pressure air. The process is noisy and difficult to control. Usually, the carbon electrode is held in holder. The holder is provided with an air valve. The high-pressure air blows away the molten metal. Besides removing unwanted welded items, it is also used for preparing weld joints.
4. Plasma arc gouging—This method uses high temperature plasma gas to remove excess material from ferrous and nonferrous plates or assemblies.

Brazing

It is a process of permanently joining two similar or dissimilar metal components by heating and using a brazing filler metal. Brazing provides leak-proof joints. In brazing process, the parent materials do not melt. This process is used for assembling hydraulic fittings, gas valves, automotive radiators, bicycle, jewelry, and heat exchangers. Brazing is also used for assembling carbide metal, cutting inserts with steel toolholders for manual and CNC lathes.

Brazing is done by electric induction, gas, and in a vacuum furnace. Plumbers use brazing to assemble copper components with copper tubing.

Before brazing, parts are cleaned by sanding or brushing and provided with a proper clearance at the mating surface. Beside filler metals, also included is the application of flux to the joint. The flux is applied to remove metal oxides from the parts. Flux helps in making the filler metal flow into the gap between two parts and prevents oxidation of metal during the brazing process.

The parts are heated together around 840°F in the presence of filler metal and flux. Due to capillary action, the molten filler metal is drawn into the gap between two parts. The clearance between the two parts is around 0.002" to 0.004". For proper assembly, the parts to be brazed should be held in a fixture.

The heating of both parts can be done by propane gas, acetylene, or induction heating. Induction heating system is used with a suitable power source, a coil of proper kilowatt, and suitable electric frequency.

The following websites can further help in finding more information about brazing:

1. https://www.lucasmilhaupt.com/—This website provides information about basic brazing, joint design, and filler metals.
2. www.fusion-inc.com—This Company builds brazing equipment, filler metals, fluxes, and pastes for brazing.
3. https://www.solvay.us/en/binaries/NOCOLOK_Brazing_Process-en-de-179520.pdf—This is for large-scale brazing aluminum heat exchangers.
4. http://www.teksonsradiators.com/products.html—Teksons based in India is a user of brazing systems for heat exchangers.

Welding Cost

The cost of welding usually consists of the following factors:

1. Cost of flux, wire, electrodes per pound, and gas volume
2. Cost of power per kilowatt hour
3. Metal deposited in pounds
4. Wages of welder per hour
5. Time spent for each assembly
6. Overhead cost (includes rent, supervisory, and other salary employees)
7. Complete cost (includes the cost of material and the scrap factor)

Heat-Treating of Welded Assemblies

During the preparation of welded assemblies, some of the parts are cut by oxy-fuel and plasma cutting processes. In the cutting operation, the temperature of around the cut edge can increase to 2,500 to 2,700°F. This high-cutting temperature, changes the microstructure of cut metal. Also, the welding process changes the hardness and properties of the surrounding area. The completed weldment has built in stresses and has to be removed by heat treatment. This operation can be carried out by outside vendors or in-house stress relieving furnace.

Quality Check of Welds

Depending on the size of welded item and number of parts to be made, the quality control supervisor has to decide the inspection method.

The weld can have anyone of the following imperfections:

1. Poor penetration
2. Cracked welds
3. Warpage
4. Poor appearance
5. Splatter
6. Poor fusion

The above quality problems can result from wrong electrode, not enough gas shield coverage, fast welding speed, and low current.

The quality control inspector can use nondestructive procedures or destructive procedure to check the flaws in the welds. Besides checking the cracks visually by a magnifying glass, following are some of the nondestructive testing methods:

1. Liquid penetrant testing—This method could be used for ferrous or nonferrous metals, which have surface flaws. Prior to applying the penetrant, the part is thoroughly cleaned to remove

dust and grease. The area to be inspected is either sprayed or dipped into brightly colored liquid penetrant.

The part is dried, and the area is sprayed with powder. The liquid in the cracks attracts the powder. This is a simple way of finding cracks in welds or parent material.

2. Fluorescent penetrant testing—In this method, special fluorescent penetrant is used.

   The fluorescent liquid glows when exposed to ultraviolet light or black light.

   Both methods are very effective for checking welds in steel, aluminum, and stainless steel.

For more information, visit www.ndtsupply.com and www.chemtool.com and Spectronics Corp. (www.spectroline.com).

3. Magnetic particle inspection—This method can be used to check cracks and porosity in ferrous metals. The process consists of applying special iron powder on the surface of welded joint. After spraying the powder, two electrodes are used to induce electric current between the ends of the welded section. The induced direct current creates circular magnetic field. The ferrous powder is clearly visible in areas which have flaws.

The system consists of power source, with electrodes and iron powder. For magnetic particle information visit Parker research Corp. at www.parkerndt.com.

4. Radiographic Testing—This method uses an X-ray equipment to take picture of the welded joint on a radiographic film. The newer radiography systems display the joint picture on a computer screen.

For more information, visit the following companies that provide radiographic services:

> https://jgarantmc.com/industrial-ct-scanning-services/
> https://www.americanmetaltesting.com/radiographic-metal-testing

5. Ultrasonic testing—This method is also used to check flaws in welded and machined parts. Using a piezoelectric transducer (also called probe) and special fluid, Ultrasonic unit is used to expose the area with high frequency sound waves. The system can find flaws on under and over the surface. The ultrasonic unit consists of as oscillograph which displays of the internal flaw in the part.

An average welding shop may not have access to all above tools; however, tools such as dye penetrant and magnetic particle testing are easy to procure.

You can visit Berg Engineering at www.bergeng.com for nondestructive testing products. At a recent show in Chicago, a Chinese company displayed some of their instruments for nondestructive testing. You can check their website (www.solidnde.com) for details.

For large quantities, the QC can conduct sample tests with following procedures:

1. Bend test
2. Tensile strength test
3. Impact toughness test

Depending on the application, the design engineer of the welded products must address the expectation of the quality of the welds.

The welding process creates sparks, fumes, vapors, and debris during weld cleaning. Take the following steps to create a safe environment for the welder and the coworkers:

1. Follow safety regulations recommended by Occupational Safety and Health Administration and Center for devices and Radiological Health for laser usage.
2. Remove any combustible mineral fluid, paper, and cloth from the welding area to prevent fire.
3. Use welding helmet for operators and provide other workers with safety eye glasses with side shields to prevent eye injury from arc welding and laser and weld grinding.
4. Provide proper ventilation for fumes and respiratory protection.
5. Clean welding slag from the floor periodically to prevent slipping.
6. Monitor noise near the welding area, and if required, provide hearing protection to welder and coworkers.
7. Use leather cover for body and arms to minimize UV effect from welding.

For more information on weld industry, visit the following websites:

www.millerwelds.com (Miller Electric Mfg. Co.)
www.lincolnelectric.com
www.aws.org (American Welding Society)
For five volumes of welding information, visit the following: https://www.aws.org/publications/weldinghandbook
www.hobartbrothers.com
https://ewi.org/about/ (The Edison Welding institute) www.aws.org/publications/weldingjournal
www.esabna.com-visit (ESAB Knowledge Center)
www.thermatool.com (for welders and heat treat systems)
www.hypertherm.com (for plasma air-oxygen cutting and water-jet cutting)
www.thermal-dynamics.com (plasma cutting systems)
www.polysoude.com (for TIG, pipe, and orbital welding)
www.arcspecialties.com (for automation systems for GTAW, GMAW, laser, and robotic integration of cutting, handling, assembling, and finishing cells)

www.pemamek.com (PEMA welding solutions from Finland)
PEMA builds welding and production systems for ship building, wind energy, oil, and gas. The company provides the following welding products:

1. External and internal longitudinal pipe welding
2. External circumferential, large and small diameter pipe welding
3. Positioners and roller beds for welding dish for pressure vessels
   www.read-tpi.com (Tube Products International)

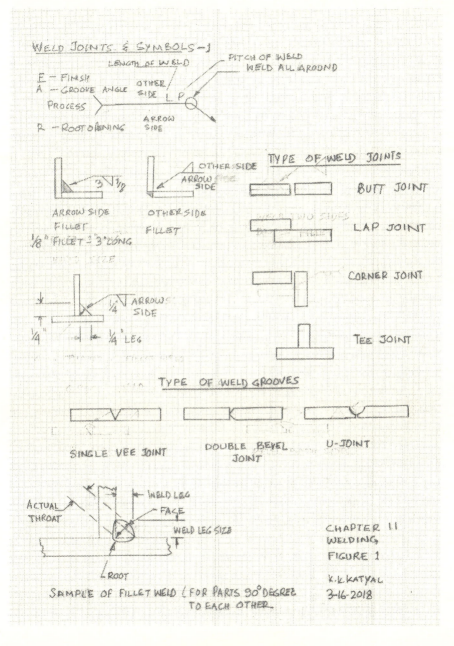

Fig. 1—Welding joints

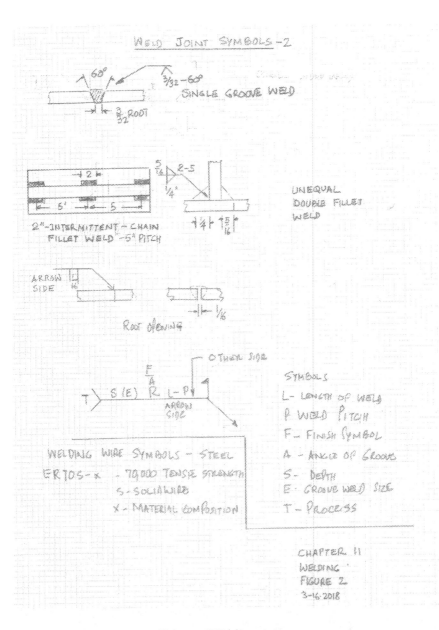

Fig. 2—Welding joints

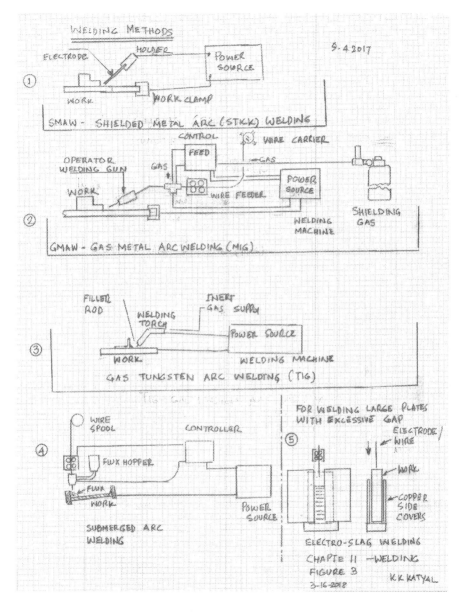

Fig.3—Welding methods'

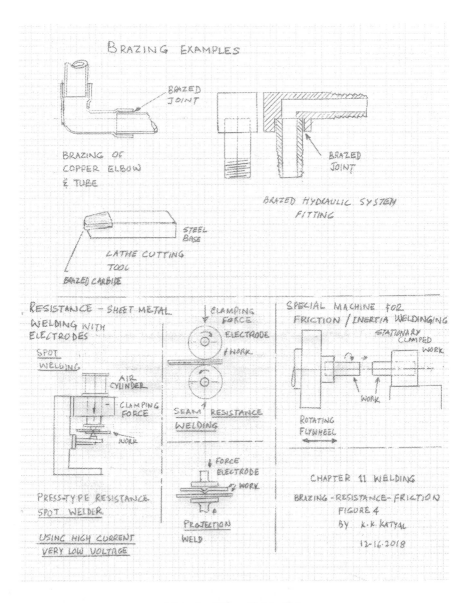

Fig. 4—Braz-Resis-Fric

CHAPTER 12

Machining and Related Processes

Topics covered are machining of round parts, blocks and castings, CNC controls, drilling, tools for deep hole drilling, electric discharge machining (EDM), micro hole drilling, sawing, cutting fluids, water miscible coolants, straight cutting oil, glimpse of coolant and filter manufacturers; cutting tools for turning and milling, glimpse of tool manufacturers, tool coatings, turning on lathe and CNC lathe manufacturers, Swiss-type turning centers, CNC control builders, multiple spindle turning centers and tools for turning; manual and CNC vertical mills, large CNC machining services and equipment builders, hard milling, grinding, centerless grinding, glimpse of grinding wheel manufacturer; burnishing, honing system, direct metal laser sintering (DMLS), stereolithography, flexible manufacturing systems, high-volume production machines, automated assembly machines, robots in industry, collaborative robots or cobots, 3-D printing, production efficiency, return on investment on capital equipment, laser-alignment systems, glimpse of DATRON CNC milling machines, glimpse of major US and international machine builders, machine safety, metal finishing, common electroplating methods, powder coating, galvanizing, and source for used machinery.

MACHINING IS THE process of shaping the unfinished metal into a usable shape and utilizing cutting tools and suitable machinery. Before machining, the raw material for any work piece is given extra allowance. Machining process removes this excess allowance from the following:

- Rough forgings
- Rough castings
- Round, flat, hex, or a block of material

There are various types of manual, automatic, and CNC machines, which are used to finish the work piece. The finished piece finally becomes a part of ship, airplane, machine tools, bridge, automobile, locomotives, power generation equipment, or oil-producing well.

Machines help in making shafts, threaded parts, gears, and dies for injection molding and finished castings.

Machining Round Parts

Cylindrical parts are usually made from round bars, forgings, castings, or hex bars using manual or CNC lathes. For repeatable jobs and high productivity, screw machines and CNC lathes are very efficient.

Machining of Large Blocks and Castings

Milling is a process used for machining auto, truck, locomotives, ships, and aerospace metal parts. Mills are used to shape, drill, tap, and slot parts. This is an important tool to make dies for plastic, forgings, and nonferrous casting industry. The major categories of machines used for large and small parts are drilling, electric discharge machining (EDM), sawing, turning, milling, grinding, gear making, honing, etc.

For high productivity, conventional manual machines are being substituted with an equivalent computer numerically controlled units. CNC machines are excellent for large production runs as well as small lots. These machines help in reducing cost and improve accuracy of the work.

Computer Numerical Control

CNC controls are built for machines such as lathes, drills, and milling machines. To improve performance, CNC controls are applied to band saws, robots, grinders, gear cutters, wood working, plastic sheet cutters, plastic routers, laser, and water-jet cutting systems.

Another bigger application of CNC technology is for coordinate measuring machines. These machines are used to inspect fully machined and nonmachined parts. Also, there are CNC machines built with measurement probe to inspect the machined parts.

In the CNC system, the part to be machined is located using Cartesian coordinates. In case of vertical milling machine, the point of origin is the point where two horizontal axes (X and Y) and one vertical spindle (Z) axis meet. CNC machines are built in 2, 3, and 5 axes models. They are based on closed-loop system. All axes motors are built with angle and position sensors. The machine travel is based on digital data entered into the control via manual keyboard, data from tape, and disk loaded through a personal computer or downloaded by company's digital network.

There are three major axes in a CNC milling machines. They are based on three fingers. The X axis is represented by thumb, the Y axis by index finger, and Z by middle finger. The following are additional axes:

Axis A rotates about X, axis U is parallel to X
Axis B rotates about Y, axis V is parallel to Y
Axis C rotates about Z, axis W is parallel to Z

The following are typical movements in three dimensions:

1. Point-to-point control in which three axes can move simultaneously
2. Straight movement in one direction only

3. Linear movement, where the tool moves straight in more than one axis
4. Circular interpolation

Program

In 1970s, most of CNC machines were fitted with punched tape reader. The machining program was punched on paper or synthetic material tapes. The operational sequence was represented with a row of punched holes. There were a few machine companies that had their own CNC programming language. These days, most machine builders have their computer language with common *G* and *M* commands. Also, some machine builders are used for conversational programming.

Beside perforated tapes, the older CNC machines were also equipped with magnetic tapes, cassette tapes, and floppy disks. The newer machines have solid-state memory and can download the machine programs from a personal computer or from a remote network.

Based on the engineering print, the operator of the CNC-controlled machine enters the data consisting of numbers and letters. The following are some of the commands used for writing the CNC program for a machine:

G00—Rapid traverse
G01—Linear or straight line move
G02—Circular interpolation
G78—Threading
N—Block number (00–999)
G94—Feed in inches per minute
X and *Z* axes dimensions
F—Feed rate
T—Tool number in use
M00—Program stop
M03—Spindle on
M05—Spindle off
M30—End of program

Many machine tool builders also offer conversational programming. The following are some of the machines built with CNC controls:

1. Vertical and horizontal surface milling machines with high degree of automation—These machines can have three- to five-axis interpolation capabilities.
2. Traveling column and gantry milling machines—These are available for machining large parts.
3. Special high-speed machines for tool and die.
4. Laser cutting and electron-beam welding machines.
5. Water-jet, plasma, and oxy-fuel, natural gas cutting machines.
6. Band saws.
7. Tube bending machines.
8. Tool grinders.
9. Robots.
10. Coordinate measuring machines.
11. Electric discharge machines (EDM).
12. Routers.

CNC machine safety: CNC machines' cutting tools can collide with fixtures and parts if not programmed properly. Any collision during machining can cost a lot of money and time for repair.

The machines are provided with E-stop, safety enclosures, light curtains, and infrared cameras. The owners of the machines should enforce that the machine operator cannot bypass machine interlocks and programmed soft limits.

Drilling

Drilling can be done with a portable electric drill and dedicated, stand-alone vertical drill. Drilling machines are available with hydraulic, pneumatic, deep hole capability and with CNC automation.

For accuracy purposes, the part to be drilled must be held in a vice or fixture before drilling. The following are some of the drilling tools:

- Twist drill—This is made of high-speed steel or carbide tipped tool steel with 3 to 4 flutes.
- Carbide-brazed tools—This can drill deeper holes (ejector drill and gun drill).
- Coolant-through drill—<u>This is</u> used for deep-hole drilling.
- Spade drill—<u>It is</u> with a replaceable carbide tip. It is stronger and creates less pressure on parts and provides better chip control.
- Indexable carbide-insert drill—It can run at very high speed and can provide more life to the drill.
- Half-round drill—<u>It is</u> for brass, copper, and nonferrous alloys.
- Combination drill and reamer.
- Subland drill—It can combine drilling of two diameters.
- Spot drill—By using this tool prior to drilling, you eliminate sharp edges around the hole.

Drill sizes are expressed as follows:

Twist drills consist of a shank and body. The main drill could have two or three flutes or helical grooves. The drill could have straight shank or taper shank. Drills below ½" have straight shank and some taper shank, while drills above ½" diameter have taper shank. This taper is called Morse taper. The drill with taper shank is held in the female taper part of the machine spindle.

Drills are marketed in the following categories:

Number series: no. 80 (0.0135") to no. 1 (0.228")
Letter series: *A* (0.234") to *Z* (0.413")
Fraction sizes: 1/64 to 63/64" and 3–1/2"
Metric series with increment from 0.015 mm

For drilling speed, machinery handbooks are provided with charts, which help in selecting the right speed for the metals. This is about the speed required to drill holes in certain metals using high-speed steel drills and carbide-tipped drills.

Machines for Drilling

Presently, for accuracy purposes, most parts are drilled on vertical or horizontal CNC mills, CNC drills, and tapping machines. Gun drills or ejector drills are used for parts requiring deep holes.

Besides CNC drilling machines, the following kind of drilling equipment are still being used in the industry:

- Bench-type drill press with manual speed adjustment
- Single-column drilling machine
- Gang drilling (machine set up with common work-holding table)
- Radial drill
- Multiple spindle drilling machine
- Pneumatic drill
- Electric spindle with hydraulic feed
- Deep-hole drilling

The drilling machines are also used for reaming, countersinking, and spot-facing the holes. The drills for these operations may have taper shank holders.

Air and hydraulic drilling power units are available. Also, special ball screw–actuated CNC-controlled special drilling machines can be designed and built. CNC drills provide faster cycle time. Programmable drill head provides accurate holes. For information, contact Zagar Inc. of Cleveland, Ohio. Also, you can contact https://createch-design.com/Home.aspxct (Createch Machine and Design) for special drilling and tapping machines.

Deep-hole drilling is required for automotive and construction products. Depth of deep holes are usually 10 to 100 times the diameter of the holes. The main problem during the operation is the removal of broken chips. It is necessary to remove chips to avoid bad surface finish. Sandvik Coromant builds several drilling tools and options to remove broken chips.

For machinery for deep-hole drilling, visit www.unisig.com, www.kays-dehoff.com and www.technidrillsystems.com.

For deep-hole drilling, visit www.sandvik.coromant.com and look at information under drilling tools for CoroDrill models 801, 808, 818, and gun drill.

Coolant for drilling: Mineral oil–based and water-based coolants are available for both drilling and milling operations. For deep-hole drilling, the machine manufacturers recommend mineral oil–based coolants.

For more information on other drilling machines, visit www.zagar.com, www.sugino.com, www.aaaproducts.com, www.autodrill.com, and www.govro.com.

Electric Discharge Machining

This process is used for very precise cutting of any conducting material (steel, stainless, tungsten, tool steel, graphite, etc.) by discharging capacitors' stored electric current.

The electric discharge takes place between an electrode (cathode) and a work piece (anode) to erode the metal. In the presence of dielectric fluid (deionized water), the spark takes place between the work and the cutting metal wire. The spark vaporizes the metal surface. In EDM, there is no physical contact between the wire and the part. As compared to regular machining, EDM does not create any chips and leave any burr on the parts. Also, the part to be cut does not require any heavy fixturing, which is usually required on a CNC mill.

EDM machines are used for drilling very small holes in aircraft engine blades, making molds for plastics, die-casting, stamping dies, and cutting hardened metal. EDM is also used for medical components, such as screws for bone repair and shaping needles for dental surgery. EDM machines provide very high tolerance.

There are three kinds of EDM machines:

1. Wire-cut EDM—It uses brass or copper wire with a diameter from 0.02 mm to 0.33 mm (per GF Machines) to cut the material. These machines have three to five axes to cut angular holes.

The wire is charged electrically with correct voltage. The spark jumps the gap and melts small portion of work piece. The part to be cut is submerged in deionized water. The very small diameter of electric wire is held between upper and lower guides. The wire electrode cuts the conductive material. The deionized water flushes the removed material. Wire EDM can cut material up to 16" thick and provide burr-free cut surface.

2. Ram-type die sinker EDM—This machine uses shaped graphite electrodes to form desired contour in metals for die-casting and plastic mold-making. It makes pockets and holes by burning downward.
3. Hole-drilling EDM—Brass or copper tubes are used to drill holes in conductive material. Electrodes as small as 0.3 mm are used to drill holes.

EDM process is an excellent tool for parts that are very small, have low volume, and have complex shape. They need very high precision and are made from very high hard conductive material.

EDM machines are specified according to the travels of axes X, Y, and Z, maximum workpiece dimensions, maximum weight of the part the machine table can carry, maximum angle of conical cut, wire diameter, and maximum cutting speed.

For more information on machines, visit www Sodick.com, www.mcmachinery.com, www.gfms.com, www.onaedm.com, www.kentusa.com, and www.chmer.com.

For EDM services, visit www.xactedm.com, www.njpt.com, www.noujaimtools.com, and www.applegateedm.com.

Glimpse of EDM consumable supplier:

Saturn Industries (www.saturnedm.com) supplies the following:

- EDM copper, tungsten, brass, and graphite electrodes
- EDM filters, dielectric fluids, wire, ceramic wire guides, and rollers

Micro hole Drilling

For drilling holes in material up to 1 millimeter thick and 0.004 inches diameter in carbon steel, ceramics, silicon, and other hard materials, the following methods are considered:

Diode pumped solid-state laser (DPSSL) by Ladda Physik may be considered. Similar laser techniques are used in drilling into gas turbine blades. These lasers have short wavelength and provide less heat. Visit www.laserage.com and www.rache.com for more information.

Laser does not require any drilling tube. Laser can be used for nonconducting material, while EDM is good for conducting materials. Laser drilling is faster and less expensive.

Electron-beam drilling can also be used for holes from 0.004" to 0.040" diameter for conductive and nonconductive materials. This process was developed in Germany to drill holes in jewels of watches. For more information, visit www.ebdrilling.com.

EDM process is extensively used to drill small holes in metals. EDM (electric discharge machining) process can drill micro holes using ram-type EDM for conductive material. The process uses tungsten carbide electrode for the process. The process uses stereo microscope for positioning the electrodes.

For more information, visit www.americanwireedm.com, www.edmlabs.com, www.adron.com, and www.rsprecision.com.

For micro drills, contact www.richardsmicrotool.com and for service visit www.najet.com

Glimpse from websites of EDM equipment manufacturers:

1. www.currentedm.com
   EDM drill ST400 manual
   X travel-16", Y travel 12", and Z travel-16"
2. www.mcmachinery.com
   Mitsubishi EDM MV1200—S advance type 800
   X travel 15.7", Y-11.8", and Z-8.7", wide angle taper 45 degrees, wire diameter 0.004"–0.0012"
3. www.sodick.com
   Wire EDM specifications (from brochure at 2018 IMTS Show)
   Specs. model ALN400G and ALN600G
   X-axis travel 15.75" 23.62"
   Y-axis travel 11.81" 15.75"
   Z-axis travel 9.84" 13.78"
   Taper angle +/- 25 degrees +/- 25
   Wire dia. 0.004" -0.012" 0.004" -0.012"

Sawing

Before the parts could be machined by lathe or milling machine, the raw material has to be cut from solid round, hex tubing, pipe, and flat bars. Heavy fabrication shops frequently saw beams, heavy wall tubing, and heavy bundles of bars and tubes. Band saws and cold saws are critical parts of any manufacturing operation.

For a busy manufacturing shop, an automatic band saw is an essential part of the setup. There are three kinds of saws:

1. Band saw (horizontal and vertical)
2. Circular cut-off saw (cold)
3. Abrasive saw

Band saws are equipped with blades from 1–1/4" width to 3" width. The blade thickness can range from 0.040" to 0.060". These blades experience shock while cutting uneven surfaces. The most common blades used on band saws are bimetal. The blade consists of high-speed steel welded to high-strength strip. The following are a few types of band saw blades:

1. Bimetal—Here, high-speed steel cutting edge is welded to spring steel back. Bimetal blades are economical. These blades can cut both ferrous and nonferrous steel.
2. Carbide tipped (tungsten carbide)—Solid carbide teeth welded to spring steel back. Use this blade for cutting high alloy steel and abrasive material. These blades can withstand high heat.
3. Carbide grit blade—This is used for cutting abrasive material, reinforced fiber plastic, and heat-treated steel.
4. Diamond grit blade—This is used for cutting stone, ceramic, and fiber glass.
5. Carbon steel blade—This low-cost blade is for general band saw cutting of low-carbon steel.

Lenox Tools sells an extreme cutting blade. It is coated in aluminum, titanium, and nitrogen (AlTiN) coatings.

Band saw blades are further classified according to the number of teeth per inch, tooth rake angle, tooth pitch (distance between two teeth), blade thickness, and blade width.

Blades are manufactured with constant pitch and variable pitch. Use blades with more teeth per inch (fine pitch) to cut thin sections. Use blades with coarser pitch (less teeth per inch) to cut thicker sections or heavy wall products.

To reduce vibration and noise, use variable-pitch blade to cut heavy wall metals.

Carbide tipped and bi-metal blades provide more life and productivity.

For more information on blades, visit www.doallsaws.com, www.mkmorse.com, www.starret.com, and www.lenoxtools.com.

Band saws are available in horizontal pivot type, double column, horizontal and vertical column type saws. These saws are provided with automatic feed loading tables and vise to grip to hold round, hex, square bars tubes, and bundles.

To provide good cutting, the following options should be there in an automatic saw:

1. Use about 3 degree angle of blade.
2. Saw should index automatically so that it moves the material forward for the next cut.
3. Variable vice pressure to reduce crushing of tubing.
4. Split front vise so that it grips the material at both side of the cut.
5. Use multiple pitches saw blades to reduce vibration.
6. Have about four teeth per inch of the blade or use multiple pitches.
7. Assure at least three teeth are in contact with the work all the time.
8. Use bundle cutting for multiple bars.
9. Use proper ratio of water and coolant during the saw operation.
10. Use manufacturers' recommended pitch of blades for tube and solid material.
11. A wide band blade provides high-beam strength.
12. Use proper surface feet per minute speed for the blades.

Above suggestions were made by Cliff Dixon in an article published in April/May 2001 in Tube Journal. I had a chance to meet him in late 1970s when I worked as a tool engineer with the Electro Motive Division of General Motors (manufacturer of diesel electric locomotives).

Circular or Cold Saws

These saws use round high-speed steel or carbide tipped blades. A user must conduct testing about the productivity of cold saw before deciding to buy these cutting machines. For more information on cold saws, visit www.patmooneysaws.com (distributor) and other manufacturers.

Abrasive Saws

These saws are mostly used with a manual saw operation. They are used for both dry and wet cutting. This system could be used to cut hydraulic hose, steel reinforcing bars, and wire rope. In dry cutting, these saws create excessive metal dust. At the time of purchase, the user must add exhaust dust collector to the cutting machine. For more information about abrasive saws, visit www.everettindustries.com.

Saw manufacturers: www.hydmech.com, www.behringersaws.com, www.amadamt.com (Amada Machine tool America), www.kasto.com, and www.coldsawstore.com.

Glimpse from websites of band saw manufacturers:

1. www.doallsaws.com
   DoALL Saw DC 1,000NC Dual column CNC band saw
   Band saw blade 2.64"×0.063"
   Saw capacity 33.5x40" round tube or solid holding size
2. DoALL cut off / cold circular saw model SC 150A
   Capacity 2.64"-4 ×2.64-4" and round tube 6"
3. www.behringersaws.com
   HBP Series Automatic Band saw—Dual column
   Capacity 47.2"×31.5"

Visit www.sawcalc.com from Lenoxtools.com for correct blade recommendation for a specific band saw.

Cutting Fluids

For machining operations such as drilling, sawing, turning, milling, tapping, sawing, grinding, and thread rolling, it is necessary to use a fluid to provide lubricity, eliminate rust, and remove heat from the operation. A good supply of coolant (mixed with water) or cutting oil are required for these operations. In addition, operations such as cold forming, cold rolling, roll forming, tube bending, and wire drawing also need either water-based or oil-based fluids.

Also, required are special draw compounds for metal forming or press operations and dielectric fluids for electric discharge machining (EDM). Special fluids are required for cleaning, heat treatment, honing, and super finishing and surface protection.

For selection of cutting fluid, the machining supervisor should check what material has to be processed (e.g., carbon steel, alloy steel, cast iron, aluminum or stainless steel, etc.). Check with coolant manufacture, which is right coolant for the metal.

There are three kinds of cutting oils:

1. Straight and soluble oil
2. Semisynthetic
3. Synthetic

Water Miscible Coolants (Semisynthetic and Synthetic)

For sawing, turning, milling, grinding, and tapping about 5% concentrated coolant is mixed with 95% clean water. Once mixed, the resultant solution has milky appearance. Usually, most machines are provided with 50- to 60-gallon tank for carrying the coolant. During the machining operation, the coolant evaporates. The machine operator has to maintain the level of water and adjust its concentration by replenishing the coolant and water.

Care of coolant:

1. The operator should be provided with a portable instrument to check the concentration of coolant and water mixture. This instrument is called a refractometer. Most coolant manufacturers suggest concentration numbers for the refractometer.
2. Keep sump clean using a coolant filter and keep metal chips out of tank. Plan to clean the coolant tank periodically.
3. The older CNC mills and lathes do drain some lubricating oils from ways into the coolant tank. This floating oil from the surface of coolant must be removed. Commercially available belt and disk skimmer system should be used to remove tramp oil

out of coolant. For more information about tramp oil skimmers, visit www.zebraskimmers.com.
4. Use a mixing valve to mix suitable amount of coolant with water.
5. Check with coolant manufacturers about the suitable pH value and hardness of mixing water. To prevent rancidity of coolant, run the coolant pump at different intervals. Drain coolant tank if the machine is shut down for a few weeks.
6. If possible, look into using deionized water for mixing with concentrated coolant.
7. If the company has centralized coolant system, develop guidelines to maintain the cleanliness of tanks.

Water Quality

In the US cities, the water supply is hard and may contain salts and minerals. The water may have dissolved sodium, potassium, calcium, and magnesium. Hard water can degrade machine coolant performance and may leave salt residue on drying. In addition, these minerals have ill effect on the life of machinery systems. If possible, check the hardness of water supply and compare with information provided by www.culligan.com from the Department of Interior and Water Quality Association:

A. Soft water has maximum 60mg/L of calcium carbonate
B. Moderately hard water has 61–120 mg/L of calcium carbonate
C. Hard water has 121–180 mg/L of calcium carbonate
D. Very hard water has over 180mg/L of calcium carbonate

According to William Sluhan of www.masterfluidsolutions.com, the performance of water-based coolant is degraded by its hardness. Calcium and magnesium which dissolves as mineral in water causes hardness of water. Minerals such as sodium chloride and sodium sulfate create corrosion, rust, and leave residue on machine ways and switches.

To prevent rust, insoluble scum, and bacteria, look into the use of deionized water for coolant. According to www.waterandmorehub.com, deionized water has been treated to remove most minerals. The system dissolves all mineral from the water. Deionized water has no residue. As such, it leaves no marks on evaporation.

Due to superior properties, deionized water is used for microelectronics, printed circuit boards, and pharmacies.

In May 2001, *Tooling and Production* magazine, Jim Lorincz wrote an article "A World of Choice in Metalworking Fluids." Jim covered metal working fluid Cimcool, which is made by Milacron Co. of Cincinnati, Ohio. Jim suggests additional few steps to improve metal working fluids:

1. Acidity/alkalinity—He suggests that the mixture should have pH value between 8.8 and 9.2.
2. Amount of dirt—The amount of dirt in coolant affects tooling life and finish. It should be removed by filtering the coolant.
3. Percentage of free oil in the coolant—He recommends the oil to be less than 0.5%.
4. Dissolved minerals-The city water has calcium, magnesium, sodium, and sodium chloride. These minerals cause residue on the machine components. He suggests using treated soft water.
5. Offensive odors—It is caused by bacteria in the fluid. Frequent changes and filtering can reduce the odor in the coolant.

Straight Cutting Oil

For screw machines, threading and gun drilling, most companies use straight cutting oil. The oil provides high lubricity but less heat-removing property.

About the problems with coolants sometimes you need to find out what are the root cause of foaming, rusting, tool life, odor, skin irritation, and residue on machine. In all these cases, check for coolant concentration, water hardness, and pH value of the mixture.

For clean recirculating coolant, all machines are provided with some kind of settlement tank and filtering system. Most common items for filtering are screen to keep debris out of the coolant pump, paper or cloth filter on roll, magnetic drum (provided mostly used with grinding machines), cyclone filter, and centrifugal filter.

Beside fixed filtering system, it is a good practice to periodically use a portable coolant filtering system to filter the coolant. The coolant should be replaced if it has lot of mixed lubricants and hydraulic oils. If drained, the tank should be fully cleaned and the used coolant should be disposed through certified hazardous material disposal service.

It is important to follow federal, state, and local laws for disposal of used coolant.

The following are major US coolant and other chemical manufacturers: www.cimcool.com, www.hangsterfers.com, www.houghtonintl.com, www.blaser.com, www.koolrite.com, and www.masterfluidsolutions.com.

Glimpse of www.houghtonintl.com. The company manufactures the chemicals for cleaning, heat treatment, metal surface finish, metal forming, metal protection, metal removal, hydraulic fluids, and steel mills.

Glimpse of Prab Inc. (www.prab.com). The company manufactures the following:

1. Conveyors, metal scrap processing equipment, waste water solutions
2. Guardian coolant recycling system
3. Paper bed filters
4. Drum-type scrap separators
5. Magnetic separator
6. Vacuum filtration

Glimpse of Industrial Filters Manufacturing Company at www.indfilco.com. The company manufactures coolant filters, deep bed filter, roll tray filter, filter fabric, and magnetic filter.

Cutting Tools for Turning and Milling

Before we cover, the major CNC turning and milling machines, we would like to cover briefly carbide cutting tools, indexable inserts, super abrasive PCD, and PCBN alternates.

All machining tool cutters for milling, drilling, and turning use inserts, which are made from tungsten carbide. These inserts are made with cobalt as binder. The raw material uses wolframite ore for tungsten. The ore is converted to tungsten carbide.

Cemented carbide cutting inserts and drills are used in the machining operation. Powder metal techniques are used by mixing metal carbide, binders, and tungsten carbide (WC) to make inserts. The powder of tantalum and titanium are also used.

The indexable carbide and PCD (polycrystalline diamond) inserts are classified by ANSI (American National Standard Institute) and ISO (International Organization of Standards Codes). For cutting tools, the ANSI code is adopted by US industry, while European and Asian countries have adopted ISO codes.

About ten alphanumeric codes are used by ANSI to specify the shape of carbide cutting inserts. The following are some of the designations:

Round insert are specified by letter *R*, square insert is specified by *S*, triangular insert is specified by letter *T*, and pentagon insert is specified by letter *P*. The other nomenclatures are A, B, E, F, C, D, M, and V.

According to "Cracking the Code" article in June 1995 issue of *Cutting Tool Engineering*, the following is an example of how a cutting insert is specified:

Example: ANSI description TNMG-432-C-LF

Here, *T* stands for triangle, *N* stands for relief angle, *M* stands for tolerance class, *G* stands if there is a hole, 4 is the size, 3 stands for the thickness, while 2 stands for the shape of cutting tool corners.

The ISO nomenclature for inserts is similar to ANSI standard except for cutting edge, cutting direction, and length of cutting edge.

The cutting inserts are different for turning and milling machines. For specific purpose, the cutting insert may have multiple coatings, special substrate and special chip breaker form. The coatings include

TiCN, TiN, TiAlN, and ZrTiN. The TicN coating is very hard while TiN offers lowest coefficient of friction.

For more information on cutting tools and carbide inserts, visit: www.secotools.com, www.iscarmetals.com, www.hornusa.com, www.mitsubishicarbide.com, www.kyoceraprecisiontools.com, and www.greenleafcorporation.com.

As a glimpse of products from www.kyocera precisiontools.com, the company manufactures indexable milling cutters with 45, 75, and 90 degrees lead angle, turning inserts, drilling, grooving, and threading inserts.

As a glimpse of www.kennametal.com, the company manufactures indexable milling cutters, solid carbide end mills, indexable drilling and counter boring tools, OD/ID turning and threading tools.

As a glimpse of www.sandvik.coromant.com, the company manufactures the following tools: turning tools, parting and grooving tools, threading tools, milling tools, drilling tools (indexable insert drill, solid carbide drills, exchangeable tip drill, and deep-hole machining drill), boring and reaming tooling systems, and inserts and solid round tools.

Tool Coatings

Several coatings are available to extend the life of tools used for turning, milling, cold-heading tools, and punch tools. These coatings increase the hardness of carbide inserts and drills. Per Balzers coating company, PVD reduces cutting friction and tool wear.

The coatings are also used to extend the life of deep draw dies and turret press punches for sheet metal stamping and fabrication industry. According to an article in *Cutting Tool Engineering* in February 1990, Transmatic Co. of Holland Michigan increased the life of their deep drawing punches and dies by 100% by coating them with titanium nitride by CVD process. The coatings were done by Richter Precision of East Petersburg, Pennsylvania.

Coating helps in preventing abrasive wear. The coatings also prevent galling or cold welding of material to punches.

The tool coatings are done in high-temperature atmosphere in the presence of mixture of gases. The constituents of decomposed gases adhere to the tool or the surface to be coated.

There are two major kind of hard coatings:

CVD (Chemical vapor deposition)
PVD (Physical vapor deposition)

CVD operation is carried out at high temperature of about 900 to 1,050°C and the process deposit several layers of titanium nitride. The thickness of the coating is around 0.0003". CVD is a gaseous process and used mostly for tooling for stamping industry for forming die components. Since the CVD coated parts are subjected to high temperature, it may be necessary to post heat treat the tools to restore their mechanical properties. For metals, titanium carbide (TiC) is a most common coating. A second layer of titanium nitride (TiN) is also applied.

PVD coatings are applied in a vacuum chamber between 180 and 600°C. The solid material is used to condense on the surface of the tool. PVD is a low-temperature process, and coated pieces do not pose any distortion concerns. For cutting tools, the popular PVD coatings are titanium nitride (TiN), titanium carbo nitride (TiCN), titanium aluminum nitride (TiAIN), and aluminum titanium nitride (AITiN).

IonBond, a Swiss Co. with plants in the US and other countries, provides decorative as well as PVD, CVD, PACVD (plasma assist chemical vapor deposition), and laser hardening services.

For more information, visit www.ionbond.com, www.richter precision.com, and www.oerlikon.com/balzers coatings.

Turning on Lathe

This process involves the holding of the work piece in a chuck and turning at high speed against a cutting tool. Machining could be carried out by cutting tool with a carbide insert. Lathe helps in removing layer of material from outside or inside of tube. The lathes are available in forms, such as manual/engine lathe, CNC lathe, and screw machine.

The lathes are used for turning the outside, boring inside diameter, cutting internal and external threads, chamfering, facing, reaming, knurling, boring, and polishing. Following are different types of lathes:

1. Manual or engine lathe
2. Horizontal turret Lathe
3. Vertical Turret lathe
4. Single spindle Automatic Lathe
5. Multi spindle bar lathe
6. CNC Lathe

A manual lathe holds one cutting tool. A *turret lathes* has a Hex Turret which can hold six different tools for finishing several steps on the part. Horizontal manual Turret lathes are now more or less obsolete. They were designed for high production turning and drilling. Turret concept of carrying multiple tools is being used by slant bed CNC lathes and older vertical turning machines as Bullard.

Manual or CNC lathes are specified by the horsepower—the largest diameter of the piece it could turn and the length of part it can machine. Lathes have the following major parts:

- Headstock that holds the spindle, chuck, and gearbox for changing speed.
- Lead screw that provides longitudinal movement to tool post called X axis.
- Cross slide that provides Z axis to cutting tool.

Tailstock helps in holding the other ends of longer parts for machining purpose. Tailstock does not rotate but is able to slide on the hardened ways.

Lathe carriage holds the tool post and the cutting tools on engine lathes.

Chuck could have three jaws and four jaws and could be pneumatic or hydraulically operated.

For general purpose and for making a few turned pieces, a manual or engine lathe will do the work.

For high-volume production, computer numerically controlled lathes are very essential to survive in this manufacturing environment. A lathe controlled by CNC cuts machining time. Program is developed on the CNC lathe before the part could be machined.

A CNC lathe uses X and Z axes. The Z axis is parallel to spindle. This axis is used in machining the length of the part. The X axis is perpendicular to Z axes. This is controlled to machining the outside diameter of the part.

CNC lathes are provided with an indexable tool changer. The tool changers are designed to hold drills, threading tool, turning ID, and OD tool. In addition, some of the CNC lathes are provided an automatic bar feeder, high-pressure coolant system, and a chip conveyor.

The following are some of the manual and CNC lathes manufacturers:

> www.davenportmachine.com—This company builds multiple spindle chucking machines. These machines besides turning can do cross drilling, cross tapping, slotting, milling, thread rolling, and fly cutting.

> www.bardonsoliver.com—This company builds pipe and tube cut off and turning lathes.

> www.lagun.com—This company builds lathes, grinders, vertical mills, robotics, and acrylic polishing machines.

> www.Hasscnc.com
> www.toolmex.com
> www.southbendlathe.com
> www.romiusa.com

www.knuth-usa.com
www.mazakusa.com
www.emag.com
www.bourn-koch.com
Cincinnati Machine Co.

Swiss-type turning centers are extensively used for components, which need to be highly precise, small, and complex. Parts are made from a bar stock, which is fed through a hollow spindle. The older Swiss-type machines are cam operated and need skilled operators. The newer CNC machines are multitasking, and as such, they are provided with several tool attachments. Swiss-type screw machines are used for parts, which are less than 1-1/2" diameter. Once programmed, these machines run untended.

The following are some of the companies that make Swiss-type turning centers for small parts:

www.marucit.com/cincom.html (Marubeni Citizen Cincom)
www.tornos.com
www.maier-machine.de
www.remsales.com (Tsugami/Rem Sales)
www.indextraub.com
www.starcnc.com

CNC machines have the following advantages:

1. High-production output due to reduced cycle time
2. A low-skilled person can run the machine
3. High accuracy and consistency
4. For a long machining cycle parts, the operator can program and run other machines in a cell.

In a large machining facility, CNC machines are controlled by DNC software. This software and hardware can help download machine programs from a desktop computer to multiple machines.

Beside basic CNC machining software, some companies make computer-aided manufacturing software. This software simulates the actual cutting to prevent any tool crashes and obstruction with fixtures. The following are some of the software manufacturers: www.espiritcam.com, www.nccs.com, www.gibbscam.com, and www.mastercam.com.

Following are three CNC control builders and their key products:

1. www.fagorautomation.com (for CNC, feedback, and digital readout systems)
2. www.fanucamerica.com—Fanuc builds CNC-controlled equipment to assist in following processes:
   a. Arc welding using robots
   b. Assembly with robots
   c. CNC milling using multi axis control
   d. CNC motion control for 32 axis simultaneously
   e. CNC turning
   f. Machine tending—loading and unloading parts on machinery
   g. Spot welding robots
   h. Painting robots
   i. Part transfer robots with load capacity from 0.5kg to 2300 kg.
   j. Integrated CO_2 laser system from 1,000 to 6,000 watts for cutting sheet metal up to 32 mm thickness
3. www.usa.siemens.com/cnc and https://www.industry.usa.siemens.com/drives/us/en/cnc/applications/Pages/milling.aspx—Beside CNC controllers for mills and lathes builds the company makes drives, motors, generators, and motion control solutions.

Sample Multiple Spindle Screw Machine Companies

Based on their website, the following two companies can provide machining services: www.jessenmfg.com and www.ashleyward.com.

Manual Milling Machines

These are still widely available. The most common knee-manual mill was made by Bridgeport Machine Co. (www.bpt.com). These machines are designed to hold small parts on the table for drilling and milling operation. Similar manual machines are made by Cincinnati Machine Co. This company is now part of www.fivesgroup.com.

For manual milling machines, visit www.southbendlathe.com and www.sharp-industries.com.

CNC Vertical Milling Machines

These are used to drill, tap, and machine excess material using special toolholders and fixtures. These machines are available in three to six axes. These machines are available with several tool-changing pockets. These machines use milling tool cutters, which have round or square replaceable carbide inserts.

For a vertical milling machine, the horizontal left and right travel axis is called X. The Y axis is in and out, and Z is assigned to vertical spindle axis. A person with little machining background can learn CNC programming in a matter of few weeks.

These days, it is very common to have a five-axis milling machine where the spindle head could tilt and swivel for jobs, which require the making of molds. For more information on machine axes, visit www.engineering.com and see five-axis milling machines by Haas, Mazak, and Mandelli.

The CNC control takes advantage of computer-aided manufacturing program (CAM) to machine the parts. CNC mills are available to machine metals, woods, and plastics.

Beside vertical machines, CNC mills are also available as

A. horizontal mills,

B. bridge/Gantry mills, and
C. traveling column mills.

The following are some of the major manufacturers of CNC mills: www.emco-mecof.it, www.en.pama.it, www.snkamerica.com, www.mikromat.wzm.de, www.datron.com, www.toyodausa.com, http://us.pama.it, and http://www.mag-ias.com/web/en/produkte/produktseite.php. ....

Other companies:

> www.camozzimachinetools.com—It is the builder of large machining centers, consisting of Camozzi, Innse-Berardi, and Ingersoll Machine tools. Ingersoll Machine Co. of Rockford, Illinois, USA, before being acquired by Camozzi in 2003, was a builder of very large machining systems for locomotive and aerospace companies. I made several visits to Ingersoll Machine Co. in mid-80s to build a custom machine for a locomotive welded housing. Also, I had a chance to see in action several large Ingersoll machines at major aerospace customer (Boeing) in Oregon, USA.
>
> www.weingartner.com—This company is a builder of lathes with milling head for crankshaft, whirling machines for plastic extruder and cavity pumps screws.
>
> www.fivesgroup.com—This company comprises of Gidding and Lewis, Cincinnati Machines, Forest Line, Liné Machines, and Rouchaud.
>
> www.okuma.com
> www.doosanmachinetools.com
> www.dmscncrouters.com
> www.hardingus.com
> www.toyoda.com

www.us.dmgmori.com
www.heller.biz
www.okk.com
www.mightyviper.com
www.haascnc.com
www.mitsuiseiki.com
www.mikron.com

Large Machines

The major large machine builders are Cincinnati Machines, Pama, Fives Group, Cammozi, Mazak, Toshiba, and Pietro Carnaghi, USA Inc. In September 2018 issue of *Fabricating and Metalworking* magazine, the editor covered Mazak Versatech V-140N 5-axis mill installed at R-Tech Tool and Machine located at Wamego, KS 66547.

1. www.mazakusa.com— Below are specifications of their two models:

	Mazak Versatech V-140N/440	Versatech V100N/160
Max work diameter	10,000 meter	3000 mm
Height of work	3100 mm	2100 mm
Number of tools	30	30
Spindle type	60	60
Spindle tilt	200 degrees	200 degrees
X, Y, and Z travel	11,000, 4,600, and 710mm	4,000, 3,600, and 710mm

2. www.fivesgroup.com for Gidding and Lewis Boring Mills and Vertical Turning centers and https://metal-cutting-composites.fivesgroup.com/products/turning/giddings-lewis-vtc-series-5-8m.html.

3. www.pietrocarnaghi.com—The following are their major machine building capabilities:
   a. Big dimension vertical lathe—max. Turning diameter 126-700"
   b. Movable portal gantry milling machine—Distance between columns 138" to 550"
   (Source: their advertisement in Illinois Manufacturers Directory 2017)

Personally, I had an opportunity to work with Toyoda Machine Co. and visit Mazak and PAMA Machine Tool Company factories. At the end of this chapter, see a glimpse of DATRON's high-speed milling machines for aluminum and plastics.

Machining of Heavy and Large Pieces

Bill Kennedy covered the "Turning of Big Stuff" in the June 2004 issue of *Cutting Tool Engineering* magazine. I am listing a few companies that were listed in the article, and a few additional companies that can machine large components:

1. Grand Valley Manufacturing Co. (www.grandvalleymfg.com)—This company can machine parts with ID of 30" and length of 70 feet. The company can mill 17' x 14' x 8' workpiece.
2. Camco Machine Inc. (www.camcomachine/com)—This company can turn 40" diameter and eight feet high workpiece.
3. www.akrongear.com
4. www.machinecraftcompany.com
5. www.witherstool.com—The company, besides milling and turning, can also do large surface grinding.
6. www.three-m.com
7. www.retechtool.com

Tools for Turning and Milling

Carbide inserts are used extensively to machine outside and inside diameter of parts. For machining hard material, alumina and silicon nitride inserts are used.

The following companies provide cutting tools and toolholders for turning and milling:

>   www.Greenleafglobalsupport.com
>   www.bigkaiser.com
>   www.Kennametal.com--metalworking
>   www.brineytooling.com
>   www.sandvik.coromant.com
>   www.kyocera-sgstool.com
>   www.iscar.com

Each of the above manufacturers have their own carbide grades.

Hard Milling

It is being used for machining pre hardened materials using ceramics and PCBN cutting tools. It is a process of removing small amount of hard material (RC 42 or higher) on lathes and 3-, 4-, and 5-axis milling machines at a very high speed. In some instances, hard turning is being replaced for grinding operation. Since the grinding operation is slow, hard turning speeds up the machining operation.

Inserts made of cubic boron nitride (CBN) and polycrystalline cubic boron nitride (PCBN) are good for machining pre hardened material. This machining process will be successful if the machine is rigid to control vibrations. Also, if liquid nitrogen is sprayed during hard-material machining, the life of CBN and PCBN will increase. The liquid nitrogen will bring the temperature down to -320°F. For more information on ceramics and PCBN inserts, check with Sandvik-Coromant Company.

Grinding

This is a process of removing small amount of material from metals by using abrasive belts, discs, diamonds, and cBN wheels. These abrasive tools are used in toolrooms and manufacturing to do the following:

1. Sharpen drills, taps, reamers, and cutting tools
2. Sharpening steel dies for thread rolling
3. Polishing molds for die-casting and injection molding
4. Grinding outside diameter for bars and tubes

The most common grinding machines in a shop are surface grinder, tool and cutter grinder, cylindrical grinder, centerless grinder, drill and reamer sharpener, and bench and pedestal grinder.

Surface grinder has a horizontal spindle and a reciprocating table. The work to be ground is set up on a vise or magnetic table. The table could be moved by hand or by a motor drive.

- ❖ Tool and cutter grinder could be manual or CNC controlled. They are used for sharpening taps, end mills, and special tools.
- ❖ Cylindrical grinder is used to grind OD of round parts, which is held between two centers.

Centerless Grinding

The round bar material required for screw machines and thread rolling application has to be purely smooth and uniform. The commercially available material sometimes is not uniform.

Centerless grinding is used to smooth out the not-so-round bar material. The grinding wheel provides accurate and cleaner finish. The work is held on a blade in between the grinding wheel and the regulating wheel.

The unfinished bar is fed through between a regulating (rubber bonded) wheel, which is set about three degrees and the grinding wheel.

There are two major versions of these grinders—through feed and end feed. The end feed is used for taper and plunge grinding.

Per www.maxgrind.com website, centerless grinding has the following advantages:

1. More productivity
2. Less setup time
3. Removes less material
4. Provides stability to the work

Grinding wheels are made from aluminum oxide, silicon carbide, diamonds, and cBN materials. See more information about their specifications is under glimpse of Norton Abrasives website.

Cubic Boron Nitride (CBN) Grinding Wheels

CBN wheels provide superior life and finish when used for high-speed and alloy steel components. These wheels are very effective on machines, which are supplied with water- or oil-based coolants. CBN grains have higher hardness and abrasive resistance than aluminum oxide wheels, which get dull faster.

Glimpse of grinding machines manufacturer (www.sharp-industries.com).

1. Cylindrical grinder for OD and ID—8.6" diameter and 20" length
2. Manual surface grinder—6"×18" table
3. CNC cylindrical grinder—18" swing and 80" between centers
4. Double column surface grinder

Drill sharpeners are special dedicated machines for sharpening tips of small and large diameter drills. For drill sharpening machine, visit www.rushmachinery.com.

Glimpse of Rush Machinery Product Line

The company builds wheel truing machine, drill and tool grinder, grinding oil filtration system, cutoff machines for carbide rod, and PCD tool grinding machine.

Grinding wheels are used to grind steel, nonferrous metals, tool steel, carbide, and ceramic. The grinding wheels are made from aluminum oxide, silicon carbide, boron nitride, and diamond.

Grinding wheels are available in different sizes. They as specified by diameter, width, and size of an arbor hole. They could be a thin and flat cutoff type. In addition, they are specified by grit size, grade, and bond-and-grain type.

For more information on specifying grinding wheels, visit the following website: www.nortonabrasives.com, www.cgwcamel.com, www.aaabrasives.com, and www.buffaloabrasives.com.

As a glimpse of grinding wheel manufacturer www.nortonabrasives.com, the company manufacturers:

1. Precision grinding wheels
2. Rough grinding wheels
3. Cutoff wheels
4. Diamond and cBN products
5. Wheel dressing products

For full-line abrasive products, visit their catalog no. 7362. Their grinding wheels are specified according to the following:

1. Type of abrasive such as alumina, alumina oxide, and silicon carbide
2. Grit range—Extra coarse (XC), coarse (C), medium (m), and fine (F)
3. Grit size—XC- (24-36), C-(50 to 80), and F (180-220)
4. Density—2 (soft) to (9) harder, which gives better finish
5. Bond-type resin-B, shellac-E, plastic-P, rubber-R, and vitrified-V

For toolroom application, visit their page on Vitrified Wheels and Norton Diamond / cBN stock wheels.

For grinding machinery, visit www.maxgrind.com, www.trutechsystems.com (3-axis grinding machines), www.studer.com (United Grinding Technologies), www.clausing-industrial.com (surface grinders), www.hardingeus.com, www.chevalierusa.com, and www.kentusa.com.

For centerless grinding service, visit www.bostoncenterless.com and www.minnesotagrinding.com.

Burnishing

After the boring or drilling operation, the machined inside diameter of any hole has peaks and valleys. The surface of the hole is not totally smooth.

To improve the surface finish, a process called roller burnishing is employed. The burnishing tool consists of a set of hardened steel rollers. These planetary rollers are forced against the inside diameter of the machined hole.

The pressure of tool compresses or displaces the metals. The peaks are pushed into the valley. This flow of metal improves the surface finish. Usually, the ductile material could be burnished easily.

Burnishing can improve the inside diameter finish of connecting rods (for internal combustion engine pistons), valves, air and hydraulic cylinder, and brake system holes.

Honing Systems

This process is used to improve the quality of machined hole. Honing improves the quality of the small and large engines cylinders, gear holes, hydraulic valves, and pumps.

Rotating honing abrasive tool puts inside pressure on the hole. This improves the roundness and straightness of the hole. The process removes very little stock.

For honing, two to three spindle machines are designed for valves, pumps, and engine blocks.

For more information, visit www.sunnen.com and www.engis.com for honing equipment for piston hydraulic pumps, two stroke small engines, fuel injectors, and cylinder liners.

According to an article in August 2006 issue of *Products Finishing*, Brush Research Mfg. Co. makes ball-style hones for bore finishing. Ball hones replace stone hones, which are used in bore finishing. Ball hones create cross hatching, which results in good lubrication for piston rings.

For more applications on honing, visit www.pfonline.com, and for information on flex hones, visit www.brushreasearch.com.

Direct Metal Laser Sintering (DMLS)

This is a 3-D method to make prototype of smaller parts using a three-dimensional CAD drawing.

This equipment uses fiber optic laser to sinter or bond the metal powder stock together. The part is built one layer at a time. It creates dense prototype of the powder material from cobalt chromium, aluminum, and nonferrous alloys. For more information visit www.temcotool.com.

Stereolithography

This is another method of making 3-D plastic parts. It uses photo sensitive plastic resin, which responds to UV radiation. In this process, a new layer of melted plastic resin is laid on top of already cured layer. The three-dimensional part is created by successive layers of plastic resin.

This method is used to make concept parts. The process is also used for master pattern for investment castings. For more information visit www.temcotool.com.

Flexible Manufacturing Systems (FMS)

This involves use of several CNC machines, which are connected together with a set of conveyors to machine parts.

These systems are designed to machine same family of parts for agriculture, mining, automobile, and earth-moving component manufacturers.

The CNC machines are programmed to partially mill and drill parts. The parts are inspected by an in-process probe to check the quality of parts. After inspection, the part is sent to another machine or station, which can finish the parts. Flexible system uses a set of pallets, which hold the parts on special fixtures. Pallets wait in a programmed sequence to finish the parts. A host computer is used to control conveyors and CNC machines. For flexible manufacturing systems, visit www.pietrocarnaghi.com.

High-volume Production Machines

If your business manufactures very high volume small round, hex brass, zinc, and other cast or forged components for cars, trucks, defense, water, fire hoses, locks, and pneumatic and hydraulic industry, then you should look for transfer machines and multispindle machines.

These machines allow machining two to four sides of the parts simultaneously after first clamping. These machines are designed to cut machining time. Based on information picked at September 2018 IMTS show, please visit www.buffoli.com (Buffoli Transfer SpA) and http://www.btb.it/en/machines-types/linea-trod (BTB Transfer SpA) and look at their capabilities.

Automated Assembly Machines

There are several builders of assembling and packaging equipment for consumer and medical products. Visit a builder's website at www.arthurgrussell.com (The Arthur G. Russell Co.)

Robots in Industry

Similar to CNC machines, robots are programmed to assist the handling of material, welding, and other assembly functions in manufacturing. Due to their flexibility, robots can be integrated in a manufacturing cell. This integration is accomplished with the sensors and exchanging of signals.

Robots are reprogrammable and use electric servo drives for the movement of their several manipulating axes. Each joint of the robots have a degree of freedom. Robots are provided with grippers for conducting different tasks.

Robots can be provided with mechanical, pneumatic, suction, magnetic, and needle grippers or end effectors. Robots are also used for routing, grinding, MIG, and spot welding. The major manufacturers of robots are: Fanuc, Yaskawa, ABB, Kawasaki, Epson, Nachi, Denso, Kuka, Mitsubishi, Comau, and Foxconn.

According to A3Automate.org (October 2018), 381,000 robots were sold worldwide in 2017. Japan is the world's biggest producers of robots. Also, the reports note that the biggest users of robots are in China, Japan, South Korea, Germany, and United States.

As per Robotics and Automation (January 11, 2018) website, Fanuc has installed over 400,000 and Yaskawa sold over 360,000 robots worldwide. For more information, visit

www.roboticsandautomation.com,
www.robotics tomorrow.com,
www.abb.com/robotics,
www.fanucamerica.com,
https://www.intelligentactuator.com/productoverview-new/,
www.yrginc.com, and www.motoman.com (Yaskawa).

Glimpse of the website www.yrginc.com (YRG Robotics Systems) as they provide the following systems:

1. High-speed pick and place
2. Single-axis cartesian
3. Multi axis articulated

4. Multi axis cartesian
5. Scara series

Glimpse of www.motoman.com website: Motoman builds 150 types of robots for carrying out welding, machine tending, painting, packaging, and palletizing.

Collaborative Robots or Cobots

In October 2018 issue of *Medical Manufacturing and Machining*, Brian Dillman of Universal Robots of Odense, Denmark covers the advantages of cobots. According to Brian, they are designed to handle parts, which are less than ten kg. The following are key advantages of collaborative robots:

1. They have very small footprints and can be installed in limited and tight spaces.
2. From safety point of view, these robots are designed to stop if they feel obstruction.
3. They are lightweight and are easy to relocate.
4. They do not require extensive fencing and mounting base.
5. They can locate the parts within +/- 0.004".

According to their website, they have over 25,000 installations worldwide. They are being used for injection molding, machine loading/unloading, assembly (pick and place application), and welding and assembly operations. According to Brian, in the US, Universal Robots are being used by Dynamic Group of Minnesota and Tegra Medical products of Massachusetts.

According to www.universal-robots.com website, about one hundred cobots are being used by Bajaj Motorcycle Co. of Pune, India, for repetitive work.

Following are additional related websites for equipment and training:

www.techspex.com (Lists machine manufacturers, distributors, work holding systems, and tools)
www.cncci.com (source for CNC training)
www.machinetoolhelp.com
www.mms.gibbscam.com (CNC programming for turning, milling, wire EDM-2–5 axis milling)
https://www.vision-systems.com/index.html

3-D Printing

This phenomenon of making prototype parts from 3 dimensional CAD prints is being adopted by every industry, which needs plastic or metal components. The following is a source of suppliers: https://3d.markforged.com/3-D-Printing-Buyers-Guide-for-Manufacturing.html?mfa=man.

Production Efficiency

Once a company invests substantial capital in machinery, the aim of the owner should be to utilize the equipment 24 hours a day. The aim should be to minimize downtime for any reason. The following are some of the areas where you can improve productivity:

1. Loading and unloading of the parts (look into robotic part handling or dedicated loader)
2. Machine should be able to change the tooling quickly (similar to ATC arms on CNC mills).
3. Make sure gauges and tools are available at the machine or have QC inspector available.
4. Arrangement to load the part while other part is machined.
5. Have high-pressure coolant system available on CNC mills and lathes.
6. Have bar feeders available on CNC lathes
7. Have dual pallet system for CNC mills

8. If possible, buy equipment with built-in gaging probes to inspect complete piece
9. Scheduled time for machine preventive maintenance

Return on Investment on Capital Equipment

Before buying a major piece of equipment, every owner of business should look into return on investment. The owner/ manager must compare productivity of the present equipment with the new equipment he or she intends to purchase. They should look at labor savings and additional productivity from the new equipment.

Use the following simple formula to estimate return on your investment:

= (Estimated annual savings by new equipment + annual depreciation of new equipment based on 5 or 10 years life) / (Total investment- salvage value of existing old equipment to be replaced)

Laser-Alignment Systems

Functioning machinery can go out of specifications. The equipment loses accuracy and needs to be calibrated to make parts. Although there are mechanical means to fine-tune the equipment; however, laser alignment is the most accurate to calibrate the equipment. These equipment have very low laser power (1mw). The following are some of the areas where laser can help:

1. Machinery such as CNC lathes, CNC mills, and grinders
2. Roll alignment for paper mill, printing, and textile equipment
3. Power generation such as alignment of steam turbines
4. Shaft alignment between pump and motor
5. Steel fabrication
6. Bore alignment etc.
7. Calibrate plastic extruders

For more information, visit www.hamarlaser.com.

Glimpse of CNC equipment:

1. DATRON milling machines: I met Steve Carter, brand manager of DATRON Dynamics of Milford, New Hampshire, on September 11, 2018, at the International Machine Tool Show in Chicago. Steve authorized me to include the pictures of his equipment and two white papers on high-speed machining and batch machining. The following are major specifications of their CNC mills:

DATRON M8 Cube CNC high-speed milling machine for aluminum and plastics

> Travel-X-40", Y-28" and Z-9", 30 tool—automatic tool changer
> Spindle 48000 to 60,000 RPM with cast polymer concrete bed
> Window-based control software—4 and 5 axes option

DATRON M10 Pro-CNC high-speed milling machine

> Travel—X-41", Y-28.35" Z-9.44"
> Spindle 3 Kw-40,000 RPM
> Solid granite machining table
> Microsoft Window based CNC 3- to 6-axis option

Note: DATRON has two following white papers on their website (www.datron.com).

1. Batch machining
2. High-speed machining

Note for tooling high-speed machining:
In December 2002, an article "Fast and Light" by Steve Piscopo and Peter Mesa of Sandvik Cormant appeared in www.toolingandproduction.com.

The article discusses the use of CoroMill 790 cutter for high productivity of machining. This cutter can cut pockets in aluminum by helical interpolation.

Glimpse of major US machine builder:

www.cinmac.com (Cincinnati machine)—Types of machines built by them:

1. Surface grinders, way grinders, rotary surface grinders, centerless, blanchard, and tool and cutter grinder
2. Engine lathe
3. Radial drill, multiple spindle gantry drill
4. Deep-hole Drilling
5. Vertical machining centers and knee mills

www.haascnc.com (Haas machine company builds)
Vertical Mills, Horizontal Mills, and Rotary Indexers

US-based www.toyoda.com builds CNC horizontal and vertical mills, grinders, and turning centers.

Machinery Safety

The manufacturers of machines usually provide guarding to protect the machine operator from any injury. Also, it is the responsibility of machine operator not to circumvent any safety interlocks and guards during operation of the machine.

In US, the Department of Labor's Occupational Safety and Health Administration can look into any unsafe practices of any company. For any maintenance of the equipment, the company management must use lockout/tagout method to service the equipment. This method involves attaching a special lock to machine control power disconnect, which prevents the operator to start the machine.

Every person who is exposed to any machining, welding, metal cutting and grinding must wear safety glasses to protect his or her eyes.

Metal Finishing

Somehow this area of product decoration does not belong under this chapter, but I feel is necessary to discuss brief sources of these services:

A good source of product finishing information is available at www.pfonline.com. I was subscriber to their journal for several years. The website and its publication covers electroplating, powder coating, cleaning and pretreatment, vacuum coating, liquid coating, anodizing, and mechanical finish.

Common Electroplating Methods

The following are the most common methods of Plating:

1. Copper plating
2. Hard chromium plating
3. Decorative chrome plating
4. Nickel plating
5. Electroless nickel plating
6. Zinc plating
7. Tin plating
8. Silver plating
9. Gold plating

Glimpse of www.fmcallahan.com: An article titled "The Ins and Outs of Electroplating" was written about F. M. Callahan and Son of Malden, Massachusetts (www.fmcallahan.com) by Barbara Donohue of www.todaysmachiningworld.com sometime between 2006 and 2009. The Callahan Co. provides the following finishing services: precious metal plating (gold and silver), zinc, copper, bright nickel, electroless nickel, and tin plating. Also, they provide anodizing for aluminum.

Powder Coating

Components for appliance, automotive, building, electrical, furniture, lawn, and garden industry are being finished with powder. It is a dry finishing process, where fine particles of pigment and resin are charged electrically and sprayed on the grounded part. The freshly powder-coated part is passed through a curing oven. The fine powder melts and provides a smooth surface on the part.

The powder does not contain any volatile organic compounds. The air used in the powder spraying cycle could recirculate in the plant. As compared to liquid painting, powder coatings are environmentally safe method providing corrosion protection and please appearance.

Thermoplastic and thermoset are two kinds of powder coatings. Thermoplastic coatings use materials such as polyethylene, polypropylene, nylon, and polyvinyl. Thermoset powder coatings use epoxy, polyester, acrylic, and silicon.

Epoxy coating is used extensively for coating reinforcing metal rebars and other metal products used in road and concrete bridge construction.

For more information on powder coating industry, visit www.powdercoating.org. The site provides buyers' guide for all related to powder and equipment supplies.

Galvanizing

To prevent atmospheric corrosion, machined and fabricated steel components (including nuts and bolts), which are used in open, should be galvanized. Galvanizing coating prolongs the life of these metal components.

The most common method is called hot-dip galvanizing. Prior to galvanizing, the parts are cleaned by heated alkaline bath or acid pickling. The process is carried by dipping cleaned parts in a melted zinc tank called kettle. The melted zinc reacts metallurgically with steel to form tight coating.

According to American Galvanizers Association, more than 600,000 tons of zinc is used every year in North America for hot-dip galvanizing. For more information and suggestion for design of the product for galvanizing, visit https://galvanizeit.org/hot-dip-galvanizing/what-is-galvanizing.

Used Machinery

There are situations where you do not want to invest in new equipment. The following websites will help you find used equipment to fit your business:

1. Machinery Dealers National Association—https://mdna.org
2. Surplus Record—https://surplusrecord.com/
3. https://www.locatoronline.com/

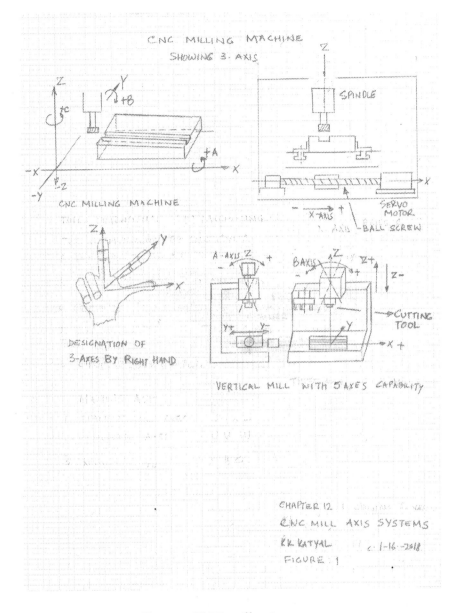

Fig. 1—CNC mill axis system

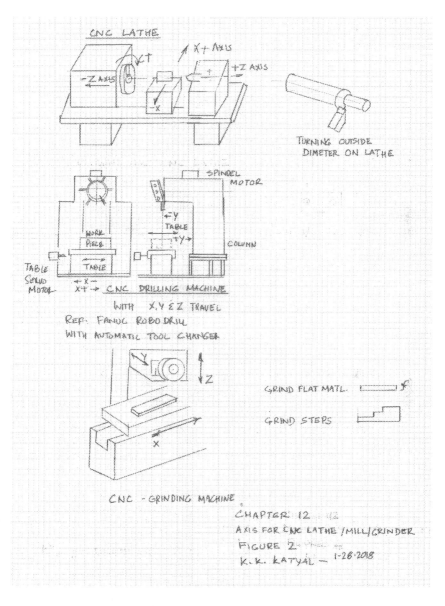

Fig. 2—CNC lathe and grinder

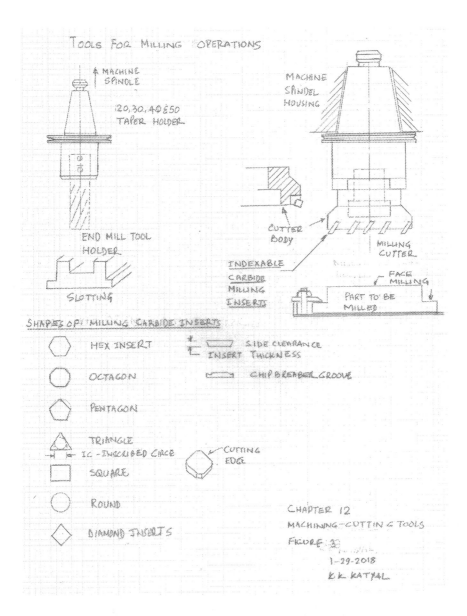

Fig. 3—Mach cutting tools

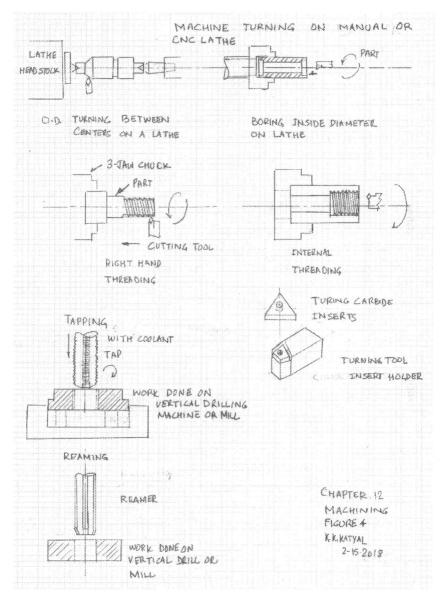

Fig. 4—Turn-thread-tap

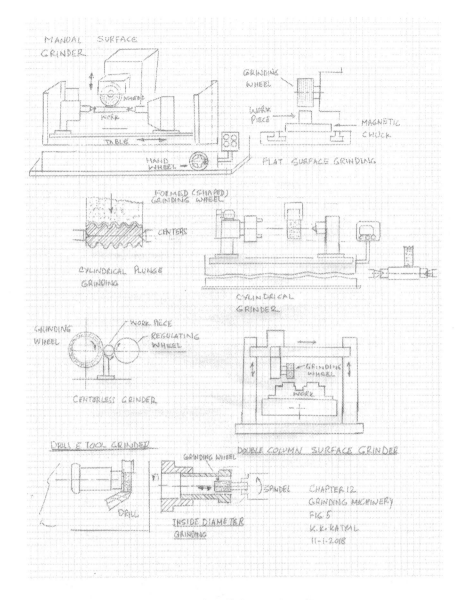

Fig. 5—Grinding equipment

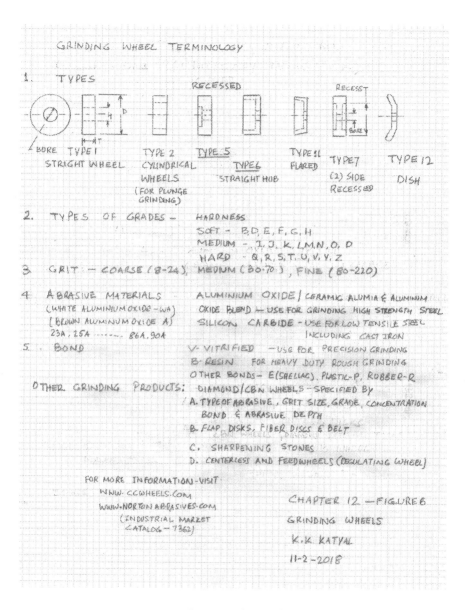

Fig. 6—Grinding wheel

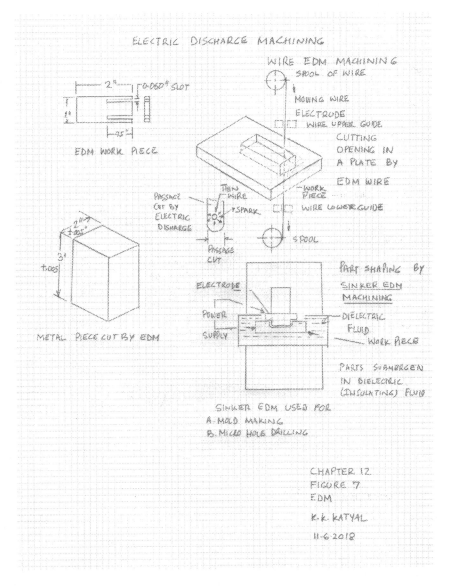

Fig. 7—Electric discharge machining

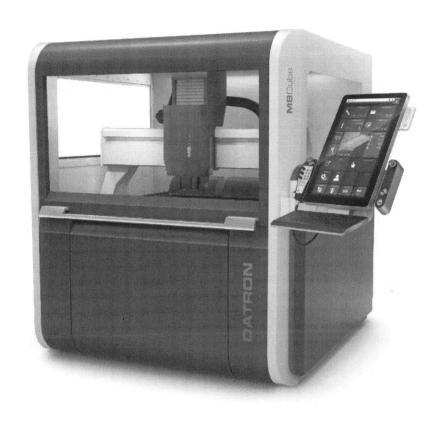

DATRON M8C Cube CNC mill

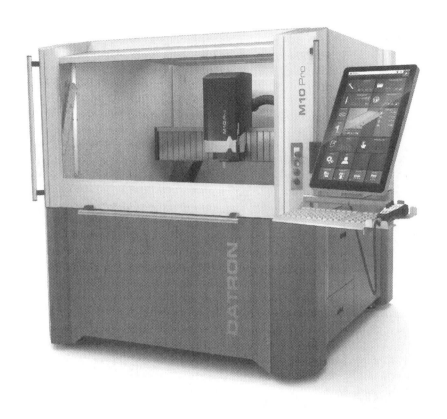

DATRON M10 Pro CNC mill

CHAPTER 13

Machinery Components and Electrical Systems

Topics covered are bearings, ball screw, lead screw, belts, clutch and brake, chain, springs, gears, gear motors, linear and rotary tables, rack and pinion, pulleys, linear actuators, AC motors, adjustable speed drives, DC motors, servomotors, stepper motors, HMI graphics board, limit switch, LVDT sensors, proximity and photoelectric sensors, encoders, RFID tags, wiring, control panel, and schematics and programmable logic controller.

GENERAL AND SPECIAL machinery used in industry consist of several mechanical, electrical, hydraulic, pneumatic, and lubrication subsystems.

It is important that we familiarize these components. Hydraulic and pneumatic systems are group under fluid power.

Mechanical Components

The frames of all machines are usually made from one of the following materials:

A. Cast iron
B. Steel fabrication
C. Aluminum frame
D. Sheet metal

The other major components are as follows:

Bearings

Bearings reduces rotational friction between shaft and the housing. It also helps in bearing radial and axial loads. The following are a few categories of bearings:

1. *Ball bearings* are made of balls, which are located between inner and outer race. They are used for light load and high-speed application.
2. *Roller or cylindrical bearings* are used for heavy-load and slow-speed application.
3. *Needle bearings* are used for heavier loads. They are used for tight-space application.
4. *Thrust bearings* are helpful where slight shaft misalignment could be a problem.
5. *Tapered roller bearings* are used for radial and axial loads. These bearings have tapered inner and outer ring raceways.
6. *Spherical roller bearings* can tolerate some misalignment of shaft.

Bearing Failures

The bearings should be selected based on axial and radial loading, speed, temperature, heat, sealing arrangement, and lubrication. Bearings can fail due to shock loading, high force, improper alignment, too tight and loose mounting, lack of lubricant, improper viscosity, and wrong selection of lubricating oil or grease.

Due to internal clearance between the raceways, balls and rollers, preloading of the bearings is necessary. Bearings can also fail because of lack of preload. To keep the metal and dirt particles out of raceways, proper shields and seal should be part of the design.

Major bearing manufacturers are www.koyo.com/en, www.nskamericas.com, www.timken.com, www.schaeffler.com, www.thk.com, www.amroll.com, www.aurorabearing.com, www.rexnord.

com-bearings, and http://www.skf.com/us/knowledge-centre/media-library/index.html.

Graphite sleeve bearings can be used where the machine is exposed to vibration, grit and high temperature, and if it needs frequent wash down. For information on graphite bearings, visit www.graphalloy.com (Graphite Metalizing Corp.)

Ball Screws

They are used to convert rotary motion into straight motion. In other words, ball screw provides linear motion. It consists of set of balls inside a nut with helical groove and a machined screw shaft. The rolling of balls eliminates sliding friction. Ball screws can take heavy thrust loads. Rotary stepper motors and servomotors are usually attached to ball screws. This assembly helps in positioning or transporting loads. The torque to drive ball screw is one third of lead screw design. Almost all CNC vertical and horizontal mills are attached to ball screws assembly to provide X-, Y-, and Z-axis travels.

The Tool carriage of slant bed CNC Lathe is attached to a ball screw. Ball screw provides precise positioning to light and heavy loads. Ball screws do need frequent lubrication during its working life.

Major manufacturers of ball screws are www.hiwin.com, www.schneeberger.com, www.steinmeyer.com, www.thk.com, www.haydonkerk.com, and www.dynatect.com.

Lead Screws

They also provide linear motion. They do not have any recirculating balls. The lead screw system is used where efficiency, rigidity, and accuracy are not of concern. Due to large surface contact between the nut and the screw shaft, lead screw can take heavy loads. Most manual lathes have lead screws to engage the saddle, which holds cutting tools. Lead screws are designed with acme, buttress, and square threads. The friction with the engaging nut is higher than the ball screw nut. Due to this reason lead screws are not efficient for micro movement and do bind because of dirt and chips on the screw shaft.

Lead screws are manufactured either by machining or thread rolling. The leads crews made by thread rolling are much stronger. And if necessary, they could be ground for better accuracy.

Belts

Belts are usually quiet. Most of the belts are reinforced by cords. The materials for belts are polyester, fiberglass, polyurethane, and carbon fiber.

Toothed belts are made for pulleys with teeth. And V-belts are used for V-pulley. For more information, visit www.martinsprocket.com, www.fptgroup.com (Fenner), www.sdp-si.com (for timing belts and gears), and www.brecoflex.com. For timing pulleys, visit www.cmtco.com.

Electromagnetic Clutch and Brakes

Clutch is used to engage and disengage the load from the main driving motor. Clutch helps in rapid cycling of the load. Clutch can help in cycling the load more frequently than a motor. Single clutch is also used in machine gearbox to start and stop different functions.

Brakes are used in conjunction with clutch to stop the mechanical part from moving. It also holds the moving part. Brakes are also used to slow down in winding and unwinding of cable drums. Clutch and brakes are also used in power presses. Clutch-and-brake combination is used on packaging machines and conveyors. This combination also reduces the stress on the motors. The following are major manufacturers: www.kbamerica.com (Permanent magnet brakes), www.altramotion.com, www.placidindustries.com, www.cjmco.com (Carlyle Johnson), www.warnerelectric.com, and www.rexnord.com (PT dive components).

Note: Clutch and brake manufacturers recommend their use with motors driven by variable frequency drive controller.

Couplings

They are used to connect electric motor output shaft to conveyors, gearboxes, pumps, and fans. Couplings are available in rigid and flexible design. Some of the common manufacturers are www.zero-max.com, www.lovejoy-inc.com, www.ringfeder.com, and www.nbk1560.com, www.reuland.com.

As a glimpse from the website www.reuland.com, these are the types of their couplings:

1. Beam coupling
2. Bellows coupling
3. Control flex coupling
4. Oldham coupling
5. Disc coupling
6. Jaw coupling

Glimpse of www.lovejoy-inc.com website, as they make the following couplings, such as jaw, S-flex, gear, torsional, and quick. Also, they make variable speed pulleys.

Chain

Roller chains are used to transmit the power from motor sprocket to a machine spindle or driven sprocket. They are used in completely covered environment and open condition with practically no lubrication. All components of chain are hardened to provide long life. It consists of roller link plates, pins, and bushings. According to the chain selection article in June 2004 issue of *Motion System Design*, the following are the key criteria for its usage:

1. Minimum recommended number of teeth on smaller sprocket should be nine.
2. Maximum number of teeth on large sprocket should be 120.
3. Minimum speed ratio should be three to one.

4. The smaller sprocket should have a minimum 120 degrees wrap.
5. Minimum center distance between smaller and larger sprockets should be the sum of their diameters.

For more information on chains, visit www.rexnord.com, www.skf.com-transmissionchains, www.martinsprocket.com, www.fptgoup.com (Fenner), and www.tsubakimoto.com.

The other critical parts for machines are the following:

1. Springs
2. Gears (spur, helical, bevel, worm, hypoid, etc.)—For more information, visit the following suppliers' websites: www.khkgears.us, www.excelgear.com, and www.imsgear.com.
3. Gearboxes—These are speed reducers, which multiply the torque. They are integrated with AC and DC motors and run at constant speed. Gearbox could be face- or foot-mounted. They could be right angle, worm, or parallel shaft. The following are some of the suppliers for gearboxes: www.dieuqa.com, www.harmonicdrivegearhead.com, www.bodine-electric.com, www.newgartusa.com, www.sewdrive.com, www.groschopp.com, www.bisongear.com, and www.forestcitygear.com.
4. Gear head / gear motors—They are speed reducers and allow large load to control with small motors. They are available foot-mounted and face-mounted with AC and DC motors. Gear heads are used with servomotors, which frequently accelerate and decelerate. Some gear heads have low backlash for very accurate positioning. Planetary gear heads can multiply torque and provide very accurate positioning specially for tapping and other machining.

Gear motors are available with spur, helical, or worm design. Worm and helical gearbox are more efficient. They are also available with brush and brushless options. Brushless motors can run at higher speed and are more reliable. Brush motors are prone to electrical shorting due to wearing out of carbon brushes. A gear motor reduces number of parts and misalignment between motor and gearbox. For more information, visit www.baldor.com (for AC/DC motors, gearboxes, and drives) and www.parker.com (electromechanical drives—North America).

5. Positioning stages—Linear or rotary tables are used as a subassembly for holding parts or fixtures. For more information, visit www.aerotech.com, www.hiwin.com, and www.festo.com.
6. Rack and pinion sets—These are used for linear motion. They are used for small packaging machines to large traveling column CNC milling machines. The pinions (gear or roller) are usually driven by servomotor for accuracy. For more information, visit www.nexengroup.com.
7. Pulleys—They are used to transmit power and reduce and increase number of revolutions per minute. Pulleys are available for flat, V, and toothed belts. Pulleys are made of steel and plastic composites.

To lighten the weight of the equipment, pulleys with plastic composites are available with embedded fibers, such as glass, carbon, and aramid. Pulleys are available both for thermoset and thermoplastic materials. For improved mounting, the composite pulleys can be provided with oil-impregnated sintered bushings. Plastic pulleys are good for equipment that needs to be washed down.

Linear Motion

Linear actuators are used in machines to provide straight line motion. The most common actuators are the following:

1. Pneumatic cylinder
2. Hydraulic cylinder
3. Electric linear actuator

The pneumatic cylinder provides fast and simple movement. But it does not provide accurate feedback of its travel in mid stoke or partial location.

Electric linear actuator provides a very accurate way of positioning machine slides. Direct-driven linear actuators eliminate gears, cams, belts, pulleys, and ball screws.

Electrical System and Components

AC Electric Motors

The alternating current–driven electric motors drive pumps for water, hydraulic pumps, gearboxes, and other units using special couplings.

The electric winding of AC motors is located in the stator (outside shell). The outer stator induces the rotation in the rotor. As such, no brushes are attached to the rotor of the AC motor. AC motors are suitable for wet and corrosive environment. They are widely available through manufacturers and distributors. There are two kinds of AC motors: induction and synchronous.

For many years, there was no simple technology to vary the speed of AC motors. For a long time, DC motors was the choice for locomotives, plastic extruders, lift trucks, and many other machines. The new development in microprocessors has created new-cheaper variable speed controller.

From the maintenance point, AC motors have no commutators, spring and brushes, which results in less breakdown of the equipment. Also, AC motors run cool as compared to DC motors. AC motor drives are replacing DC motors on lift trucks, locomotives, ships, and machine tools. According to the article "GE Stays on Track by Rebuilding Locomotives" in *Assembly Magazine* of August 2018 by Austin Weber, the traction motors of older DC-powered locomotives are being replaced with AC motors. The newer technology provides better controls to the wheels.

The following factors should be considered for the servicing or selection of AC motor:

1. Voltage—They could be a single phase with a voltage of 110V or 3 phase with 230 or 460 volts with 60 hertz frequency.
2. RPM—Typical standard AC motors are designed to run at 900, 1,200, and 1,800 revolutions per minute.
3. Horsepower
4. Frame size, location of junction box, and type of mounting (hinged or feet)
5. Enclosure—The common motor enclosures are open-drip proof (indoor application), totally enclosed fan cooled (used for conveyors), totally enclosed nonventilated, totally enclosed blower cooled, and explosion proof fan cooled.
6. Hazardous location—Check if explosive gas, dust, and vapors are present. Look for manufacturers suitable code letters, *A* to *G*, and class 1 and class 11 ratings for the right application.
7. If the motor selected is suitable with variable speed controller.

Motors fail in field due to overheating and unbalanced voltages. For motor maintenance, make sure the motors are not exposed to outside heat. And at the same time, using digital multimeter, check the voltage in each electrical phase. Also, check voltage between phase to phase in a 3-phase supply.

For more information, visit www.leeson.com (for 1- or 3-phase motors), www.kamanautomation.com (Minarik AC/DC drives), www.baldor.com, and www.magtrol.com (for motor testing equipment).

Adjustable Speed Drives

Three-phase AC motors can run at one speed using magnetic motor controller. Most of the applications these days require variable speed due to change of loads. AC drives (electronic controlled) are available for variable speed application. This controller is called variable frequency drive. To avoid heavy in rush of current, these drives start with low frequency and low current.

In machinery building, the engineer has to decide the application of the motor such as the following:

A. Variable torque
B. Constant torque
C. Constant horsepower
D. Speed range
E. Open-loop or closed-loop feedback

The adjustable drives can be used for conveyors, fans, pumps, blowers, cranes, compressors, cut-to-length lines, extruders, and mixing machines. Some CNC milling machine spindles use vector drive, which provides large speed range and good torque.

Adjustable speed drives can also be replace old DC drives on plastic extruders. Depending on simple application, they can be installed without feedback encoder.

For more information, visit www.controlsys.org and www.controldesign.com, www.yaskawa.com, www.baldor.com, www.fanuc.com, www.schneider-electric.us/en, www.industry.usa.siemens.com/drives, www.usmotors.com, www.seweurodrive.com, and www.danahermotion.com.

DC Motors

In DC motors, the main rotational field winding is located on the rotor. The rotating armature is supplied power through brushes. DC motors are known to be very high starting torque as such as they have been preferred for locomotives and plastic extruders. However, failures do happen on DC motors if carbon brushes are not changed periodically.

For more information visit: www.torquesystems.com/dynetic (Montevideo Technology Inc.), www.leeson.com, and www.kaman automation.com.

For miniature motors, visit www.micromo.com, www.faulhaber.com, and www.hsi-inc.com (Haydon Switch).

Servomotors

All CNC mills and lathes use servomotors on all axes. These motors are used when requirements such as incremental positioning, deceleration, and acceleration are required. These motors are provided with closed-loop devices such as encoder or resolver to provide precise speed and torque. These motors are sold in DC or AC versions. Brushless DC servomotors provide high reliability. To reduce the size motor and increase the torque output, servomotors are paired with a gearbox.

Stepper Motors

They are used for open-loop application where feedback from encoder is not required. These motors can start and stop for a fraction of a degree. These motors are designed to take fraction of a step without using any feedback such as encoder or resolver. These motors are programmed to provide certain amount travel to a slide block or a tool. For more information, visit www.linengineering.com.

These motors are specified according to output torque, step angle, speed, and rotor inertia.

For more information on servomotors and stepper motors, visit www.micromo.com, www.electrocraft.com, www.kollmorgen.com, and www.fanuc.com.

HMI Graphics Panel

Human machine interface panels consist of LCD screen. They serve the function of inputting commands to operate the machine. They replace push buttons and knobs on the machines. According to

National Electric Code and October 2017 "Control Design" article by Dave Perkow, HMI graphics panels are not safe for explosive atmosphere applications. For more information, visit www.maplesystems.com.

Sensors

In designing automation systems, there is a need of several sensors to sense linear displacement and angular position. Real-time feedback is necessary for PLCs and microcontrollers. Sensors are also required for gas turbines, steam turbines, diesel engines, gas engines, and collision warning for automobiles. According to "Machine Design" article published in July 8, 2004, some of the sensors are resistive (potentiometer), capacitive, inductive (AC-LVDT, DC-LVDT, LVRT, and LVIT), magnetic (hall effect, magneto resistive and magneto strictive, ultrasonic, laser, and pulse encoder) and optical.

The following are additional sensors and switches:

Limit switches. These are very common switches on automatic machines. These are mechanical devices. The switch has a rocker arm and an adjustable screw. Machines are programmed to stop with the actuation of these switches. For more info, visit www.euchner.com, www.wilbrechtledco.com, and www.schneider-electric.us.

Position sensors. The servomotors and AC motors provide rotary and linear motion to machine components. It is important to provide feedback to motor and controller about the angular and linear position of the mechanical device.

The following are some of the commercially available position sensors:

LVDT sensor. It is used for feedback for linear motion. LVDT is an abbreviation for Linear variable differential transformer. It can operate in extreme machine surroundings. It is a non contacting transducer and provides signal to controller about the location of mechanical system. For more information, visit www.keyence.com/LVDT, www.microstrain.com (Lord Sensing), www.positek.com and www.rdpe.com, www.cw-industrialgroup.com (Curtiss Wright-Penny and Giles Sensors), and www.evrtp.com (Everight Position Technologies).

Inductive proximity sensors. There are small cylindrical. They are designed to sense the presence of metal objects. They can stand in shock and vibration. When powered, they emit radio-frequency signal. The presence of a metal object in its magnetic field sends a signal to machine controller.

Capacitive sensors. They can sense metal and nonmetal objects. Both inductive and capacitive sensors are designed to sense objects for distance of about two inches. For targets from 2" to 100 ft. LED and laser sensors could be a good fit.

Photoelectric sensors. They are used to sense the presence of conducting and non conducting parts or items. It is a two-part system. One part is a LED or laser light source. The other part is reflector or detector, which mounted opposite the light beam. To prevent accidental closing of car garage door in the US homes, a photoelectric sensor is mounted at the sides. Packaging industry is one of the biggest uses of these sensors.

Ultrasonic sensors. These could be used for sensing height of liquid or grease inside tanks.

For more information on proximity, photoelectric, laser, ultrasonic, and fiber optics sensors, visit the following websites: www.keyence.com, www.bannerengineering.com, www.micro-epsilon.com, www.sick.com, www.omega.com, www.pepperl-fuchs.com, www.gavazzi-automation.com or www.gavazzionline.com, and www.rockwellautomation.com.

The other special sensors are used to monitor pressure, voltage, temperature, and vibration of engines for aircraft and locomotives using special software. For information on sensors for force, torque, and acceleration, visit www.kistler.com.

Encoders

They are transducers, which sense the position of shaft during rotation. Encoders are used in high-speed motors and robotics. It is a sensing device, which transmits the electric signal to programmable logic control or counters. There are two kind of encoders—linear and rotary. For more information, visit www.encoder.com, https.//kuebler.com, www.usdigital.com, www.beisensors.com (optical and magnetic rotary encoders), www.heidenhain.com (linear, angle, and rotary encoders—length gauge), and www.newall.com.

Potentiometers provide analog feedback to controller.
Resolvers provide analog feedback of mechanical motion.

RFID TAGS

Bar code or universal product code (UPC) are used in manufacturing to process parts. Also, UPC code is used in retail business environment. For the last few years, radio frequency identification device (RFID) is being used to identify metal and plastic parts. This is a non contacting method of tracking the assemblies and components. RFID labeled parts or assemblies could be sensed from a distance.

Wiring

For wiring the machine control panels, motors, and switches, we need to adhere the guidelines outlined by National Fire Protection Association. Look for 2015 or newer NFPA 79, Electrical standard for Industrial Machinery.

Also, follow American wire gauge size for their current carrying capability. Common machine control uses 14, 16, and 18 AWG wires. No. 14 AWG is popular size that can carry 20 amperes of current. Also, check the voltage-carrying capacity of the wires and markings by approval agencies such as Underwriters Laboratories.

For power distribution, consult *Modern Commercial Wiring* book written by Harvey Holzman.

Control Panel Schematics

Dave Perkow, technical editor of *Control Design*, wrote an excellent article about the design of electrical schematics for machine control panel in September 2016. Electrical schematic is a diagram, which depicts all functions and the electrical items inside and outside the panel.

The control panel houses the main power disconnect, motor starters, PLC, variable speed controller for motors, safety relays, timers, and other items.

The electric schematic (drawn by hand or computer-aided design) becomes a blueprint for wiring the machine. It also provides us with bill of material of the components in the system. The bill material also lists NEMA enclosures.

The main input voltage to the control panel could be 110 V, 240 V, or three phase 480 V AC. The schematic must follow all UL/NFPA/NEC codes.

The newer panels are designed with an option to connect to internet.

Programmable Logic Controller Sequence

These controllers are software based. *PLCs* were introduced for controlling the machines in early 1970s in the US. This concept brought flexibility to all kinds of equipment. To actuate various systems of an automatic machine, a programmable logic control systems is used. The designer (usually electrical engineer) writes a program to enable actuators to perform their functions. This program is called ladder logic.

The ladder Logic sequence provides the following:

A. Machine start
B. machine pause/stop
C. Automation or manual mode

For a typical robot, these steps could spell the sequence of picking the part, assembling with other parts.

Usually, each manufacturer of PLC has its own set of guidelines.

To enhance productivity and getting real-time performance, PLCs are being replaced by program automation controller (PAC), which uses the power of personal computer. This system helps in communicating with sensors and industrial internet of things (IIOT). For more information about PLC and PAC, visit the following website: https://www.arnoldmachine.com/plc-vs-pac-whats-difference/.

Control Cabinet

In a typical machine control cabinet, we have the following components:

1. Power disconnect (depending on voltage and current)
2. Control transformer rated in kVA
3. Fuses
4. Circuit breakers
5. On the door of cabinets (items such as push buttons, selector switches on membrane switches are located)

6. Relays and programmable logic controller
7. Motor controllers if required

For control panel components, visit www.schneider-electric.com, www.new.ABB.com,

www.eaton.com, www.cooperindustries.com, www.rockwellautomation.com, www.siemens.com, www.euchner.com, www.idec.com, and www.hms-networks.com.

For further reading on mechanical devices consult the following:

1. *Machine Devices and Components* by Robert O. Parmley, PE, which is published by McGraw-Hill books.
2. Related magazines: www.powertransmission.com and www.machinedesign.com

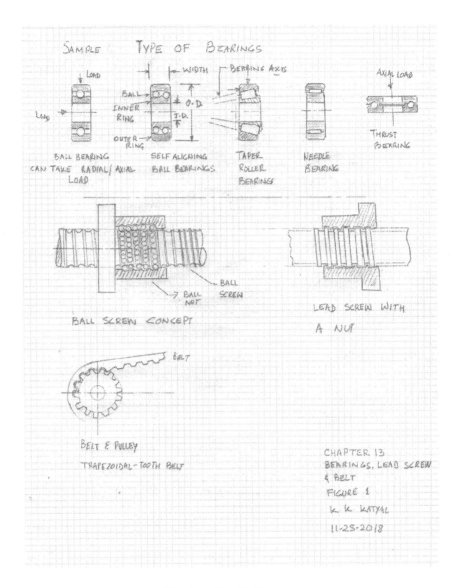

Fig. 1—Brg-Ball screw

CHAPTER 14

Fluid Power Systems

Hydraulics and Pneumatics Systems

Topics covered are hydraulics and pneumatic systems difference, air/oil filter specifications; air tanks, air dryers, air system components, plastic connectors, air valves and vacuum system; hydraulic components—fittings, metric threads; hydraulic fluids—viscosity, fire resistant fluids; hydraulic oil tank, oil filters, tank breathers; hydraulic hoses; valves—flow control, pressure control, and directional control; hydraulic—pumps, motors, gauges; sources for hydraulics and pneumatics components; fluid power graphic symbols; preventive maintenance tools, and fluid power training sources.

Fluid Power

IN FLUID POWER, we have two systems—hydraulics and pneumatics. Hydraulics uses high-pressure oil from its pumps to actuate cylinders and motors. Hydraulic systems use pressures from 300 to 10,000 psi. On other hand, pneumatics uses low-pressure, compressed air (100 to 125 psi) to actuate components of packaging and other processing equipment.

Hydraulic system is a closed-circuit system. It needs two lines for each valve—one line has pressure flow from the pump, while the other line takes the oil back to tank.

While for pneumatic system, the source of air is plant's compressor system. The pneumatic valves need one air pressure line. The air from other side exhausts to atmosphere. The pneumatic systems provide fast response and used for light load capacity.

Hydraulic Systems

These are more expensive than a pneumatic system. Hydraulic components are used for aerospace, construction, agriculture, lawn and garden, mining, oil and gas, material handling, trucks, machine tools, and paper and plastics equipment. In a typical CNC horizontal mill, hydraulics are used to actuate tool changer and locking of the indexing table. At the same time, air is used to keep spindle clean from dirt.

Hydraulics provide very high forces to actuate systems on commercial aircrafts, hydraulic presses, equipment to pull steel-reinforcing cables for concrete bridges, mobile construction, and agriculture equipment. Hydraulic equipment is based on Pascal law. The law states that when pressure is applied in a closed loop system, it is transmitted equally in all direction. The force is calculated by multiplying hydraulic or pneumatic pressure with surface area. Large cylinder diameter will have more force than smaller cylinders.

Basic hydraulic system for any equipment consists of a power unit. The power unit contains hydraulic oil, reservoir, prefilters, heat exchanger, oil distribution manifolds, pump (gear, vane, or piston) with attached electric motor, and pressure relief valves.

The power unit is further connected to actuating cylinders or hydraulic motors with a set of manual or electrically actuated 2, 3, or 4 way solenoid valves. The valves and power units are connected with high-pressure steel tubing, special fittings, and flexible hoses to actuators.

More sophisticated hydraulic systems are provided with servo-controlled valves, which provide very accurate movement to cylinders and motors. In addition, hydraulic units are provided digital indicators for oil pressure, temperature, level, valve actuation, and condition of filter.

The other common applications of hydraulics are earth-moving machines, waste collection trucks (https://www.heil.com/products/automated-front-loaders), band saws, CNC lathes, and special equipment to fixture parts on the machine.

Filters

The following information is about filter specifications:

Filters are required to protect the components of pneumatic and hydraulic systems. The filtration is a process of pushing liquid or gas through a medium, which can clean the fluids.

Air systems use paper and porous powder metal filter to clean the air. While oil filters are made of metal or plastic screens, string wound cellulose acetate, viscous rayon, and polypropylene cartridges.

Filters are classified according to micron size.

One micron is equal to 0.000039" or 0.001 mm (10 raise to power -6 meter)

Human hair diameter is 0.0035" or 0.0889 mm or could be from 50 to 70 microns). For information sake, the following are typical particle micron sizes:

Table salt	100 micron (100µm)
Red blood cell	8 micron (8µm)
Bacteria	2 micron (2µm)
Smoke particle	0.5µm, aerosol particle—0.05µm
Naked eye can see	40 micron

Hydraulic intake oil filter usually have 50 to 100 mesh screens. The following are common mesh screens:

US mesh	Inches	Micron
20	0.0331	841
40	0.0165	420
50	0.0117	297

ESSENTIAL GUIDE TO METALS AND MANUFACTURING

100	0.0059	149 micron
230	0.0024	63 micron
400	0.0015	37 micron

Note: To prevent failure of the hydraulic pumps and pneumatic valves, the manufacturers recommend to use a very specific small micron oil and air filter. In the September/October 2018 issue of *Fluid Power Journal*, Donald C. Krause of Flow Ezy Filters recommends to use the following suction line micron size filters:

Piston pump—low pressure (250 to 500 psi—149 micron)
high pressure (1000 to 2000 psi—74 micron)
Vane pump—low pressure (250-500 psi—238 micron)
high pressure (1,000-5,000 psi—149 micron)

Note: For the long operational life of hydraulic pumps, motors, and valves, please follow the manufacturers' recommendations.

Pneumatic Systems

Pneumatic components are used for building equipment for machine tools, packaging machinery, food processing, medical equipment, semiconductors, and other special equipment. Most of the pneumatic components use air from 90 to 125 psi (pound per square inch). The air is used for the following functions:

1. Actuating air motors, air valves, and air cylinders
2. Power transmission
3. Portable pneumatic drills and sanders
4. Painting guns, tire spreader, grease guns, and tire inflators
5. Lift tables
6. Air chucks to hold parts and cleaning spindles of CNC mills
7. Large grease pumping systems
8. Clamping and marking

Air Compressors

Air compressors are required by many industries as well as on ships and submarines. Compressors are manufactured as diaphragm, oil less reciprocating (piston), rotary screw, rotary vane, and vacuum pump.

The normal air in the atmosphere has a pressure of 14.7 psi or 101.3 kPa at 68°F at zero feet altitude on earth. The atmospheric pressure of 14.7 psi is equivalent to barometric pressure of 29.92" of mercury, 1.013 bar and 0.986 atmosphere. The atmosphere pressure is lower at the altitude of 5,000 ft.

A typical manufacturing plant has one or more air compressors with air lines all over inside of the property. The compressors are designed to run from 100 to 125 psi. Kaeser Compressor Company builds their rotary screw machines up to 600 HP and 217 psi pressure output. Common piston-type compressor has 80 gallon tank and 5 HP electric motor. It delivers 10–13 CFM air. Piston-type compressors are good for short-term application.

The air output of compressor is expressed in SCFM (standard cubic feet per minute) and pressure. The major two kinds of compressors are rotary screw type and reciprocating (piston) type. Depending on the size, their motors could be wired for 115 V single phase to 3 phases with voltages from 230 to 460 V. The compressor is selected based on highest air demand (CFM), pressure, size of storage tank, and duty cycle. Common air pressure is set around 115 psig.

Air compressors are fitted with the following:

1. Air receiver (tank) with relief valve and automatic drain to store clean, dry air
2. Air line filter
3. Refrigerated air dryer
4. Oil removal filters
5. Air lines throughout the plant
6. Air drops behind every machine with filter, regulators, and lubricator (if required) and manual shut-off valve. Some operations may have 4" ID pipe with 1 degree inclination

throughout the plant to distribute air. To keep the moisture out from the machine, the air supply tube or pipe leading to machine should be taken up ward and then directed down. The water in line should be removed by filters with automatic drain.

Air (Tank) Receivers

They are attached or located next to air compressors. Make sure they are fitted with maximum pressure relief valve. These tanks improve the efficiency of air distribution system in a plant. It supplies immediate air requirement to the system and dampens the pulses in the air line.

Air Dryers

A typical manufacturing plant has one or more air compressors. Air from the compressor is hot, laden with moisture, and with dust particles. Based on dew point, the air starts condensing in the tank and also in distribution pipe lines.

The water in the system is detrimental to air cylinders in machine tools and portable air-operated shop tools.

To remove water, compressor feeds into air dryer.

There are three kinds of air dryers—refrigerated, desiccant, and heat of compression. They are further subdivided as cycling and nonrecycling dryers.

Dryers are selected based on the following:

1. Air consumption
2. Amount of dryness expected from the unit
3. Match air output with the compressor

As published in March/April 2018 issue *Fluid Power Journal*, Ron Marshall of Marshall Compressed Air Consulting wrote, "Every 20°F increase in air temperature doubles the amount of water in system." He recommends both compressor and dryer must be located in open and cool place to dissipate heat. Based on humidity levels, compressed air has certain level of moisture. An automatic water draining system is very helpful in removing moisture from after air coolers, filters, dryers, and tanks.

Some of the air dryer manufacturers are www.atlascopco.us, www.norgren.com, www.laman.com, and www.saharahenderson.com.

Some of the air compressor manufacturers are www.atlascopco.us, www.gardnerdenver.com, wwwbauercomp.com, www.us.kaeser.com, www.quincycompressor.com, www.ingersollandproducts.com, and www.origin.atlascopcogroup.com, www.sauercompressor.com (Germany).

Air System Components

Air Filter, Regulator, Lubricator, Gauge Unit (FRL)

For any machine, which requires compressed air, it must be provided with this modular FRL unit. They are available in 1/8", ¼", and 3/8" NPT sizes.

In this combined unit, air up to 150 psi enters the filtering unit. This combination of air filter, regulator, and pressure gauge is required for machine tools. These units clean the air as well as lower the pressure. The filter has element that can clean the air from 5μm and 40μm particle sizes. These units are also available up to 12 bar (175 psi) of pressure settings.

Need of Lubricator for Air Systems

The pneumatic system for a machine may have valves, cylinders, pneumatic chucks, drills, or a clamping system. To prevent leaks, they have rubber or synthetic seals. To maintain proper sealing, these seals need some lubricant in the form of oil vapors. Air line lubricators are designed to mix a drop of oil at some intervals. Lubricators are available with manual and no drain. Before periodic lubricator filling, check recommended viscosity of oil.

Some of the major manufacturers of air filter, regulator, and lubricators are www.imi-precision.com, www.masterpneumatic.com, www.kelleypneumatics.com, www.arrowpneumatics.com, www.aventtics.com/us/en (pneumatic valves and cylinders).

Plastic and other Connectors for Pneumatics

Quick-connecting plastic connectors are being used for low-pressure (125 psi or less) air lines. These connectors normally use flexible plastic (nylon) tubing between air valves, cylinders, and regulators.

Plastic connectors are also being used for machine tools and low-temperature (less than 200°F) medical applications. Before selecting plastic connectors, consider the temperature range, pressure, flow rate, and the media to be conveyed.

Typical material used for plastic connectors are polyethylene, polycarbonate, polyamide (nylon), ABS, acetyl, PTFE, and PVDF.

For small pneumatic system, 6 mm OD nylon tubing is used with straight and 90-degree elbows.

Connectors made of brass, zinc, and stainless steel can be used for high-temperature application. Black steel pipes with NPT threads are used to interconnect air supply lines from compressor. Metal or plastic barbs and quick-disconnect couplings are used for connecting machines to main air line or filter-lubricator and regulator modules.

For fittings, visit www.camozzi-usa.com, www.andersonmetals.com, www.imi-precision.com, www.aignepusa.com, www.smcpneumatics.com, https://www.swagelok.com/en/Services, and www.parker.com.

Actuators for Pneumatics

Primarily, there are air cylinders that provide speed and force for automation. They could provide straight and angular motion

Actuators could by compact, rodless, or heavy duty. They are available in single-acting and double-acting versions. Rotary actuators can provide angular motion with rack and pinion.

Pneumatic motors provide low torque and used for high-speed drilling. The other industrial tools such as grinder, screw driver, welding slag remover, impact wrench, and chipping hammer use pneumatic motors.

Ingersoll Company builds air starters for several equipment, visit them at https://www.ingersollrandproducts.com/en-us/power-tools/products/air-starters/air-starters.html.

Valves for Pneumatics

Manual and solenoid actuated valves are available to control airflow. The pneumatic valves have an exhaust port, while in the hydraulic valves, the oil returns tank. The following are the categories of the valves:

1. Subplate mounted
2. In line
3. Proportional valve (Flow control is adjusted by current or voltage control.)
4. Flow control
5. Nonreturn valve

Directional valves may have 2, 3, 4, or 5 ports. They can be manually, solenoid, or pilot operated.

Pneumatic solenoid valves are also used in medical devices. Usually, they are used for high-performance oxygen delivery, diagnostic equipment, patient monitors, ventilators, and respirators. The air pressure for the medical valves is about one to two bars. These valves are lightweight and compact.

The following are other components used in pneumatic systems:

- Speed control valve—It is sold as in built, in fittings, or separately.
- Check valve—It is a nonreturn valve and allows media to flow in one direction

- Pressure—It has vacuum switch, flow switch, after-cooler, and noise-reducing muffler.

More information about pneumatics components is available at https://www.arozone.com/en/products/pneumatic-valves-and-cylinders.html, www.smcpneumatics.com, www.imi-precision.com, and www.parker.com/pneumatics.

According to Aro Pneumatics (www.arozone.com) website, they make the following air operated products:

1. Filter, regulator, and lubricators
2. Air-operated diaphragm pumps
3. Piston pumps
4. Lubrication pumps
5. Pneumatic valves and cylinders

Vacuum System

High-pressure air is used to create vacuum for picking up small objects in the packaging industry. The vacuum systems consist of pumps, cups, bellows, and switches. Vacuum is used in industries such as sign-making and glass and automotive trims. CNC router and heavy fabric cutting use vacuum to hold the material. The vacuum causes suction force to hold the material during cutting.

For more information on vacuum system builders, visit vacuforce.com, www.smcpneumatics.com, and https://www.piab.com/en-US/.

Hydraulic Components and Systems

In most applications, the hydraulic system consist of a suitable clean metal tank that contains petroleum-based special oil (exception in some cases water), filter, electric motor (AC/DC), pump, electric or manual valve, piping, cylinder, or hydraulic motor.

In the hydraulic system, the force or energy is transferred through oil or water. The force created by a pump is transmitted equally in the closed loop system. In some cases, once initiated the power to hold, the load stays with the use of gas-charged accumulator.

In the US, the hydraulic system follows National Fluid Power Association (NFPA—www.nfpa.com) guidelines, including the following:

1. American National Standard Association (ANSI)
2. American Petroleum Institute (API)
3. Society of Automotive Engineers (SAE)

Hydraulic Fittings

Fittings are chosen based on pressure, vibration, and temperature. To achieve leak-proof joint, metal-to-metal contact is essential. They are chosen based on the size of tube, wall thickness, flare, bite type (flareless), and *O*-ring. The *O*-ring fitting provides leak-proof joint by compressing an elastomeric seal.

According to John Joyce of Brennan Industries, most of the hydraulic fittings are made from seamless stainless steel tubing. The fittings could be flared or flareless (compression). Flared fittings are used in earth movers and construction equipment. Metal-to-metal contact reduces leakage. Medium- to high-pressure system (3000 psi) uses compression (flareless). Also, they use O-ring fittings for leak-tight connections.

Flare-type fittings are used for thin and medium thick tubing. Flareless fittings could be used for thick-walled tubing. Fittings with *O*-ring are being preferred for high-pressure systems.

For low-pressure pneumatic system, the selection of material for fittings could be stainless steel, aluminum, or brass. For hydraulic application, forged corrosion resistant alloys and stainless steel materials are used.

The following are the major categories of threads:

- UN/UNF, NPT/NPTF—In US, thread forms for hydraulic fitting follow NPT, SAE straight thread, and UNC guidelines. Wherever the hydraulic components are taken apart frequently, the uses of fittings with NPT or pipe threads should be avoided. NPT threads are prone to leak for high-pressure oil system.

Please note what each letter stands for—*N* stands for national, *P* for pipe, *T* for tapered thread, *F* for fuel, *S* for straight thread, and *M* for mechanical joint.
- BSPP (parallel), BSPT (tapered), British Standard or BS (British standard parallel pipe and British standard taper pipe)—Please note that NPT threads have 60-degree angle, while BSPT has 55-degree angle. Also, NPTF thread is not interchangeable with BSPT thread (source: Gates Rubber Co.).

Also, note that Japanese-tapered pipe thread is fully interchangeable with BSPT. Japanese 30-degree flare parallel thread is not interchangeable with BSPP threads.

Metric Threads

Some of the standards for metric threads are metric parallel, metric tapered (International Standard Organization or ISO), Deutsche Industrial Norme (DIN), IEC, and Japanese Industrial Standard (JIS).

Hydraulic Fluids

The function of hydraulic fluid is to transmit power; lubricate pump moving parts, cylinder, and valve parts; and provide lubricity to seals and dissipate the heat. Water is not a proper fluid for hydraulic system. Water evaporates when heated. Also, it freezes and rusts the parts. Water-based system are used in some mining and steel mill equipment applications.

Hydraulic fluids are very sensitive to the temperature. The life of hydraulic fluids is affected above 140°F. The fluids can be become corrosive above 160°F.

Viscosity

It is oil's measure of the resistant to flow at a given temperature. The ability to pump the fluid depends on its viscosity. Higher viscosity oils are sluggish and take longer to flow. If the viscosity is too high, the flow is sluggish, and the system generates heat and increases pressure drop. If the viscosity is too low, the oil will leak through seals and not provide lubricity to moving parts.

Viscosity is expressed as kinematic viscosity in cSt (centistokes), in Saybolt universal second (SUS), and dynamic viscosity (centipoises—cP) units. Most common hydraulic oils have an ISO viscosity range from VG 22 to 68 numbers.

Commercial manufacturers (Mobil, Chevron, and BP or British Petroleum) of hydraulic oils specify their products according to ISO viscosity grades. The most common descriptions are grades AW 32, 46, and 68.

Here, AW stands for antiwear and ISO grade 32 stands for viscosity in centistokes (cSt). For other lubricants, standards are laid down by SAE, AGMA, and ISO.

Green biobased hydraulic fluids are being preferred by equipment users in the national forest service. This is to prevent the forest from being contaminated by petroleum-based fluids.

Most of the commercial hydraulic oil manufactures recommend using ISO grade 32, 46, and 68 products. For a specific requirement, you must follow the machine manufacturer's recommendation. If you are building a new equipment, evaluate the following properties of hydraulic fluid:

1. Viscosity grade (cSt at 40°C)
2. Pour point (the lowest temperature at which oil will flow)
3. Flash point (the temperature at which it gives enough gas to flash)
4. Fire point (the temperature at which oil will catch fire
5. Resistant to oxidation (prevent making of sludge)
6. Fluid (should be able to transmit force, conduct heat, and lubricate moving parts)
7. Wear

For more information on oils, visit the websites of Shell, Mobil, BP, Chevron, Hydrex, and Lubriplate Companies:

1. https://www.shell.us/business-customers/lubricants-for-business/lube-space.html
2. https://www.shell.us/business-customers/lubricants-for-business/lube-space.html (major hydraulic oil manufacturers)
3. https://www.mobil.com/en/industrial/lubricants/applications/hydraulics
4. https://www.chevronlubricants.com/en_us/home/products/product_category/hydraulic_oils/industrial.html
5. www.lubriplate.com
6. https://www.bp.com/en_au/australia/products-services/lubricants/hydraulic-flulid.html
7. Hydrex hydraulic oil-wwwlubricants.petro-canada.ca

Fire Resistant Hydraulic Fluids

A ruptured hose on a hydraulically operated machine can cause fire. A fire-resistant hydraulic fluid can prevent the propagation of fire. The following synthetic fire resistant fluids are available:

1. High water-base fluids
2. Water in oil emulsion
3. Water—glycol hydraulic fluids (HFC)
4. Synthetic fluids

Peter Skoog of Quaker Chemical Corporation in September/October 2018 issue of *Fluid Power Journal* recommended the use of three kinds of fire resistant Quintolubric hydraulic fluids. For more information on fire resistant fluids, visit their website at www.quakerchem.com.

Hydraulic System Major Components

Oil reservoir stores and protect the oil from contamination. The tank is a part of the closed-circuit system. The tank size should be minimum three to eight times the pump output. The steel tank should be large enough to dissipate heat and allow dirt and contaminants to settle down.

The tank should be large enough to release entrapped air. Most tanks are made of steel and provided with pump inlet, return line, suction line oil strainer, breather filter, sight glass, and a magnet plug to catch fine steel particles.

The life of hydraulic pump can increase if you increase the size of the tank. The larger tank also provides dwell time to escaping trapped air. Air trapped in hydraulic system can cause noise level to increase, heat load, and oxidation, and thermal degradation of fluid.

Oil filtration. Many of the failures in hydraulic systems occur due to dirt and contaminants. The following are sources of contaminants:

1. Newly fabricated steel tank and hoses
2. Rust, paint, dust, and metal chips
3. Lint from cleaning cloth
4. Moisture from air breather mounted on tanks
5. Oil oxidation
6. Fine chips from valves and pumps

Society of Automotive Engineers (SAE) classifies oil quality from 0 to 6. Class *0* has least amount of contaminants. The oil with *6* contaminants may be suitable for system where extreme cleanliness is not necessary. Oil with Class 0 has 2,700 particles in 1,000 cc. of fluid while class 6 has 12,8000 particles in 1000 cc. Class 0 oil is filtered through 5µ element. Class 6 oil is filtered through 40µ cleaning element.

Filtering medias. Usually paper filters are good up to 150 psi, while stainless steel can work up to 4500 psi. The other common filtration media's are the following:

1. Porous media
2. Wire cloth, polyester, and metal fiber
3. Woven filter (stainless steel wire, or nylon fiber)

A 100 mesh filter has 100 strands per inch. Also, a 100-mesh (1 sq. inch with 10,000 squares) screen has 149μ (micron) opening. A 325-mesh screen has 44 μ (micron) openings.

Filters are located at pump suction line as well as in pressure line. Pressure line filters are not common. For higher flow, 100 to 60 micron filters are installed in suction line. Suction filters are located inside the oil tank.

Return line filters are used very frequently. A 10- to 20-micron filter is located in the return line of a hydraulic system.

Filler breathers. These are usually mounted on top of oil tank. They provide dual functions of filling the fluids and also act as a breathing device for the tank. It allows air to flow in and out of tank. They are also provided with foam or other filter media to catch dust particles in air. The filtering media can catch particles up to 40 micron.

Hydraulic hoses. Flexible hydraulic hoses are used to connect pumps and valves to cylinders and hydraulic motors. Hoses are manufactured according to SAEJ517 and European (EN) standards and rated for certain pressures.

Usually hose manufacturers supply their own end fittings. The fittings are swaged or crimped to the ends of cut hoses. To resist abrasion, the hoses are covered by wire spring, spiral steel, and polywraps.

Most hoses on equipment fail due to temperature and age. Consider changing the hose if it leaks, abrades, and develops bulges or blisters. For replacing the old hose, check its inside and outside diameter, pressure rating, temperature rating, and end-fittings sizes. For more information on hoses, visit https://www.gates.com/us/en/fluid-power/c/102.

Flow-control valves. Valves are used to direct the flow rate of oil to regulate the speed of actuators. The following are a few kinds of valves:

- Check valve—This valve allows the flow in one direction only.
- Flow control valve—It allows change of speed of hydraulic actuator by an adjustable orifice. This provides free flow in one direction and reverses check in other direction.
- Pilot-operated check valve—This valve allows the flow in one direction in normal condition. It is provided with another port for pressure signal to mechanically open the flow in reverse direction.

Pressure-control valves. They are used to keep hydraulic system safe. They are available as the following:

- Relief valve—It is used to limit maximum pressure in the hydraulic circuit.
- Pressure reducing valve—This valve is used to reduce the pressure of oil in the secondary circuit.
- Sequence valve—Depending on pressure, this valve is used to sequence the other parts of the circuit.
- Pressure limiting valve—This is used to limit pressure in the secondary circuit.

Directional valves. These valves direct the flow of oil in the hydraulic circuit. They may contain a spool or piston to divert the flow. These valves can be actuated manually by electric solenoid or by a pilot pressure line. These valves are available in two positions or three positions and with four ports.

These valves are mounted independently on manifold or on subplate. A four-way valve ports are labeled as pressure (P), T-tank, and A and B. The oil can flow from pressure P to A and B ports.

These valves are available as spring centered with electric solenoid on one or two sides.

Some valves are provided with manual handle and detent for a specific position. Also, these valves can be purchased with servo or proportional options.

- Proportional valves—These valves can vary pressure, flow, and direction from a remote position.
- Servo valves—These valves provide internal feedback and operate in a control loop. They are used to control the actuation of cylinder or motor very precisely.

Hydraulic pumps. Pumps usually are driven by electric motor. The motor's electric energy is converted to hydraulic energy. The pump output is expressed as gallons per minute or liters per minute. The output is also expressed as cubic inches per revolution of the shaft.

The pumps are available with positive and nonpositive displacement (centrifugal). Hydraulic pumps with positive displacement are available as gear, vane, and piston.

The piston pumps are available as radial or axial designs.

Hydraulic motors. They are used as prime movers for agriculture, garbage truck, aerospace, and industrial equipment. They are supplied by high-pressure hydraulic fluid. The following are some types of hydraulic motors:

1. External gear motor
2. Internal gear motor
3. Gerotor motor
4. Vane motor
5. Radial piston motor
6. Axial piston motor

Hydraulic motors are selected based on torque, speed, and the available supply pressure.

For hydraulic pumps and motors, visit www.parker.com, www.eaton.com, www.enerpac.com, and www.nachiamerica.com.

Pressure gauges. Gauges are different for air lines and hydraulic tubing. Gauges contain C-shaped spiral and helical Bourdon tube. Beside pressure, they are specified by connection size with male or female thread. Also, they are specified as male and female with bottom or back mounting.

The dial of pressure gauge is calibrated in bar, psi, or kPa. The cover of gauge could be glass or plastic. Some liquid gauges are filled with glycerin to dampen shock and vibration.

Digital pressure gauges with strain gauge are also available. They have LED or LCD readout with battery backup.

Gauge isolator. It is used between the gauge and the hydraulic circuit to protect it from pulsations in line.

Flow meter—a nonpermanent device—is used to check the flow in the system. It is used temporarily to check the amount of flow.

For more information on air and hydraulics systems, visit the following websites:

> www.hydraulicspneumatics.com (magazine)
> www.nfpa.com (National Fluid Power Association)
> www.fluidpowerjournal.com (magazine)
> www.ifps.org (International Fluid Power Society)

Hydraulic Component Sources

- http://www.hydraulics.eaton.com/ (for hoses, filters, cylinders, power sources, valves, motors, etc.)

- www.unitedalloy.com and www.ifhgroup.com (for hydraulic tanks)
- https://www.enerpac.com/en-us/e/USProducts (Enerpac provides work holding pumps, cylinders, jacks, and air and hydraulic manual valves)
- www.webtec.com-pumps/motors/and/valves.
- www.schydraulic.com-Hyd (test cart)
- www.mpfiltriusa.com (filters)
- www.danfoss.com (valves, switches and electric controls, filter cart) www.sevennorthindustries.com

Following is the website of Parker Company for fluid power products:

- http://www.parker.com/hydraulicvalve/accumulator/actuator/cylinder/finitefilter/and/gear pump

Following is a link to Bosch Rexroth industrial hydraulics components:

- https://www.boschrexroth.com/en/us/products/product-groups/industrial-hydraulics/onoff-valves/standard-hydraulic-valve-overview/index

Pneumatic Products Sources

- https://www.smcpneumatics.com/SMC (Pneumatics provides the following components for air: directional control valves, air cylinders, rotary actuators, vacuum equipment, lubrication equipment, fittings and combined filter, lubricator, and regulator)
- www.clippard.com and www.anchorfluidpower.com (air valves)
- www.aventtics.com/us/en (pneumatic valves and cylinders)
- https://www.festo.com/cat/en-us_us/products

Air Compressor Sources

- www.us.kaeser.com
- www.hiigroup.com
- www.quincycompressor.com
- www.ingersollandproducts.com
- www.origin.atlascopcogroup.com

For air fittings, visit the following:

- www.andersonmetals.com
- www.camozzi-usa.com
- www.veljan.in (pneumatic and hydraulic components)
- http://www.tompkinsind.com/products/brass-adapters-and-fittings
- http://www.parker.com/pneumatics

Fluid Power Graphic Symbol Sources

- https://advancedfluidpowerinc.com/wp-content/uploads/2016/03/Fluid_Power_Symbols.pdf
- https://www.hydraulicspneumatics.com/other-technologies/chapter-4-iso-symbols
- http://cdn.norgren.com/pdf/Norgren%20Graphic%20Symbol%20Library.pdf

Predictive Maintenance Tools

Hydraulics systems, which are part of major machines, do need scheduled attention. The routine maintenance steps save time and money by early detecting potential problems. The following are key tools you can use to prevent major problems:

1. Oil analysis—It helps in determining the condition of hydraulic and lubricating oils. Use an outside contractor to make a study

of spectrochemical and wear particle analysis. For more info, visit www.dsi-ltd.com.
2. Ultrasonic measurement—This method could be used to check leaks such as air, gas, vacuum, and steam.
3. Vibration analysis—This method can pinpoint misalignment, bearing problem and out of balance conditions
4. Motor Current—Tools are available to monitor excess input current.
5. Thermography—This tool helps in scanning hot spots on the machines as well as inside the motor control panel. It can predict early failure of bearings and excess current taken by certain electrical component.

Fluid Power Training Source

According to January 2019 issue of *International Fluid Power Society Journal* (www.ifps.org), they provide the following training material for fluid power:

1. Books
2. Online training
3. Fluid power standards
4. Animated hydraulic circuits

Additional sources for fluid power training are www.nttinc.com, the Milwaukee School of Engineering, Applied Technology Center, www.nfpa.com (National Fluid Power Association), www.bfpa.co.uk (British Fluid Power Association), and www.cfcindustrialtraining.com (for hydraulic training).

Warning: All sketches and schematics are shown for the usage of components only. They are not intended to show actual function of any equipment. The users must develop their own process schematics for a specific application.

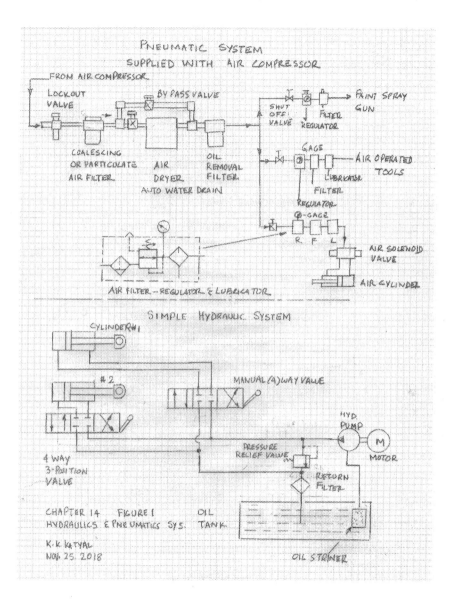

Fig.1—Pneum vs. hydrl

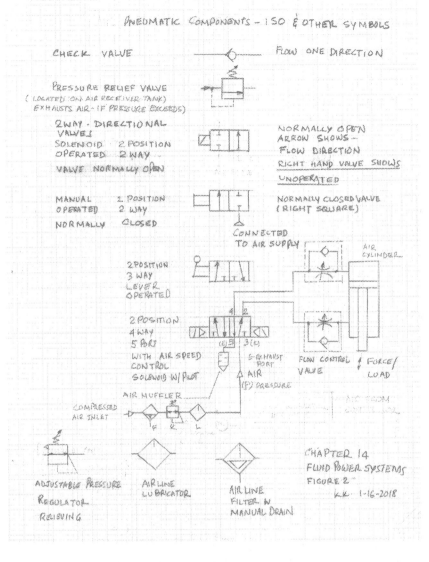

Fig. 2—Pneu components

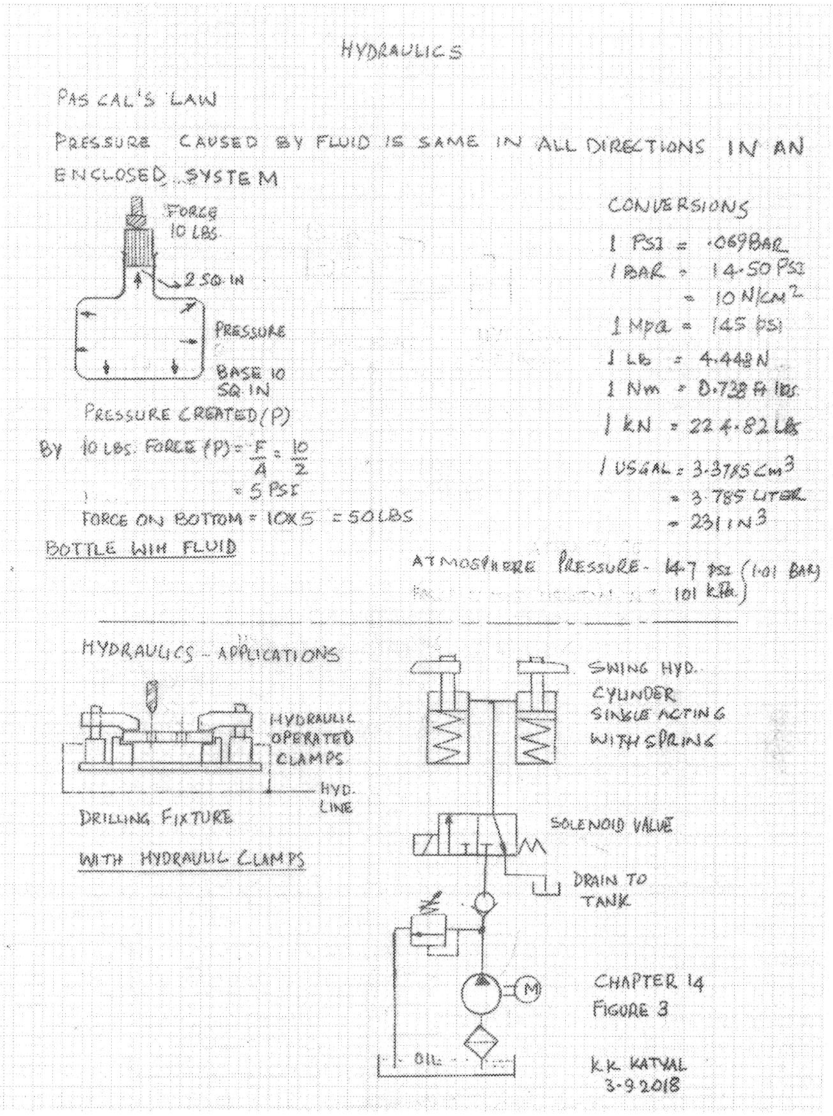

HYDRAULICS

PASCAL'S LAW

PRESSURE CAUSED BY FLUID IS SAME IN ALL DIRECTIONS IN AN ENCLOSED SYSTEM

FORCE 10 LBS.
2 SQ. IN
PRESSURE
BASE 10 SQ IN

PRESSURE CREATED (P)
BY 10 LBS. FORCE $(P) = \dfrac{F}{A} = \dfrac{10}{2}$
$= 5 \text{ PSI}$
FORCE ON BOTTOM $= 10 \times 5 = 50 \text{ LBS}$
BOTTLE WITH FLUID

CONVERSIONS

1 PSI = .069 BAR
1 BAR = 14.50 PSI
     = 10 N/CM^2
1 Mpa = 145 PSI
1 Lb = 4.448 N
1 Nm = 0.738 ft lbs
1 kN = 224.82 Lbs
1 USGAL = 3.3785 CM^3
        = 3.785 LITER
        = 231 IN^3

ATMOSPHERE PRESSURE – 14.7 PSI (1.01 BAR) 101 kPa.

HYDRAULICS – APPLICATIONS

HYDRAULIC OPERATED CLAMPS
HYD. LINE
DRILLING FIXTURE WITH HYDRAULIC CLAMPS

SWING HYD. CYLINDER SINGLE ACTING WITH SPRING
SOLENOID VALVE
DRAIN TO TANK
OIL

CHAPTER 14
FIGURE 3

K.K. KATYAL
3-9-2018

Fig. 3—Pascal-clamp

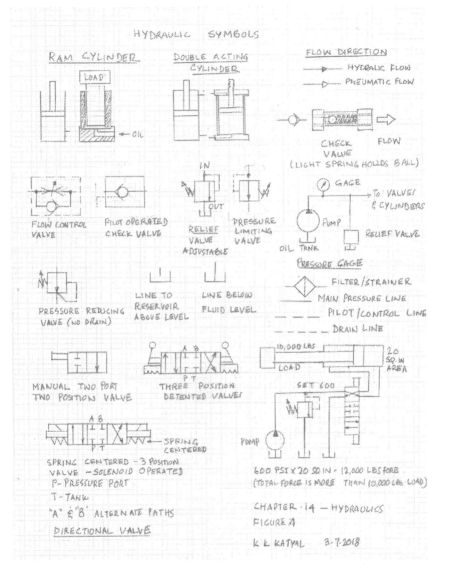

Fig. 4—Hydraulic symbols

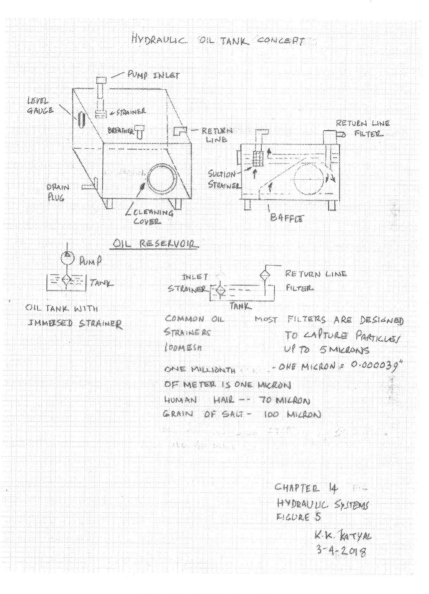

Fig. 5—Hyd oil tank

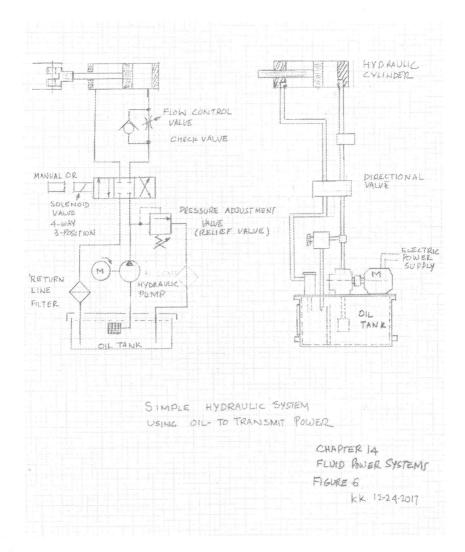

Fig 6—Simple hyd

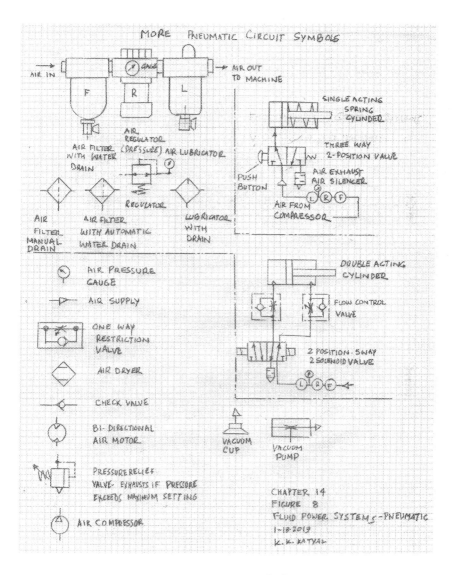

Fig. 7—Pneu symbols

CHAPTER 15

Lubrication of the Equipment

Topics covered are lubrication—hydrodynamic, hydrostatic, boundary thin film and extreme pressure; equipment that needs lubricants, lubricant selection, grease, oil lubrication, grease and oil lubricators, oil selection; glimpse of grease and oil application system manufacturers; centralized lub-systems, lubricant suppliers, sample lubricant characteristics, oil lubrication program at the plant; storing of hazardous liquids, maintenance issues; viscosity rating comparison chart; and t*hermo*plastic liner material.

TO REDUCE OR eliminate friction, machinery moving parts are supplied with some of kind of lubricant delivery system. The main purpose of lubricant is to overcome friction. The purpose of this chapter is to review those issues and provide steps to incorporate preventive maintenance to include proper lubrication for moving parts.

The purpose of lubricant is to create a layer of oil film between two sliding contact surfaces. It is also to reduce friction, wear, temperature, and corrosion. Usually, lubricants consist of oil or grease of different viscosities.

In equipment, we experience sliding friction and rolling friction. The sliding friction we see in piston inside a cylinder while rolling friction is what we experience in ball and roller bearings. The lubricant fluid film separates stationery and moving surface. Ideally, the friction should take place between the lubricant molecules and not among the metal surfaces.

To reduce friction, the present day lubricants are capable of creating 70% contact between the two surfaces.

Lubrication requirement creates the following situations:

1. Hydrodynamic lubrication—In this situation, the two mating surfaces are separated by a nonuniform thick film of lubricant. The thickness of film varies due to load, relative speed, viscosity, and the clearance between two surfaces.
2. Hydrostatic lubrication—In this situation, the external lube pump supplies enough pressure to lift the mating part and create a uniform oil film. Precision machine builders are known to provide suitable system for heavy moving parts.
3. Boundary thin film lubrication—This happens when the load is very heavy, speed is low, and the oil is not viscous to form good oil film.
4. Extreme pressure—For heavy loads, the ordinary mineral oil film is displaced easily. Suitable additives are added to oils with stand heavy loads.

Systems Needing Lubrication

The following sets of equipment are furnished with either grease or oil lubrication systems:

1. Machine tools (computer numerically controlled mills (vertical, horizontal, and boring), lathes (horizontal and vertical), band saws, drilling, thread rolling, tapping, grinding, plastic router, and special machines)
2. Construction and mining (cement trucks, wheel loaders, cranes, pavers, trenchers, scrapers, excavators, and haul trucks)
3. Windmills
4. Railroad equipment
5. Agriculture equipment
6. Heavy industry (steel, aluminum, glass, graphic, and cement mills)

Lubricant Selection

Lubricant consists of oil and grease. They are specified according to viscosity. Viscosity is the resistance to flow of the material. Water has viscosity of 1 while molasses has 15,000.

Majority of lubricants are made from the refining process of crude petroleum. The refining process improves stability, viscosity, and pour point.

Beside mineral based, manmade synthetic lubricants are very widely available. Many 2018 model new cars have synthetic oil in their crankcase. The oil change interval of these has been extended to 10,000 miles from 3,000 for mineral-based product.

Due to absence of wax, synthetic oils are good for very low temperature. Synthetic oil-based equipment runs cooler have stable viscosity index.

Grease

It is made by combining mineral oil as well as synthetic base with thickening agents. Such additives are lithium, calcium, aluminum, clay, and sodium. Also, added to grease are additives such as molybdenum disulfide to provide anti-wear, extreme-pressure, and high-temperature qualities. Some manufacturers make silicon lubricating grease with PTFE (poly-tetra-fluoro-ethylene), which is a very slippery substance. The thickening agents provide consistency to grease. Saponification process is used to make soap used for making grease.

Grease finds application where leakage of oil is not acceptable. Grease keeps dirt, dust. and water out of the critical surfaces. Grease is used for bearings, gears, slides, chains and linkages.

The most common grease uses lithium.

Grease is graded by NLGI (National Lubricating Grease Institute) system. The grade is calculated by ASTM standard D217 and D1403 methods. The test involves the use of a cone, which is dropped from a certain height. The depth of penetration at 25-degree C determines the NLGI number.

Common NLGI system grades the grease with numbers 000, 00, 0, 1, 2, 3, 4, 5, and 6. NLGI 000 number is very fluid product. Number 00 is fluid, and 1 is soft. Number 5 grease will be a very hard product. Use of NLGI grease numbers 1 and 2 are very common. For automobile wheel bearings, sometime NLGI 2 grease is recommended. It is better to check with your owner's manual about the right grease.

Grease requires less complicated system to feed moving bearings and journals. Grease is good application for heavy machinery, which does not run twenty-four hours. Machines such as pipe/tube bending, manual lathe, and large thread rolling are good application for grease.

Grease is also used in the coating of high-strength steel cables for post tensioning or prestressing of concrete slabs. The process involves coating ½" or 5/8" high-strength steel strand with grease. The coated strand is further covered by high density polyethylene (HDPE) plastic by extrusion process. These plastic-covered and grease-coated strands are held with conical wedges at both ends of the concrete slab. Concrete is poured subsequently on spaced strands for high-rise parking lots and buildings.

Oil Lubrication

Oil is used where the equipment runs at high speed and generates high temperature. This is preferred method if the need for lubrication for the components is required frequently.

There are three kinds of oils for lubrication:

1. Mineral oil
2. Synthetic oil
3. Vegetable or animal oils.

Mineral oils are refined from petroleum. Additives such as antiwear, antioxidant, antirust, and extreme pressure are added to oils. Additives such as graphite, PTFE, and molybdenum disulfide are added to improve lubricity. The extreme pressure additives are phosphorus chlorine and sulfur.

At 90°C, minerals oils oxidize rapidly. The service life of mineral oils decreases rapidly with high temperature.

Among the synthetic oils, the following are common:

1. SHS oils (synthetic hydrocarbon)—These can be used for low and high temperature.
2. PAOs ploy alpha olefins
3. Polyglycols—These can be used for high temperature application.
4. Silicone oils—These can be used for instruments.
5. Fluorinated oils
6. Dieters (low viscosity oils)—These can be used for instrument bearings.

Due to acid formation, animal and vegetable oils are not suitable for bearings. These oils are common in food industry for cooking purpose.

Oil Selection

Oils for any application are selected based on viscosity. Viscosity tables are provided d at 40 and 100°C. The viscosity does decrease with the increase in temperature. Oils are also preferred if their viscosity does not vary with fluctuation of temperature. This temperature tolerance in oil is specified as viscosity index. Oils with higher viscosity index are preferred.

Synthetic oils are preferred for high temperature (100°C and higher) application.

Oils are specified according to ISO, ASTM, IP, and DIN standards.

Wire rope Lubrication-----Typical wire rope (cable) is specified as 6x19. This cable has six strands with 19 wires in each strand. During manufacturing, wire ropes are sprayed with oil to reduce friction and prevent corrosion. New wire ropes are always oiled on the overhead crane. This reduces breaking of wires over the cable drums and sheaves.

Grease and Oil Applicators

The following major companies manufacture the grease and oil lubricators:

1. www.graco.com
2. www.bijurdelimon.com
3. www.tricocorp.com
4. http://www.skf.com/us/products/lubrication-solutions/lubrication-systems/index.html
5. www.oilrite.com
6. www.dropsa.com/en/about-us
7. www.lincolnindustrial.com

SKF has the following kinds of lubrication systems:

1. Single-point automatic lubricators
2. Multipoint automatic lubricator
3. Single-line lubrication system
4. Multiline lubricant
5. Progressive lubricators
6. Oil and air system
7. Circulation oil system
8. Grease guns and pumps

Graco supplies single line parallel, spray lube, centralized, off-road mobile, trailer, and air/oil (high-speed spindle) lubrication systems.

Bijur Delimon supplies multipoint, progressive railway chain with oil recirculating, and air-oil lubricators.

Tricor Corp. supplies constant level lubricators, automatic grease dispenser, central lubricator (with tank with positive displacement), gravity feed oilers, chain lubricator, single-point and multipoint lubricators, and oil storage system.

Oil-Rite Corp. builds the following systems:

1. Grease and oil dispenser
2. Constant level lubricators
3. Oil spray system
4. Multipoint lubrication package
5. Purge X multipoint grease applicator
6. Purge X circulating oil system

Dropsa based in Italy and US builds the following:

1. Total loss lubrication system
2. Grease lubricators
3. Air/oil lubricator
4. Oil recirculation system
5. Minimum quality lubrication for dry machining

Lincoln Industrial builds grease guns, automatic centralized system, drum and pail greasers, and other lubricators.

Centralized Lubrication Systems

Majority of the CNC mills, lathes, rolling mills, and flexible machining cells are built with centralized lubrication system. These systems create thin film of oil or grease between two moving parts. They supply precise amount of lubricant at regular intervals. This is done by programmable timer built in the main program of the machine. These systems are built for oil and grease.

The centralized systems are equipped with pressure and low-level switches to monitor the performance.

It is recommend to maintain a film of 0.001 to 0.002" thick between the two surfaces.

For more information on grease. visit www.nlgi.org (National Lubricating Grease Institute).

Lubricant Suppliers

The following are some of the major lubricant manufacturers:

1. http://www.phillips66lubricants.com/product/syncon-r-o-oil-iso-vg-32-68
2. www.castrol.com
3. www.super-lube.com (silicon lubricant grease—mineral oil with PTFE)
4. www.lubriplate.com (compressor, spray, hydraulic, multipurpose, and recirculating oils)
5. www.skf.com
6. www.gulfoilltd.com
7. https://www.mobil.com/en/industrial/lubricants

Sample Lubricants Characteristics

The following are some of the specifications of individual supplier. This information is taken from their websites on April 22, 2018.

Supplier Phillips 66, Syncon R, and O oil (ISOVG 32–68—rust and oxidation).

These are synthetic oils. They contain poly alpha olefin (PAO) chemicals. They are suitable for rotary vane and screw air compressors.

ISO Grade	32	46	68
Viscosity cSt at 40°C	32	46	68
Viscosity cSt at 100°C	5.8	7.1	9.8
Viscosity index	125	133	131

Mobil FM 101 and FM 222 grease for food equipment:

Properties	Mobil grease FM101	FM222
NLGI Grade	1	2
Color	White	White

Viscosity ASTM D445 cSt @ 40°C	100	220		
Mobil Grease for bearings SHC polyrex:				
005	221	222	462	
NLGI Grade	00	1	2	2
Viscosity @40°C –D448	220	220	220	220

Oil Lubrication Program at the Plant

If you are in-charge of maintaining several machines, you need to develop a daily, weekly, or a monthly plan for their upkeep. Note the following steps:

1. Develop one- or two-page chart of oiling and preventive maintenance plan. Also, assign an individual to check levels of oils and replenish it.
2. Assign machine operator to clean leaky oil and air lines.
3. Make a sketch for each machine indicating location of lubrication points.
4. Store all marked (labeled) lubricants at one place and assign somebody to keep drums, pumps, and funnels cleaned.
5. Use pump-operated filter cart handy to fill up small containers.
6. Store grease and grease gun in the oil drum storage area.

Storing of Hazardous Liquids

Use a separate room to store hazardous liquids if you have more than a dozen different oil drums to store. NFPA recommends separate storage room for flammable and combustible liquids. Such a separate space can prevent fire.

The companies should follow procedure recommended by NFPA (The National Fire Protection Association) and UFC (uniform fire code).

The separate storage room for oils is also recommended by Occupational Safety and Health Administration (OSHA). The separate storage room must have the following safety systems:

1. Ventilation
2. Automatic sprinkler system
3. Room designed with fire resistance components
4. Electric wiring rated per code with explosion proof switches
5. All metal drums must be grounded to prevent igniting of vapors using antistatic wire
6. Install safety vents on each drum
7. Have proper aisle width (36" to 48") and provide easy access for employees and fire fighters

Reference: *Industrial Fire Hazard* handbook, *Fire Protection* handbook, and uniform fire code.

Maintenance Issues

Some of the machine failures are attributed to lack of lubricants and dirt in their system. Clean lubricants and hydraulic oils are essential for the reliability of machines. Oil is necessary for heat removal and lubrication of power transmission. Dirty oil is one the reason machinery components fail. Components such gears, bearings, and pumps fail due to dirt.

The failure is caused by dirt and water sludge. The dirt can enter the tanks through breather caps and seals in the hydraulic cylinders. The sludge is formed by the oxidation of oil. The oxidized oils affect bearing races, piston pumps, gears, and valves.

To prevent these problems, check owner's manual of the equipment to see if you are using the following:

1. Specified lubrication and hydraulic oil with cleanliness
2. Changing filter with right filter
3. Using right oil viscosity (cSt)

If possible, drain the reservoir and put new oil and filter. For more information for lubrication, visit www.ifhgroup.com, www.hydacusa.com, www.aim4cleanoil.com, www.kleenoilusa.com, and www.y2kflluidpower.com.

Viscosity Rating Comparison Chart

Charts are available with following industrial ratings:
Saybolt second universal—SSU
International Standards Organization—ISO
American Gear Manufacturers Association—AGMA
Society of Automotive Engineers—SAE
Centistokes—cSt

The following are sample comparisons:

Viscosity per ISO	Kinematic Viscosity mm2/s at 40 Deg C	AGMA @100F	SAE	Gear	SUS 100F
ISO VG2	2.2	—	—	—	170
ISO VG 32	32	—	10W	75W	—
ISO VG 68	68	2	20W	80W	350
ISO VG 220	220	5	50W	90W	1050

Thermoplastic Material

To reduce friction between bed of machine and reciprocating table, some of the CNC milling machine builders glue a lining of Turcite and Rulon (name brands) on one side of their main table. These plastic liners with lubrication holes provide a good contact with other surface. The lubricating oil is trapped in the microsurface. This lining also helps in vibration damping.

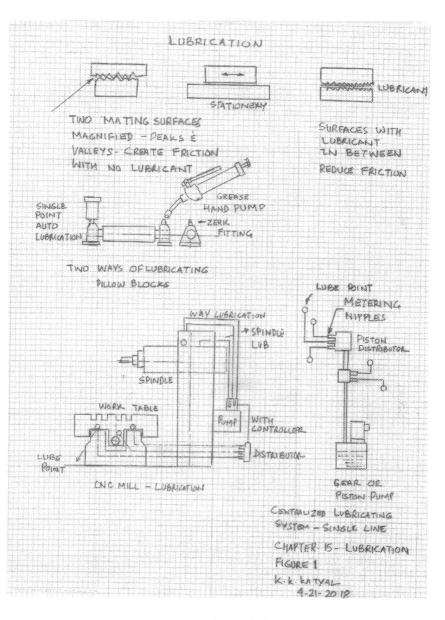

Fig. 1—Lub single line

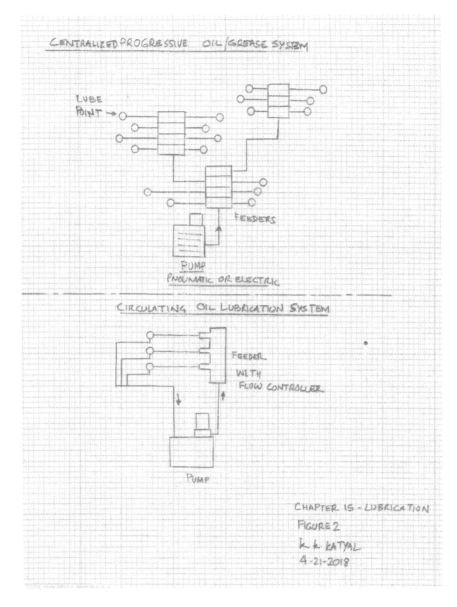

Fig. 2—Lub-progress-circul

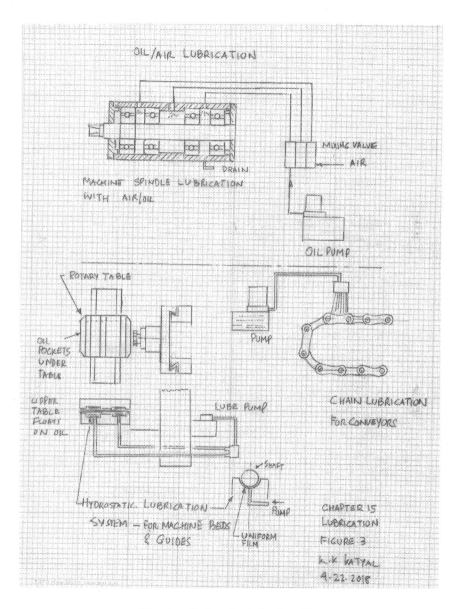

Fig. 3—Lub-oil-air hydraulic

CHAPTER 16

Plastics

Topics covered are thermosetting and thermoplastics materials, plastics advantages and disadvantages, plastics additives, key plastics processing technologies, blown film extrusion, extruder and it components, injection molding, compression molding, blow molding, thermoforming, rotational molding, plastics fabrication, selection of plastics sheet, rod and film, and recycling of plastic and its information sources.

PLASTIC MATERIALS ARE made from petroleum (benzene) and natural gas (methane). The cost of plastic materials swings with petrol or gasoline price. The term *plastic* is used for materials that could be heated and molded. Plastics are substitute for metals and wood.

Plastics polymers are long-chain molecules. Plastics are classified in three groups—thermosetting, thermoplastics, and elastomers.

- Thermosetting material—This material on heating develop a cross-link property. It is chemical bond between the long carbon chains. The process of cross-linking is irreversible. Once heated and molded, this material cannot be recycled. Typical thermoset resins are phenolic, epoxy, natural rubber, silicone, and neoprene. Thermoset parts, such as handles of pots and pans, can stand high heat. In addition, this densely cross-linked material is used for electrical switchgear.

- Thermoplastic material—This can be recycled by melting repeatedly. Thermoplastics are further divided into semicrystalline and amorphous. Amorphous plastics are transparent as glass. While semicrystalline plastics are milky in appearance. Compact discs are made from amorphous plastics.
- Elastomers (thermoplastics)—These are lightly cross-linked soft plastics. Tires and rubber seals are example of elastomers. They behave like rubber. Elastomer resins are elastic and flexible.

Plastic's advantages:

1. Plastic weighs 10% of steel.
2. It needs less energy to make product as compared to metals.
3. Due to low viscosity, it could be blow-molded, extruded, and injection-molded.
4. It provides thermal insulation for cooking utensils.
5. It provides electrical insulation for electric wires and power tools.
6. It provides transparency for certain plastics.

Plastic's disadvantages:

1. It is flammable.
2. It does not have good weather resistance.
3. It is high coefficient of thermal expansion.
4. It is very weak in tension and cannot take load.
5. Used packaging and discarded plastic has caused serious environmental problems for oceans and rivers.

All plastics are specified according to density, tensile strength, opacity, elasticity, ductility, brittleness, percent elongation before failure, hardness, impact strength, resistance to creep, and flowability.

Plastics are alloyed with other similar material to change its impact strength and flame retardation.

Additives: These are added to change mechanical properties. The following are some of the Additives:

1. Fillers (such as glass, wood, carbon black, metal powders, etc.)
2. Reinforcing fibers (nylon fibers, carbon fibers, glass fibers, etc.)
3. Others (UV stabilizers, colorants, flame retardants, etc.)

The following processes are key manufacturing areas of plastics:

1. Blown film extrusion
2. Injection molding
3. Extrusion blow molding
4. Thermoforming
5. Thermosetting (compression molding)
6. Plastic fabrication

Blown Film Extrusion

It is a process to make film for grocery bags, garbage bags, and flexible packaging. Polyethylene (PE) is a common material for these products. The process of film extrusion could be divided into blown film and cast film or flat film.

The blown film process involves extruding molten material through a vertical die in the form of a bubble. The cooling tower for the extruded bubble could be a few feet high to dissipate the heat of polymer. The bubble is controlled by extruder speed, internal air volume, and cooling rate. There are additional tools to control the film thickness.

Blown film materials:

1. Polyethylene (PE)—The specific heat of PE grades is high, and as such, it needs tall cooling tower to dissipate heat and to prevent two layers to stick together.
2. Low-density polyethylene (LDPE)—The density of LDPE lies between 0.91 to 0.93 gram/cm3. LDPE melts from 220 to 240°F. It requires less horsepower to extrude the polymer. Bags

made from LDPE are softer in touch as compared to stiff feeling from touching bags made from HDPE.
3. High-density polyethylene (HDPE)—This material has density of 0.93 to 0.96 gram/cm3. It is described to have high crystallinity or density. It melts around 265 to 275°F. HDPE bubble remains stable and has good barrier properties.
4. Linear low-density polyethylene (LLDPE)—It has density of 0.99 to 0.93 gram/cm3. It is softer to touch than LDPE.
5. Polypropylene (PP)—This material is stiffer and stronger than PE. It has high melting point and as such used for medical bags and drum liners. Due to clarity, this material is used for food packaging. It has a melting point of 330°F.
6. Polystyrene (PS)—This plastic has good clarity, high strength, and low cost. PS cools faster than PE, and the film is sensitive to damage.
7. Ethylene vinyl alcohol (EVOH)—It is copolymer of PE. It is multilayer food grade film. EVOH is water soluble and used for laundry detergent packaging.
8. Polyvinyl chloride (PVC)—PVC melts around 220°F and used for blown film extrusion. By adding plasticizers, it could be extruded rigid or flexible. It has good clarity and can be used for food wrapping and shrink wrapping of products.
9. Polyamide (nylon)—It melts at 360°F. It has high-temperature film.
10. Polyurethane (PU and TPU)—It is processed around 350 to 400°F. These films are highly elastic and tough. They are laminated to fabric and used for kayaks and inflatable bladders for rafts.

For blown films, the following additives are used:

1. To prevent stickiness, anti blocking agents are used.
2. To prevent molecular degradation, antioxidant agents are added to resins.

3. To reduce buildup of static charge, antistatic agents are added to resin.
4. For aesthetic value, different colorants are added to resin.
5. For strength reinforcement, additional reinforcement fillers are added.

Extruder

It is the most critical part of the plastic film process. The extruder heats and mixes the plastic resin into a homogeneous material. It supplies the molten material at suitable temperature and pressure to the shaping die.

Extruders are rated at different screw diameter. Majority of extruders lie between 2" and 6" in diameter. They are also rated according to pound-per-hour output.

The following are key components of extruders:

1. Motor drive system
2. Plastic resin feed system
3. Barrel and screw assembly
4. Die head assembly
5. Control system

Drive system consists of motor, speed reducer, or gearbox. The main motor has high horsepower to push molten polymer to die opening. The main driving motor could be built with variable speed DC and AC drive. The old DC motors with commutator brushes were constant source of trouble. The newer extruders are furnished with AC variable speed drive.

The electric motor is coupled to screw by a gearbox, which reduces the speed of 10 to 1 or less. The gearbox provides extra torque. Gearbox additionally protects the machine from reverse thrust from molten polymer.

Feed System

The raw material from large containers or silos is supplied to a hopper by vacuum system. Sometimes a dryer is introduced between hopper and the vacuum system. Full hopper keeps the barrel and screw properly fed.

Screw and Barrel Assembly

The barrel is covered with heating bands. Inside the barrel, we have specially machined screw. The screw is attached to the gearbox with a coupling. The screw has three sections. Those sections are feed, transition, and metering.

The depth of screw is highest in feed section while lowest in metering area. The screw performance is expressed as compression ratio.

The compression ratio is expressed as feed channel depth divided by metering channel depth.

The compression ratio varies from 2 to 1 or 4 to 1. Also, critical is the ratio of screw flight length divided by screw diameter. Most common, this ratio is 24:1. A 4" screw has a clearance of about 0.004" between the barrel inside diameter and screw outside diameter. Due to temperature and abrasion, screws are made of 4140 steel.

The barrel is made from high-strength hollow tube. The inside of tube is coated with hard alloy. The tube is aligned with the gearbox. There are several temperature zones outside the barrel. Barrels are fitted with melt thermocouple, pressure transducer, and rupture disc. The rupture disk is designed as safety valve. Rupture disc break opens from the designed pressures of 7000 to 9000 psi.

Head or Die System

This die is located at the mouth of barrel and receives the molten stream.

Die

This provides the final shape of product we are trying to make. The die opening should be highly polished.

Control for Machine

The operator control panel is designed to watch and correct hopper level, screw speed, motor current, barrel temperature zones, pressure, throat cooling area temperature, length of product, diameter, and thickness of film.

The temperature is controlled by built in PID (proportional, integral, and derivative) controller. These controllers maintain the temperature of each zone within one degree using thermocouple.

Zones

The extruder is divided in six zones. The zone under the hopper is called solid conveying zone. In between zones are melting, mixing, and degassing. The final zone is called die forming. Some of the extruders do not have degassing vent.

Hardware for Blown film

Beside the blown film die, the additional support items are bubble cooling, bubble stabilizer, collapsing frame, haul off, and winders.

A. Bubble cooling is done by large volume of air.
B. Bubble stabilizer protects the dancing by providing external devices.
C. Collapsing frame provides smooth change from round to flat shape.
D. Haul off system is provided to pull the film from die.
E. Winding of finished product is done in a form of roll.

For film specifications, finished film is checked for transparency, gloss, haze, viscosity, impact resistance, tensile strength, and elongation.

Injection Molding

The process consists of melting small pallets in a horizontal heated barrel. The heated molten polymer is injected into a mold cavity. The mold cavity is a part of the closed mold with a clamping mechanism. This process is used for thermoplastics resins.

Injection molding is the process used for making high-volume parts for appliances, window frames, bottle caps, and automotive interior and exterior parts. This is a low-cost process where the waste plastic scrap from molding, such as spree, runners, and gates are reused.

The plastic raw pallets are introduced into a heated barrel with internal variable-pitch screw. With the help of hydraulic and/or electric screw drives the pallet from hopper are carried toward the mold cavity through a nozzle. The heating bands are located on the outside of the barrel. The heat of bands and friction of the rotating screw cause the melting of resin pellets.

Beside cavity for the part to be molded, the molds are designed with sprue, runner, and gate.

A sprue is a passage where melted plastic enters the mold. From the sprue, the plastic is directed by runners to the gate of the mold. Hot and cold are two kinds of runners. On cooling, the combination of molded part, sprue and runner, are ejected from the mold.

The scrap is reground and partially used with virgin resin.

Initial prototypes for the samples could be made using 3-D printer. Injection molding has high tooling cost, and prototypes are made prior to final production.

Types of injection molding machines:

1. Hydraulic
2. Electric
3. Hybrid

Injection molding machines consist of the following:

1. Hopper
2. Barrel has three zones—The zone next to nozzle is called metering zone. The middle zone is called transition zone while around the hopper is called feed zone.
3. Screw
4. Heater
5. Ram—This creates pushing force for injection into nozzle using hydraulic cylinder.
6. Mold and part ejection system

Machine manufacturers: www.toshiba-machine.co.jp/en, www.engelglobal.com, www.arbug.com, etc.

Extrusion Systems

In the plastic process, extruders are used to produces tubes, pipes, cables, film sheets, and rods. Thermoplastics materials are used for extrusion.

Plastics manufacturers use twin-screw and single-screw extruders. To finish the shape of cable, tube or flat, the molten material exiting the dies is passed through cold water tray or spray.

The finished material is cut to length after cooling. In the manufacturing of electric or steel cable, the finished product is wound on reels.

The extruders are sold in sizes ranging from 1-1/2" to 6" diameter. More information is discussed under blown film extruders.

For machines, visit www.ptiextruders.com, www.battenfield-cincinnati.com, and www.davis-standard.com.

Compression Molding

This process is also called sheet molding compounds or structural molding compounds. The process involves forming a shape using glass fibers with a thermoset resin into a heated mold (about 300°F). The forming is done with pressure using punch and mold die. The process is used for making dining plates and electrical components.

Blow Molding

This process is used for making hollow plastic bottles for beverage, milk, and soap detergent. The process uses an extruder attached to a mold. In the vertical mold, first a tube (parison) is extruded. The extruded tube is pressurized by high-pressure hot air. The air helps in forming the bottle in the mold. The part is ejected after the cooling.

Thermoforming

This process is used for making advertising signs, appliance housings, automotive parts, aerospace parts, business machine housing, hospital beds, portable potties, and medical and consumer disposable packaging, including food containers for yogurt, cake, and cookies. The process involves heating a thermoplastics sheet or film by heaters. The heated sheet is transferred to vacuum forming or force forming stations. (See attached process sketch.)

Thermoforming may use single-sheet, twin-sheet, heavy-gauge, and pressure-forming technologies.

For thermoforming machines, visit www.brownmachinegroup.com and www.irwinreaserch.com.

For thermoform products, visit www.pactiv.com, www.wilbertplastics.com, and www.rayplastics.com.

Rotational Molding

This method is used for making low-volume, large, hollow plastic parts. It uses plastic powder, heat, and rotation of the mold to provide good wall thickness. As compared to injection molding, this method utilizes low-cost tooling. The production rate for this method is low as compared to blow and injection molding.

This method is used to make single- or double-wall bulk bins, insulated food containers, plastic pallets, playground parts, fruits and vegetables harvesting containers, agriculture tanks, health care, safety products, cargo liner for pick-up trucks, and toys.

The process uses rotational molds, which are filled up with premeasured granulated plastic resin. The closed mold is introduced to an oven. At oven, the molds are attached to the arm of a machine, which rotates in two axes (horizontal and vertical) which are 90 degrees to each other. The rotation and heat melt the plastic inside the mold and create a uniform-wall thickness.

The system uses gas-fired ovens with aluminum or sheet metal molds. After the heat cycle, the part is cooled and removed from the mold.

Some of the common materials used in rotational molding are LDPE, LLDPE, PE, HDPE, PVC, Nylon, and PP.

For more information on rotational molding, visit www.rotomolding.org, www.ferryindustries.com, www.denhertogindustries.com, www.petroflexana.com, www.apcustommolding.com, www.albertusa.com, www.rotoline.com, www.persico.com, www.sterlingrotationalmolding.com, www.bonarplastics.com, https://redlineplastics.com/about-us/, www.gemstarmfg.com, www.solarplastics.com, www.customroto.com, and www.blowmolded.com.

Plastics Fabrication

Beside the major processes discussed above, finished plastics bars and tubes are fabricated in different shapes.

Commercial fabricators build signs, point of purchase displays, brochure holders, store display cases, machine guards, hospital equipment, etc.

For these processes, materials such as acrylic, ABS, styrene, PVC, polycarbonate, and acetals are used.

The fabricators use methods as saw cutting, heat-and-cold bending, laser etching and cutting, CNC routing, CNC machining, edge polishing, welding, bonding, and assembling.

In the October 2018 issue of *Medical Manufacturing and Machining* magazine (www.medicaldesignbriefs.com), Tom Hoover of Branson Ultrasonic welding systems covered the welding of plastics. According to Tom, the most common medical plastic welding methods are the following:

A. Ultrasonic welding
B. Vibration welding
C. Clean vibration technology
D. Clean laser technology
E. Infrared technology

In another article appeared in October 2018 in *Appliance Design* on the selection of joining method of plastic parts by adhesives or ultrasonic welding. The article by Tarick Walton of Branson Co. of Emerson recommends the use of adhesives for small quantity assembly jobs and ultrasonic welding for large quantities. For more information on plastics welding, visit www.appliancedesign.com.

The following are some of the equipment builders:

www.multicam.com (CNC routers, laser, waterjet, and plasma)
www.thermwood.com (3 and 5-axis routers and large scale additives manufacturing)
www.crclarke.co.uk (thermoformers and heaters)
www.henfrickmanufacturing.com (makes routers and saws)
For information on fabricator, visit www.modernplastics.com.

Magazine for Plastics Fabrication

Plastics Distributor and Fabricated magazine (www.plasticsmag.com) covers machine builders, material suppliers, sheet thermoformers, and fabricators.

Selection of Plastic Sheet, Rod, and Film

Plastics materials are selected based on cost, tensile strength, coefficient of friction, resistance to temperature, transparency, wear, moisture absorption, and impact strength.

Finished plastics could be divided into amorphous plastics and semicrystalline plastics.

Amorphous Plastics

These are not suitable where they could be subjected to wear. They have low strength and prone to cracking. They have poor fatigue and chemical resistance. These plastics bond well with adhesive, easy to thermoform, and are transparent or translucent.

Commodity (low cost and low strength) amorphous plastics are polystyrene (PS), polyvinyl chloride (PVC), acrylic (plexiglas), cellulose acetate butyrate (CAB), acrylonitrile butadiene styrene (ABS), and polyethylene tetra phthalate glycol (PETG).

The plastics with moderate impact strength and price are polycarbonate (lexan), polypheneyle oxide, and thermoplastic polyurethane (TPU).

High-temperature resistant and high-strength plastics are plysulfone, polyetherimide, ployethersulfone, and polyphenyl sulfone.

Semicrystalline Plastics

These plastics are good for structural application and wear. These plastics are resistant to cracking, fatigue, and chemicals. These plastics are difficult to thermoform. They are opaque and difficult to bond by adhesive.

Low-strength and cost-common semicrystalline plastics are polypropylene (PP), low-density polyethylene (LDPE), high-density polyethylene (HDPE), and ultra high molecular weight polyethylene (UHMW-PE).

Slightly high-strength semicrystalline plastics are polyamide (nylon), plybutylene terephthalate (PBT), plyoxymethylene acetyl (delrin, celcon), and polyethylene terephthalate (PET).

High-cost semicrystalline plastics are plyvinylidene-chlorotrifluoroethylene (ECTFE), polyvinylidene fluoride (PVDF), and polytetrafluoroethylene (PTFE) of Teflon and RULON.

Other high-temperature and dimensionally stable plastics are polyimide and ployamide-imide.

Use of plastics

Most common plastics for medical industry are polyethylene, polypropylene, polystyrene, and polyvinyl chloride (PVC). The other materials used for medical industries are polycarbonate, polyamide, polyurethane, polyester, and ABS (acrylonitrile butadiene stryrene). PVC is used for catheters, dialysis bags, and tubings.

For more information, visit plastic websites www.plasticsnews.com, www.plasticstoday.com, www.packworld.com, and www.plasticsmachainerymagazine.com.

Recycling of Plastics

Parts made from thermoplastics materials can be remelted and recycled. Parts made from thermoset materials cannot be recycled. Thermoset parts can only be used as filler material for asphalt and concrete.

According to website www.recycleinc.com, recycled plastics could be used for making flower pots, tool boxes, garbage containers and dumpster containers.

Common recycled plastics are high-density polyethylene (HDPE), PVC, LDPE, polypropylene (PP), polystyrene (PS), and polyethylene terephthatate (PET-Polyester).

For resellers of recycled plastics, visit www.maineplastics.com, www.customcompounding.com, www.recycleinc.com, www.mcdunnough.com, and www.cprinc.com.

Related websites for equipment source are www.weima.com, www.herbold.com, www.machinexrecycling.com, and www.erema.com.

Waste-recycling magazines are www.recycling-magazine.com, www.wastetodaymagazine.com, and https://plasticsrecycling.org/.

For custom rubber-molded parts, visit www.tcmfg.com and www.trimlock.com using the following elastomeric materials (sources: TC Mfg. and Lauren Extruded Seals).

1. EPDM (ethylene-propylene-diene-monomer)
2. Viton
3. Neoprene (polychloroprene)
4. Nitrile (acrylonitrile-butadiene)
5. SBR (styrene butadiene rubber)
6. Silicone (polysiloxane)

More information on Plastic Industry

Please look into the following:

1. www.ptonline.com—This site has a knowledge center. It contains topics such as blending and dosing, plastics drying, plastics training, purging compounds, plastics conveyors, plastics feeding, and profile extrusion.
2. *Medical Device and Diagnostic Industry* magazine
3. *Understanding Injection Molding Technology* by Herbert Rees (Hanser Gardner Publishers)
4. *Successful Injection Molding* by Beaumont/Nagel/Sherman (Hanser)
5. *Plastics Extrusion Technology Handbook* by Sidney Levy and James F. Carley (Industrial Press)
6. *Blow Molding Design Guide* by Norman C. Lee (Hanser Publisher)

7. https://www.plasticsnews.com/ (trade magazine for the plastic industry)
8. http://www.plasticsmachinerymagazine.com/products/auxiliary-equipment/
9. www.iapd.com (International Association of Plastics Distribution)

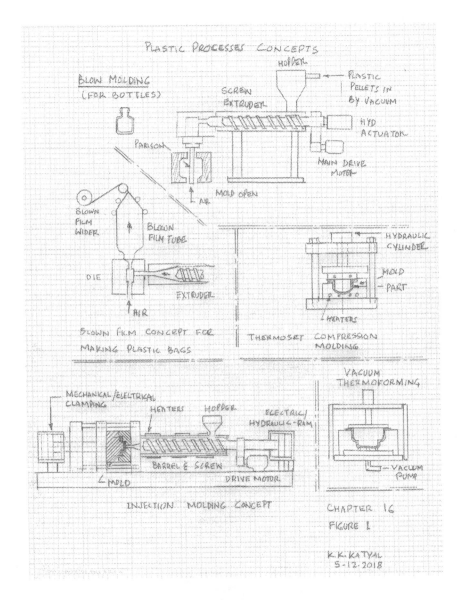

Fig.1—Plastics process

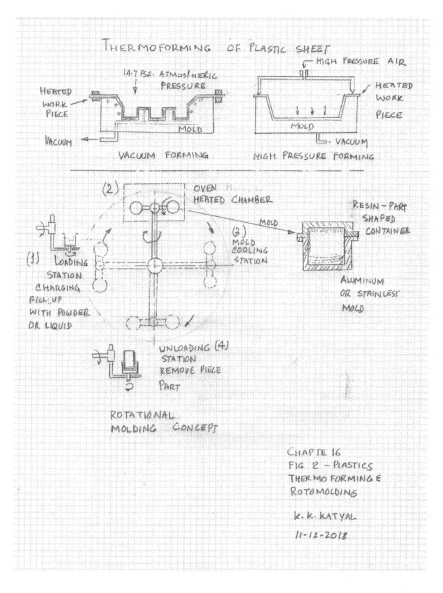

Fig. 2—Thermoforming

CHAPTER 17

Quality Control in Manufacturing

Topics covered are product and material testing, measurement tools, coordinate measuring machine, and information about nondestructive testing.

FOR A WORLD class manufacturing operation, it is essential to have an individual or an assigned group monitor the adherence to specifications laid down on the print. A typical medium-size company may have a quality manager. This manager is assisted by one or more individuals who are called quality inspectors.

It is important that the parts are made time after time consistently to the specifications. Parts will not work in assembly if they are not made to the print.

The function of the manufacturing supervisor is to assure that all necessary following steps are taken during the operation:

1. The operator has the right document or print, right material, right equipment, and gauging
2. The operator is trained to manufacture quality parts.
3. Parts are checked to every stage with proper quality tools.

Any operation cannot afford to make substandard parts. To assure, the manufacturing department is following design specifications, the quality control group must develop the following guidelines:

1. To assure that the right approved material is used
2. To assure that the parts are being made to right engineering revision
3. To assure that all tolerance on print are met
4. To frequently spot-check the production output
5. To provide suitable gauging for parts in process

Product and Material Testing

Quality control manager must assure that test certificate from the material suppliers meet the product-design guideline. If the data is not available, suitable steps must be taken by quality manager to test the material and document the results.

The finished product or assembly must be certified by the quality manager (QC). If required, an outside or an inside laboratory must be used. Quality control must also develop a plan to inspect in coming parts from an outside vendor. The parts from outside suppliers must meet the print specifications about material and tolerances. If the volume of parts from an outside supplier is high, a statistical process control may be instituted.

QC manager must also make sure that his or her department use calibrated gauges. It is the responsibility of QC manager to assure special gauges are available for machine operators and inspectors.

For small run on a machine, it is essential to develop first-piece part inspection.

For high-volume production, QC manager has to specify the number pieces to be checked for each 100, 1,000, or 10,000 number of pieces. An inspection sheet or paperless computer program must be developed to document results.

Before starting checking parts, a visual observation should be made to make sure the finished part has no dirt, rust, grease, and scratch.

Measurement Tools

The following are some of the common measuring tools:

1. Steel rule—These rulers are available in 6" and 12" lengths with or without millimeter graduations. These steel rules are available in fractions and decimal scales. These are used for checking the approximate length of a part up to 1/32 of an inch.
2. Combination square—It consists of a steel rule with square head, center head, and protractor head. This device can help find angle of parts.
3. Surface finish—It is measured in micro inches in inch standard, while checked as micron in metric system. The steps required may check roughness and waviness of machined surface. Instruments are available to check surface finish.
4. Inside and outside calipers—These can measure the part within 1/64" using steel rule. They are specified according to their mechanical joint.
5. Direct reading (inside and outside calipers)—This is a simple instrument to check the part within 1/64".
6. Calipers—There are three kinds of calipers for checking the length of parts. They can check length, depth, and inside and outside diameters.
   a. Vernier calipers—They can check the parts from 2" to 4 ft long. It can also check smaller round parts. It is provided with a Vernier scale to check the parts from 0.001" and 0.05 mm accuracy.
   b. Dial calipers—They are usually designed to check the parts up to 6". They are capable to check the parts within 0.001".
   c. Digital calipers—They are direct reading. The measurement can be seen both in inches and metric system.
7. Micrometers—They are used to check outside and inside diameter of parts within 0.0001" and 0.002 mm accuracy. They are available for parts from 1" diameter to 48" in diameter. It consists of a screw turning in a nut. Its main parts are frame,

anvil, spindle, barrel, screw, and ratchet stop. One must acquire skill to read the micrometer. It is also available in digital format.

8. Fixed gauges—Vernier, dial, digital calipers, and micrometers are used for checking final dimensions for low quantity of parts.

To speed up the checking thickness, inside diameter, outside diameter of high-volume machined parts, the following kind of fixed gauges are used:

    a. Plug gauges—These are used for checking hole size with Go / No go design
    b. Feeler gauges—These consist of blades of different thickness
    c. Ring gauge—Go / No Go gauge
    d. Snap gauge—Go / No Go gauges
    e. Radius gauge—They can be used to check internal and external radii.

9. Gauge blocks—These are standard very high accuracy blocks used for calibrating the calipers and special gauges. These are hardened and ground blocks marked with their thickness. They are kept very in clean environment. A set of gauge blocks could number up to 81. They range from sizes such as 0.101", 0.050", and 1.000" to 4.000". They are kept in a wooden box.
10. Surface plate—These level plates are flat. They are used by almost every quality department to rest the parts and conduct the checking of the height and other parameters of parts. They could be made of cast iron, granite, or glass. Granite plates are used for coordinate measuring machines. It is important to maintain cleanliness of plates for accuracy and preferably kept in an enclosed room. Height gauges, test sets with dial indicator, and V-blocks are used on surface plates.
11. Dial indicator—It looks like a clock. It is a critical part of checking unevenness of parts. It consists of round metal frame with graduated dial. The dial can move within +/-0.001" with the movement of plunger.
12. Optical comparator

The following are special gauges:

a. Indicating bore gauges
b. Gauges with several sets of dial indicators to check various diameters on a shaft
c. Continuous measurement gauge such as on-wire or cable-making machines
d. Gauges with microswitches for automatic sorting
e. Vision inspection
f. Air gauging-using compressed air for checking hole and bore condition
g. Thread gauges—Go / No Go for checking OD/ID and pitch diameter
h. Bevel protractor and inclinometer
i. Gear inspection tools
j. Surface finish measurement equipment (Mahr Inc.)

13. Coordinate measuring machine (CMM)—In mid 70s, the finished machined and fabricated parts were checked with several sets of special dedicated gauges and calipers.

While working as a tool engineer in that period, I was continually involved to make sure large weldments such as large fan housing, turbochargers housing, and engine supports are machined right. There was no way of checking accuracy except portage layout machine. The machine consist of vertical and horizontal arm assembly located on flat plate with a movable post.

Portage layout machine had a long scriber with horizontal and vertical inch scale with fraction markings. The inspectors would attach dial indicator to the layout arms to improve the measuring capability. In early 80s I was able to improve the capability of portage machine by adding a package of software and hardware probe developed by Starrett Company.

In the same period, companies such as Renishaw, DEA, Sheffield, and Bendix were developing coordinate measuring machines. These machines were breakthrough in speeding up the inspection of machined parts.

The concept of checking the parts is similar to three- to five-axis CNC milling machine.

Instead of machining, you can program or manually check machined parts. This process cuts inspection time and lower cost of the final product.

The CMM machine can speed up 100% inspection of aerospace and parts that requires utmost accuracy.

CMM consists of suitable granite plate with a traveling bridge to hold a probe-carrying vertical arm. These machines can be worked manually or programmed to run with manual or laser probe. You are able to run in X, Y, and Z directions with an articulating probe.

The process consists of setting up the part to be checked on three or four points and checking all dimensions from a reference point.

The following are a few types of coordinate measuring machines:

1. Bridge type
2. Gantry
3. Portable measuring arm
4. Horizontal arm with table

The following are the major manufacturers of coordinate measuring machines: www.zeiss.com, www.hexagonmi.com, www.mitutoyo.com, and www.helmel.com.

The following are additional tools to check the quality of material, parts, or assembly by nondestructive methods (NDT):

a. Radiography (x-ray)—This system can find hidden flaws using x-ray generators
b. Ultrasonic inspection—These systems uses high-frequency ultrasound pulse to find cracks in welds and other flaws in parts for aircraft engines.

c. Dye penetrant inspection—The equipment consists of penetrant dye, and fluorescent solvents. The area to be checked is sprayed with penetrant. Dry powder is sprayed to find cracks and pin holes in ferrous and nonferrous materials.
d. Magnetic particle inspection—This method is used to check surface flaws using metal powder and current carrying hand-held yoke.
e. Eddy current testing—It is noncontact method of finding flaws in metal components. This method consists of using electromagnetic field created by alternating current in a coil. For testing, the coil is located closed to metal parts. This technology helps find cracks, weld defects, flaws in bars and tubes, turbine blades, and quality of threads. This method can be used for inspecting low- and high-volume parts.
f. Hardness and tensile testing
g. XRF analyzers (x-ray fluorescence analyzer)—These are for detecting alloy composition of aluminum, carbon steel, Ni, Cr, alloys, stainless steel, gold, silver, platinum, rhodium, soils, and mining sediments.
h. Fiberscope—It transmits back picture using fiber bundle.
i. Videoscope and borescope
j. Bar inspection system using eddy current
k. Ultrasonic system for finding voids, porosity in welds, forgings, and turbine blades

For more information on NDT instruments, XRF Analyzers, Videoscope and microscopes, visit https://www.olympus-ims.com.

For 2-D/3-D measurement, metal thickness, and paint thickness, visit wwwmicro-epsilon.com.

In June 2004, *Quality Magazine* listed US colleges that provide training in nondestructive testing. In addition, the American Society of Nondestructive Testing provides refresher courses in NDT basics in ultrasonic, magnetic particle, radiographic testing, liquid penetrant testing, and visual testing.

The American Society of Nondestructive testing (www.asnt.org) also provides buyer's guide, which lists manufacturers of equipment for the following:

- Acoustic emission testing
- Electromagnetic testing
- Liquid penetrant testing
- Radiographic testing
- Ultrasonic testing and other methods

NDT Service Providers

For inspection and NDT services, visit https://www.industrial.ai/inspection-ndt (GE Inspection Technology global customer solution Center in Cincinnati- Ohio a Baker Hughes Co.) and http://www.magnachek.com/.

For more information on quality control products, visit https://www.qualitymag.com/directories/2169-buyers-guide and www.qualitymag.com/ndt.

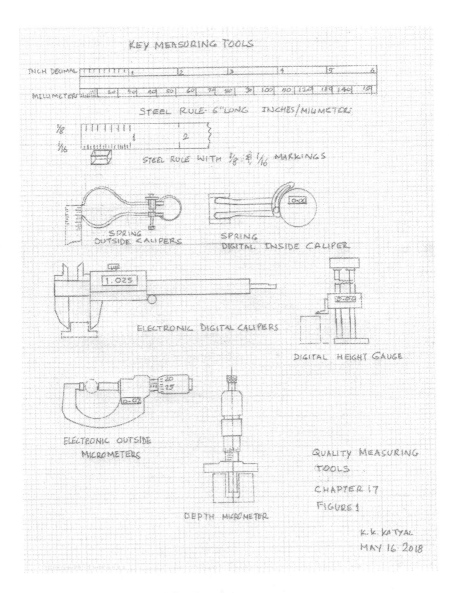

Fig. 1— Quality tools

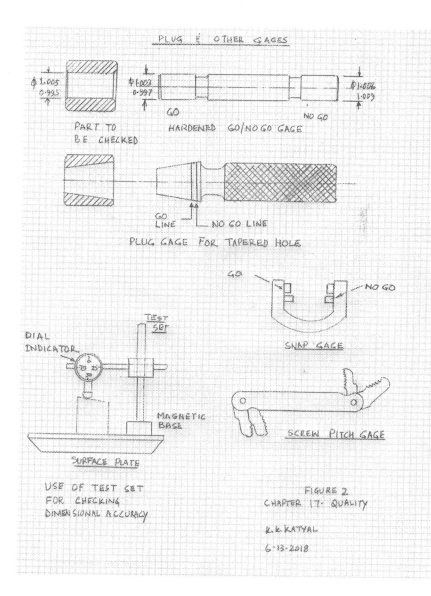

Fig. 2—Quality gauges

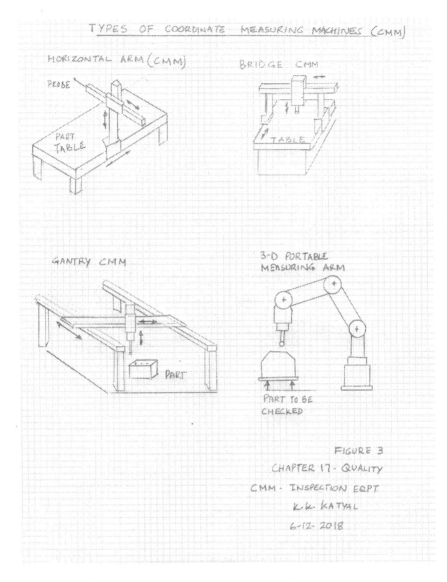

Fig. 3— Quality CMM

CHAPTER 18

Engineering Drawings

Topics covered are drafting tools, CAD software, drawing sizes, line standards, and geometric dimensioning.

BEFORE THE INTRODUCTION of computer-aided design (CAD) in 1970s, the engineering drawings were made on paper using drawing board, *T*-square, H/B lead pencils, 30- and 45-degree angles, protractors, engineering scales, lettering guide, and set of instruments to draw circles.

Before you can make a drawing, you have to have good understanding of geometry. If you want to design a component for machine or product by using drawing board or using computer-aided drafting, you ought to have knowledge of circles, arcs, angles, squares, rectangles, and materials.

In the United States, component drawings for machinery, automobile, aerospace, and general mechanical industry use the engineering standards laid down by ANSI and ASME. While ISO system is used in Europe, China, India, and Japan.

In the US, the engineering drawings are drawn according to ASME Y14.5M—1994 (www.ASME.org) dimensioning and tolerance standards. These standards also cover geometric dimensions and tolerance.

In this chapter, you will see basic information on the following topics:

1. Basic drafting tools—figure 1
2. Engineering drawing Line standards—figure 2

3. Geometric dimensioning and tolerance (GD&T)—figure 3
4. Engineering drawing and 3rd-angle projection—figures 4 and 6
5. Sample dimensioning—figure 5
6. ISO/ANSI drawing symbols and bilateral tolerance—figure 6

Drafting Tools

In early seventies, design offices were furnished with the following:

A. Drafting tables—These tables were available in 37"×60" to 38"×50" sizes (check for availability with www.mayline.com and www.westerntechnical.com)
B. Parallel slide—In combination with drafting desk, this parallel slide helped draw horizontal lines and assist triangle tools to make sloping lines.
C. Triangles are available in 30/60 and 45-degree combinations.
D. Scales are available in millimeters for metric system and in inch system. Scales in fraction and decimal are available for inch
E. Compass is used to draw circles. The most common compass are bow and beam compass
F. Other common manual tools to draw mechanical drawings are automatic pencils, erasers, French curves, erasing shields, templates for circles, squares, and letters.

For more information on mechanical drafting tools, visit www.staedtler.com (a German company).

Computer-aided drawing (CAD) uses software to generate 2-D and 3-D engineering drawings. The CAD system is integrated with computer-aided manufacturing (CAM). In the CAM software, the data from CAD is used in developing instructions for laser cutting, water-jet cutting, milling, turning, and drilling.

For more information on CAD programs, visit www.autodesk.com, www.solidworks.com, and www/solidedge.siemens.com.

Drawing Sizes

For simply reviewing, the CAD engineering drawings are reduced to 8.5"×11" by the program. To fit certain printers, standard rolls of papers for printing and drawing are available in 36 and 42" widths. The other common sizes for prints are 11x17, 17"×22", 22"×34" and 34"×44". Drawings are provided with a title block to include drawing number, scale, angle of projection, description of part, revision, and list of items. Digital printer/plotters for CAD drawings are being used extensively in the industry.

Line Standards

The following are most common types of lines:

1. Hidden line—It is a thin-dotted line to show a hidden view.
2. Center line—It consists of short dashes through the part center. It is the most common line through circles, holes, and cross sections to show the symmetry of the part.
3. Dimension and extension line—This line is used to show dimensions between the two ends. They are thin lines.
4. Leader line—This line with arrows is shown to point to welds and other critical areas inside a part.
5. Cutting lines—These lines are used to show cutting plane
6. Break lines—These lines are used for large objects, which cannot be fully shown completely.
7. Outside visible lines—They show the outside edges of the part.
8. Section lines—These lines show the area cut by a plane.
9. Phantom lines—This show the other position of a moving part.
10. Viewing plane—These lines show certain section of the part to be viewed.

Drawing Representation

With 3-D sketching, sketches are made using *isometric system* with two lines at 30 degrees to the horizontal on a graph paper. A 45-degree method is used for *oblique sketching*.

Orthogonal Projection for Technical Drawings

Orthographic projection provides two dimensional view of the object. To fully describe a mechanical part, it may be necessary to show six views on a drawing. These six views are front view, top view, left view, right view, bottom view, and rear view. Sometimes it may not be necessary to show all six views.

Geometric Dimensioning and Tolerancing

Using the equipment, the machine shop or fabrication shop makes the parts as per the tolerance shown on the drawings.

Dimensions on the part specify the length, diameter, width, thickness, angle, and symmetry from a center line.

Tolerance on the part is the allowable variation from the base dimension.

The design engineer uses the following guidelines to specify acceptable tolerances:

1. Straightness—It is specified for horizontal and vertical lines. It is the amount these lines are allowed to vary up and down without causing problem with the assembly.
2. Flatness—It is the amount of variation allowed on a flat surface.
3. Circularity—This applies to circles, cylinders, and spheres. This tolerance looks at the distance between center and outside surface of circle, cylinder, and sphere.
4. Parallelism—It specifies the tolerance limits between two parallel surfaces.

5. Cylindricity—Here, all surface points on cylinder surface must meet tolerance from the center.
6. Concentricity—It is the amount of variability allowed between two circles, which have common centers.
7. Profile of line—It is about making sure that the variability of tolerance is held from a datum point.
8. Profile surface—Here, the profile length must maintain tolerance limits.
9. Angularity—It is the angular tolerance held from the datum point.
10. Perpendicularity—It is the amount of tolerance allowed for a perpendicular line from a datum point.
11. Position tolerance—It is amount of tolerance allowed for the center of a hole from a true point.
12. Run out—It is amount of tolerance allowed to a cylindrical part over the entire length of part.
13. Total run out—The tolerance applies to a machined round part, which has several steps. The total run out may not exceed specified by tolerance.

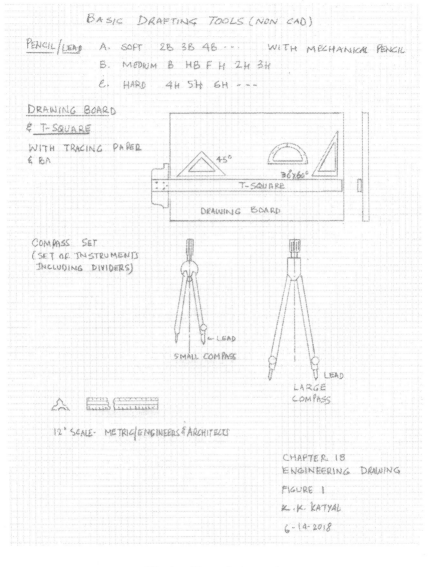

Fig.1—Eng. dwg. tools

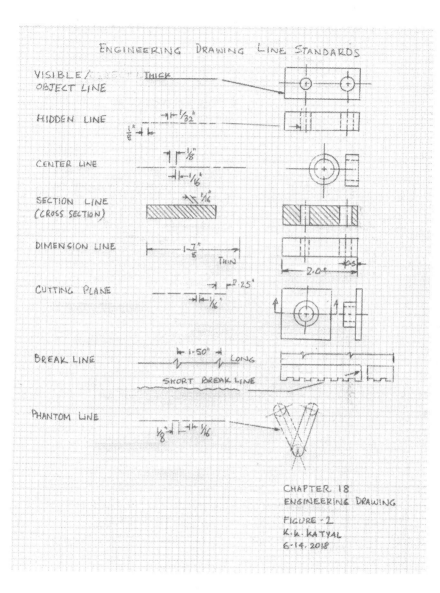

Fig. 2—Eng. dwg. line std.

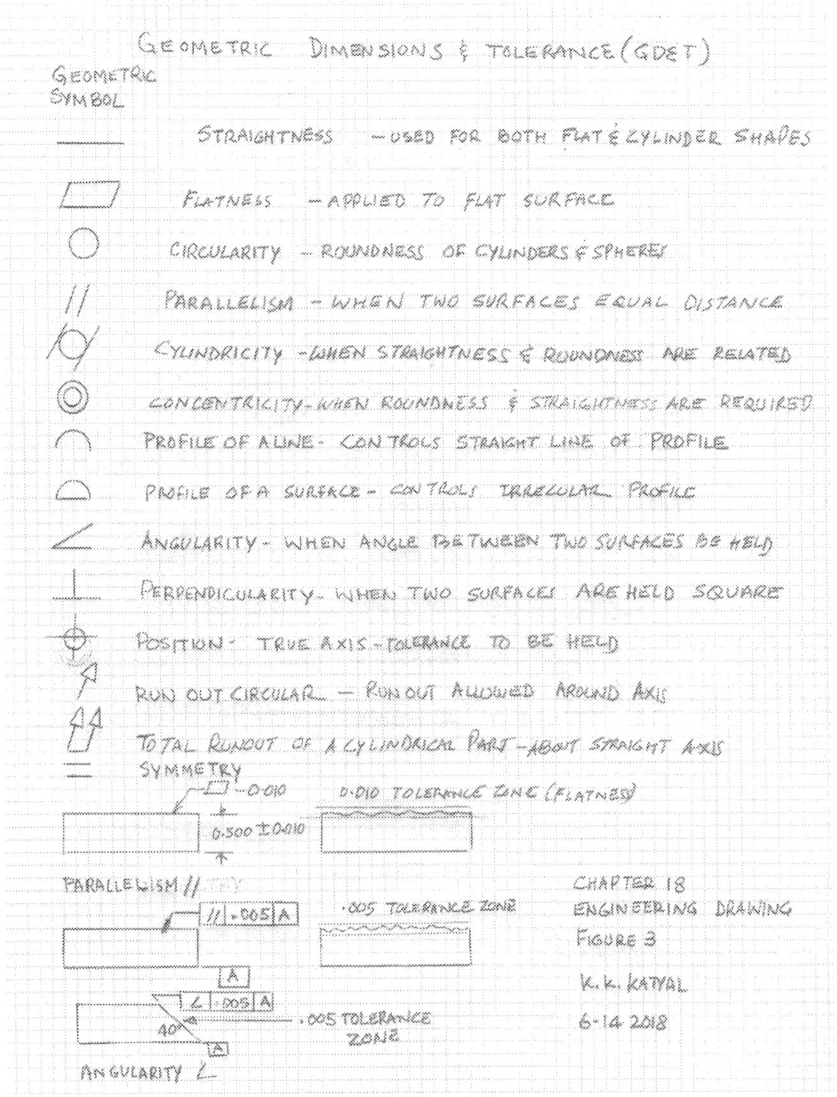

Geometric Symbol	Geometric Dimensions & Tolerance (GD&T)	
——	Straightness	— used for both flat & cylinder shapes
▱	Flatness	— applied to flat surface
○	Circularity	— roundness of cylinders & spheres
//	Parallelism	— when two surfaces equal distance
⌭	Cylindricity	— when straightness & roundness are related
◎	Concentricity	— when roundness & straightness are required
⌒	Profile of a line	— controls straight line of profile
⌒	Profile of a surface	— controls irregular profile
∠	Angularity	— when angle between two surfaces be held
⊥	Perpendicularity	— when two surfaces are held square
⌖	Position	— true axis - tolerance to be held
↗	Run out Circular	— runout allowed around axis
↗↗	Total Runout	of a cylindrical part - about straight axis
=	Symmetry	

▱ 0.010 — 0.010 tolerance zone (Flatness)
0.500 ± 0.010

Parallelism //
// .005 A — .005 tolerance zone
A

∠ .005 A — .005 tolerance zone
40°
Angularity ∠

Chapter 18
Engineering Drawing
Figure 3

K. K. Katyal
6-14-2018

Fig.3—Eng. dwg. geo. tol.

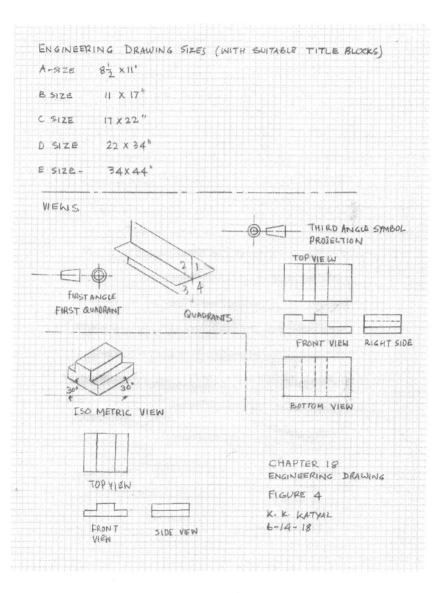

Fig. 4—Eng. dwg. size

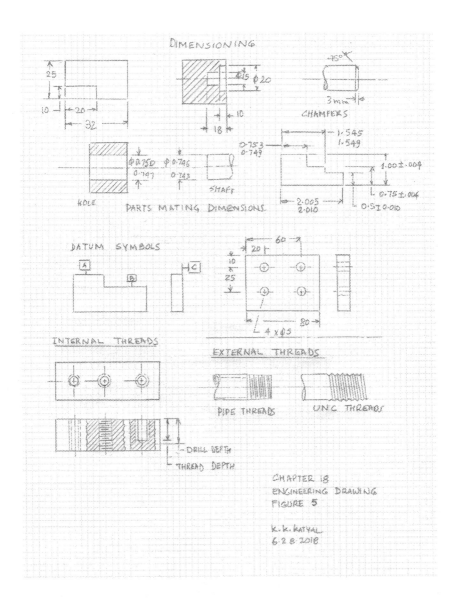

Fig. 5—Eng. dwg. dimen.

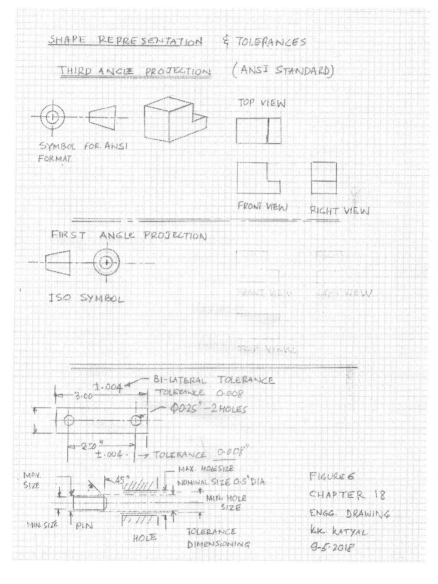

Fig. 6—Eng. dwg. views

REFERENCES

Chapter 1: Making of Iron and Steel—*Metallurgy Fundamentals* (Daniel R Brandt, J. C. Warner, 1999, Goodheart Willcox Co.), www.steel.org, www.asw-steel.com, www.worldsteel.org, www.aist.org, www.sassda.co.za, www.worldstainless.org, www.steelvaristy.org, www.slideshow.net/steelmaking, www.ikenstore.com (Mexus education), US Steel YouTube video (start to finish), *Metallurgy* (B. J. Moniz, American Technical Publishers), www.steeldynamics.com, Aiifa.org, www.wikipedia/wiki/pig-iron--/blast-furnace.

Chapter 2: Making of Cast Iron—Metallurgy Fundamentals (Daniel R. Brandt, J. C. Warner, 1999, Goodheart Willcox Co.), Materials Handbook 15th Ed. (George S. Brady, Clauser, Vaccari, McGraw Hill), Tool and Manufacturing Engineers Handbook Volume 2 (Forming, SME, Fourth Ed.), www.metalcastingdesign.com, 2011 Source Directory, Metallurgy (B. J. Moniz, American Technical Publishers), www.ferroloyinc.com.

Chapter 3: General Classification of Steels—Welding Fundamentals (Mike Gellerman), www.finkl.com, Metals Handbook Desk Ed., Metal Service Center Institute (MSCI) for steel processing terms, Practical Metallurgy and Materials for Industry (John C. Neely, Prentice Hall), Materials Handbook 15th Ed. (George S. Brady, Henry R. Clauser, John A. Vaccari. McGraw Hill), Engineering Materials Properties and Selection 3rd Ed. (Kenneth G. Budinski, Prentice Hall), "Stainless Steel Frequently Asked Questions" (www.marlinwire.com), Engineering Properties of Steel (Philip D. Harvey, editor), American Society for Metal (Metal Parks Ohio), Metallurgy by B. J. Moniz, American Technical Publishers), "Structural Steel" (www.emjmetals.com), Fundamentals of Machine Tool Technology and Manufacturing Processes (C. Thomas

Olivo), http:/en.wikipedia.org/wiki/SAE steel grades, Machine Tools and Processes for Engineers (Charles R. Hine, McGraw Hill Book Company), https://en.wikipedia.org/wiki/Iron_pillar_of_Delhi.

Chapter 4: Material Properties and Testing—Practical Metallurgy and Materials of Industry (John E. Neely, Prentice Hall), Metallurgy Fundamentals (David Brandt and J. C. Warner, Goodheart Willcox Co.), www.instron.us/en, www.sunteccorp.com, Engineering Materials Properties and Selection (Kenneth G. Budinski), "Hardness at Work" (Edmund Isakov, PhD, Cutting Tool Engineering, Jan. 2001).

Chapter 5: Nonferrous and Precious (Noble) Metals—Machine Tool Practices 9th Ed. (Richard R. Kibbe, Roland O. Meyer, John E. Neely, Warren T. White), Melting Point info (www.onlinemetals.com), Metallurgy Fundamentals (Daniel E. Brandt and J. C. Warner, Goodhearth Willcox Co.), www.hydro.com, "Noble Metals" (Machine Design, May 6, 2008), www.belmontmetals.com, www.dynacast.com, www.neymetals.com, McMaster Carr (Catalog 113 for aluminum alloys), Machine Design (May 6, 2008), Noble Metals (John C. Keefe, Alion Science and Technology), Metals Handbook Desk Ed. (Howard E. Boyer, Timothy L Gall, 1985, American Society of Metals), Ryerson Steel (Stainless Steel—www.ryerson.com).

Chapter 6: Heat Treatment of Steel—www.heattreat.net, Metal Treating Institute, www.industrialheating.com, www.forgemag.com, www.inductionheating.com, www.Metal-powder.net, www.farrarusa.com, Metallurgy for the Non-Metallurgists (Harry Chandler, ASM International), "Induction Hardness Basics" (article, June 2000), Modern Application News, Heat Treatment of Tool Steel (E. D. Tarney), Crucible Steel Service Center (Syracuse, New York), Tooling and Production magazine (May 2000), Cryogenics (William E. Bryson, Hanser Gardner Publications), Nitro Freeze Cryogenic Services (Cryogenic Institute of New England, Worcester, Massachusetts), "Shot Peening" (Design News, Sept. 2013), "Heat Treating" (Dr. Laroux K.

Gillespie, Cutting Tool Engineering, April 2008), "Controlled Dry Cryogenic Process" (www.300below.com).

Chapter 7: Ferrous and Nonferrous Metal Castings and Powder Metallurgy—Construction: Principles, Materials, and Methods (Harold B. Olin, John A. Schmidt, Walter H. Lewis, Van Nostrand Reinhold), Design 2 Part 2017 Supplier Directory, Design Solutions (Metal Powder Industry Federation), Metal Injection Molding (Barbara Donohue), Today's Machining World (Aug. 2007).

Note: For more information on powder metallurgy and isostatic pressing, see *Manufacturing, Engineering and Technology* (6th Ed.) by Serope Kalpakjian and Steven R Schmid.

Chapter 8: Metal Cutting Processes for Metal Fabrication—www.teskolaser.com, www.nmfrings.com, *Fiber Laser* (Ricky Hansson, Industrial Laser Publication), "Best Practices for Laser Cutting Tube, Pipe, Profiles" (Eric Lundin, *The Tube and Pipe Journal*, April/May 2016), *Handbook of Fabrication Processes* (O. D. Lascoe, 1988, ASM International), "The Challenges of Laser Cutting" (Jim Wollenberger, LAI Companies, *The Fabricator*, Aug. 1998), "Best Value for Cutting" (www.esbna.com).s

Chapter 9: Thread Systems—www.threadcheck.com, www.pipingdesigner.com, www.efunda.com, Materials and Process in Manufacturing 8th Ed. (E. Paul Degarmo, J. T. Black, Ronald A. Kohser, Prentice Hall), Machinery's Handbook 25 (Industrial Press Inc.), Engineering Graphics 7th Ed. (Giesecke, Mitchell, Spencer, Hill, Loving, Dygdon, and Novak, Prentice Hall), Machine Trades Blueprint Reading 2nd Ed. (David L. Taylor, Delmar/Thomson Leering), Blueprint Reading and Technical Sketching for Industry (Thomas Olivo, Delmar), Machinery Handbook 25th Ed., Audel Millwrights and Mechanics Guide 5th Ed. (Wiley Publishing Inc.), "Name that Thread" (Kenneth Korane / Burleigh Bailey, Parker Hannifin Corp.)

"Tube Fittings Columbus Ohio" (Machine Design, Oct. 21, 2004), "List of BSPP/BSPT Threads" (Metric and Multistandard Components Corp., 1990).

Chapter 10: Shaping of Materials—Forging Industry Association (USA), *Tooling and Manufacturing Engineers Handbook* (Vol. 2, Forming, Fourth Ed., Society of Manufacturing Engineers), *Handbook of Fabrication Processes* (O. D. Lascoe, 1988, ASM International), www.metalformingmagazine.com, www.americanhydroformers.com, "Introduction to Tube Hydroforming" (Gary Morphy, *The Fabricator*, June 13, 2006), *Modern Manufacturing Processes* (James Brown), Industrial Process (Hydroforming Process), "Stamping 101: Anatomy of Mechanical Press" (Dennis Cattell, *The Fabricator,* 2008), "A New Era in Press Technology" (Victor M. Cassidy, Nov. 2000, *Fabrication News*), "Roll Forming Design for Economical Mfg." (Kate Alsbrooks, Nov. 2000, *Fabrication Equipment News*), "Press Upgrades / Reducing Shock and Vibration" (Cindy Simonetti, Nov. 2000, *Fabrication Equipment News*), "A Rundown on Rolling Machine" (David Donell, 2010, *The Fabricator*), www.americanmachinetool.com, www.westwaymachinery.com, "Plate Rolls" (Francisco Massa, July 2012), "Modern Steel Construction" (www.aisc.org/modernsteel/), "Precision Cold Forming" (Barbara Donohue, Today's Machining World, 2008), www.slideshare.net/vijikammar/forging, "Metal Spinning versus Flow Forming" (Dirk Palten and Josep Mont, Nov. 2016, *The Fabricator*).

Chapter 11: Welding Methods—*How to Weld (Motorbooks Workshop)*, *Welding Fundamentals* (Mike Gellerman, Delmar Publishers), Maintenance Welding Options by Ron Holzhauer-May 8, 1995, Plant Engineering), "Selecting the Right Welder" (Ken Fisher, Miller Electric Mfg. Co., Feb. 1996, *Modern Machine Shop*), *An Introduction to Resistance Welding: From Resistance Welding Manual* (Resistance Welder Manufacturing Association in practical welding today, Sept./Oct. 1998), "The Fundamentals of Gas Tungsten Arc Welding" (Larry D. Smith, *Practical Welding Today*, July/August 1998), "Common Sense Safety Precautions for GTAW (Mike Panktatz, *Practical Welding Today*,

July/Aug. 1998), "A Tight Fit (Sizing Respirators)" (Craig E. Colton, *Practical Welding Today*, July/Aug. 2000), "Get Better Welds during Plant Maintenance" (Neal Borchert and Ken Stanzel, Miller Electric from Plant Engineering, Feb. 2007), Design 2 Part Supplier Directory (www.D2Psupplierdirectory.com), "Electric and Gas Welding" (E. F. Lindsley, Popular Science Books, Resource for Welding and Safety Supplies), "How to Estimate Direct Arc Welding Costs" (Jesse Grantham, *Practical Welding Today*, Sept./Oct. 1998), "Is Resistance Welding for You?" (Joanne Dinsmore, New Southern Resistance Welding, Pelham, Alabama, and Peter Howe, research engineer, *Practical Welding Today*, July/Aug. 1998), *Hobart Pocket Welding Guide* (1977), *Welding Basics* (Creative Publishing International), *Welding Technology Today* (Craig Stinchcomb, Prentice Hall), "Arc Welding 101 CV/CC" (Paul Cameron, *Practical Welding Today*, May/June 2011), "Why Can't I Use Stick Weld with My MIG Weld?" (Tom Meyers, www.lincolnelectric.com, www.fabricatingandwelding.com, Nov./Dec. 2013), "Resistance Welding" (*Practical Welding Today*), "Gouging: The Other Plasma Process" (Don Morong, Hypertherm Co, *Practical Welding Today*, May/June 2004), "Brazing Basics"(Adam Cort, *Assembly* magazine, 2006, www.assemblymag.com).

Chapter 12: Machining and Related Processes—Materials and Processes in Manufacturing 8th Ed. (E. Paul Degarmo, J. T. Black, and Ronald A. Kohser, Prentice Hall), "Micro Hole Drilling" (Leo Rakowski), "Non-Traditional Methods of Making Small Holes" (Modem Machine Systems, June 2002), "Sawing" (Cliff Dixon, April/May 2001, Tube Journal), "Trends in Drilling and Tapping" (John F. Zagar, Zagar Inc., Oct. 2001, Tooling and Production), "Sawing Back to Basics" (Ann Marie Rooke, July 2000, Cutting Tool Engineering), "Boring-Cutting Tool Applications" (George Schneider), "Are You Using the Right Cutting Fluid?" (Carl Kuchler, Valenite Valcool Cutting Fluids—Hass CNC Machining Winter 2002), "Pure Water Is Not Hard to Find" (William Sluhan, Master Chemicals Corp., Cutting Tool Engineering, Dec. 1996), "Choosing and Using Ball Style Hones" (Bruce Boyers, August 2006, www.PFonline.com), Grinding Basic Machining Reference

Handbook (Arthur R. Meyers and Thomas J. Slattery, Industrial Press Inc.), "Integrated CNC Machine Simulation Is Growing" (David F. Schulz, NCCS, Oct. 2005), www.toolingandproduction.com, "Medical Machining Made Simpler"(Lori Beckman, Esprit Software, Nov. 2007), "Production Machining: Success Factors for Hard Turning" (Peter Zelinski and CNC-related websites, Modern Machine Shop, Jan. 2012, Mike Lynch), "Roll to the Finish (Burnishing)" (Fred Ogburn, June 2001, Cutting Tool Engineering), CNC Handbook (Hans B. Kief and Helmut A Roschiwal, McGraw Hill), CNC Concepts: Industrial Electronics (Frank D. Petruzella-Glencoe, McGraw Hill), CNC Machining Handbook (James Madison, Industrial Press Inc.), Sandvik Coromant's Carbide Insert Technical Information (Richard Micro Tool Inc.), "PVD/CVD Coatings for Turret Punches" (Ashish Pabalkar and Bernard Janoss, June 2000), www.fabequipnews.com, "Engineering and Design Options for EDM" (Patrick Lorenz and Norm Turoff, Veridiam Inc.), Advanced EDM-MDDI Guide to Precision Technology (Sept. 2007), Surface Finish: Methods and Metrics for Production (ED Reitz), "MDDI Guide to Mechanical Precision Technology" (Sept 2007) "Cutting Fluids" (Today's Machining World, July 2008), "From Ore to Insert" (Barbara Donohue, Oct. 2006, Today's Machining World), Grinding (wwwaaabrasive.com), www.nortonabrasives.com, www.macmastercarr.com, www.mscdirect.com, http://gearsolutions.com/features/the-abcs-of-cbn-grinding/, www.etna.com-coolants.

Suggested reading on powder coating: *User's Guide to Powder Coating* by Nicholas Liberto at www.sme.org.

Chapter 13: Machinery Components and Electrical Systems—www.womackmachine.com, textbooks on hydraulics and controls, "Fluid Power Basics Fundamentals" (Peter Nachtwey, president, Delta Computer Systems, April/ May 2001), "Motion Control" (Designworldonline.com, Motioncontroltips.com, Sept. 2016), "Machine Design" (Dec. 26, 2013–2014), *OEM Engineering Handbook and Supplier Directory*, "AC Motors—The Big Five for Electric Motors" (p. 22, Oct. 2014, *Hydraulic and Pneumatics*, www.worldwideelectric.net), "Selecting the

Right Adjustable Drive" (John Malnowski, Baldor Electric, May 8, 1998, *Plant Engineering*), "Electric Wires—How to Specify" (Dave Perkow, May 2017, *Control Design* magazine), *Modern Commercial Wiring* (Harvey Holzman), "Automation Basics—Control Panel Schematics" (Dave Perkow, technical editor, *Control Design*, Sept. 2016) "How to Write a PLC Step Sequence" (Dave Perkon, Aug. 2017, *Control Design*), *Electrical Control for Machines* (Kenneth B. Rexford, Delmar Publishers), "Ball Screws vs. Lead Screws (Jan. 2008, www.motionsystemdesign.com), "Linear Motion Control" (Austin Weber, *Assembly* magazine, June 2000, www.assemblymag.com), "Planetary Gearhead" (John Mazurkiewicz, Baldor Electric, June 2008, *Motion System Design*), "Finding the Right Sensor for Linear Displacement" (Les Schaevitz), "Macro Sensors" (Edited by Stephen J. Mraz, *Machine Design*, July 8, 2004), "Hazardous Horsepower (Explosion Proof Motors)" (Cyndi Nyberg, February/March 2003, www.mrotoday.com), "Energy Cost Driving AC Drive" (Jack Smith, *Plant Engineering*, April 2008), "Troubleshooting Techniques Help Keep AC Induction Motor Running" (Timothy H. Tiebert, May 2006, *Plant Engineering*), "Composite Pulleys" (Warren Palmer, Fenner Drives Inc., *Motion System Design*, Feb. 2003), "Forum Bearings" (Larry Berardinis, *Motion System Design*, Feb. 2003), "Precision Gearmotors" (Lisa Hatch, Bayside Motion Group [now www.parker.com], Sept. 1999), "Motion Control, Optimizing Position Sensor Performance" (Dave Smallwood, Eaton Corp., *Plant Engineering*, Dec. 10, 1992), "Chain Selection" (Victor Petershack, Hitachi, Maxco, June 2004, *Motion System Design*), "Understanding AC Motors" (Gus Baldini, The Raymond Corp. (from http://www.reedlink.com), "Sensors for Machines" (Hank Hogan, *Control Design*, Jan. 2015), "Linear Motion" (Leslie Gordan, Jan. 2015), "Fundamentals of Automation Control" (Jeff Kerns, *Machine Design,* March 16, 2018, www.newequipment.com), "Motors—Modern Materials Handling (June 2005), http://www.skf.com/us/knowledge-centre/media-library/index.html.

Note: For further reading, consult *Power Transmission Handbook* published by Power Transmission Distributors Association.

Chapter 14: Fluid Power Systems—*Fluid Power Journal* (www.fluidpowerjournal.com), "Hydraulic Muscle, As Needed" (Dave Perkon, November 2017, www.controldesign.com), "Fluid Power Basics—Motion Control" (April/May 2001), "The Fundamentals of Hydraulics Motors" (*Hydraulics and Pneumatics*, July 2014, www.hydraulicspneumatics.com), *Hydraulics—Theory and Applications from Bosch* (Robert Bosch Gmbh, author, 1984, Werner Gotz), *Fluid Power Designers—Lightning Reference Handbook Fifth Ed.* (Paul Munroe, 1982, Hydraulics), "Parker Tube Fittings Installation" (Manual Bulletin 4200-B4, April 1996), "Troubleshooting Hydraulic Components" (Lawrence Schrader Jr., Parker Hannifin-Plant Eng., May 2016), "Control Air Cylinder Speed" (*Fluid Power Journal*, January/Feb. 2018, Parker Pneumatic symbols), "Hydraulic Fittings" (Le Yu, Parker Hannifin Corp., *Hydraulic & Pneumatics*, December 2012), "Filtration" T. C. Frankenfield, The Rexroth Corp. *Hydraulic & Pneumatic* magazine), "Hydraulic Hoses" (Greg Brown, Ryco Hydraulics, Houston Texas, *Machine Design*, March 2007), "Hydraulic Tank: The Hydraulic Fluid's Best Friend" (Brian Casey, www.hydraulicsupermarket.com), *Industrial Hydraulics* (P. Rohner), websites for Mobil Oil, Chevron, and British Petroleum foil Hydraulic Oil Grades), *Fluid Power with Applications* (Anthony Esposito, Prentice Hall), Enerpac—211 Work holding catalogue, *Fluid Power Journal* (March/April 2018, Fittings), Compressed air articles, "Hydraulic Symbols" (*Vickers Industrial Hydraulics Manual*, 1999, Vickers Inc.), "Predictive Maintenance" (Vlad Bacalu, Advanced Technology Services Inc., Sept. 2007), www.impomag.com, "Solenoid Valves for Medical Devices" (Paul Gant, www.mddionline.com), "Name that Thread" (Burleigh Bailey, Parker Hannifin, Columbus, Ohio, *Machine Design*, Oct. 21, 2004), *Introduction to Fluid Power* (James L. Johnson, Delmar Thomson Learning).

Chapter 15: Lubrication of the Equipment—"Oiling Program Aims for World-Class Status" (Wayne A. Vaughan, Harley Davidson Inc.), "Storing and Handling of Hazardous Liquids" (Charles Matalonis and David Evans, Justrite Mfg. Co.), Grease (www.machinerylubrication.com), Lubricating Oils (www.mobil.com), Lubrication for Industry

(Kenneth E. Banister), SKF Bearing Maintenance Handbook (1991), Willy Vogel Lubrication Systems, www.brighthubengineering.com, www.aviationpros.com, www.ilma.org.

Chapter 16: Plastics—Understanding Injection Molding (Herbert Rees, Hanser Publishers), Blow Molding Design (Norman C. Lee, Hanser Publishers), Training in Plastics Technology (Michaeli, Greif, Kaufmann, and Vosseburger, Hanser Publishers), Tooling and Manufacturing Engineers Handbook, Forming, Engineering Plastics Volume 2 Engineered Materials Handbook (ASM International), "Properties of Plastics" (Elmer Korbai), Plastics Thermoplastic Selection Guide (Plastics International), Blown Film Extrusion (Kirk Cantor, Hanser Publishers, Munich), Successful Injection Molding (Beaumont, Nagel, and Sherman, Hansers Publishers, Munich), Materials Selection in Mechanical Design (Michael A. Ashby, Elsevier), www.ptonline.com, "Plastic Rules" (Austin Weber, www.assemblymag.com), Engineering Materials Handbook Desk Ed. (ASM International), www.plasticsmag.com, Plastics Processing Technology (Edward A. Muccio, ASM International).

Chapter 17: Quality Control in Manufacturing—www.intra-corp.net (different measurement systems), www.mahr.com (Mahr Federal Inc.), Manufacturing Best Practices (Bobby Hull, John Wiley and Sons), Inspection and Gaging 6th Ed. (Kennedy, Hoffman, and Bond, Industrial Press Inc.), www.qualitymag.com, Welding Design and Fabrication 2000 Handbook Issue.

Chapter 18: Engineering Drawings—Basic Blueprint Reading (John A. Nelson, Tab Books), Welding Print Reading (John R. Walker, The Goodheart Willcox Co., Inc.), Technical Drawing (Giesecke, Mitchell, Spencer, Hill, Dygdon, and Noval, Prentice Hall), Reading Engineering Drawings (Jay Helsel and Shriver Coover), Design Dimensions and Tolerance, Blueprint Reading for the Machine Trades (Russell Schultz and Larry Smith), Printreading for Welders (Thomas E. Proctor and Jonathan F. Goose, American Technical Publishers), "Back to Basics: The Symbology of GD&T" (Mark A Curtis, Fabricating and

Metalworking, March 2007), Engineering Drawing and Design 6th Ed. (Cecil Jensen, Jay D. Helsel, and Dennis R. Short, Glencoe McGraw Hill).

Trade magazines, major trade shows, associations and associations:

www.aiche.org/cep (chemical engineering process)
https://www.aisc.org/modernsteel (steel construction)
www.ansi.org (American National Standards Institute)
https://www.ases.org/solartoday/
www.asse.org (American Society of Safety Engineers)
www.assemblymag.com
www.automationworld.com
https://www.aws.org/publications/WeldingJournal
www.controldesign.com (control design for machine builder)
www.designworldonline.com
www.fabricatingandmetalworking.com
www.fastenertech.com (Fastener Technology)
www.ctemag.com (*Cutting Tool Engineering* magazine)
www.d2pmagazine.com (*Job Shop Technology* magazine)
https://www.ffjournal.net/ (metal forming and fabricating)
www.flowcontrolnetwork.com
www.fluidpowerjournal.com
https://www.fluidpowerworld.com/
https://fsmdirect.com/issues (*Fabricating Shop* magazine)
www.gearsolutions.com
http://gomc.com/ (manufacturing confectioner)
www.hydraulicsandpneumatics.com
https://www.hydrocarbonprocessing.com/ (information on oil refining)
www.impomag.com (industrial maintenance and plant operation)
www.IMTS.com (International Machine Tool Show—Every two year held in Chicago)

www.indphotonics.com
www.jobshopcompany.com
https://www.machinedesign.com/archive/penton-media
www.medicaldesignbriefs.com
www.metalfinishing.com
www.metalformingmagazine.com
www.mmsonline.com (Modern Machine Shop)
https://www.modernmetals.com/
www.osha.gov (US government safety regulations agency)
www.pcne.eu (European suppliers for equipment and instrumentation)
www.pfonline.com
www.plasticsdecorating.com
www.plasticsmag.com (plastics distributor and fabricators)
https://pgjonline.com/ (*Pipe Line and Gas Journal*)
https://www.power-eng.com/index.html (gas / coal / hydro / nuclear and renewable energy)
https://www.powerengineeringint.com/index.html
www.powderbulksolids.com
www.processingmagazine.com
www.pump-zone.com
www.qualitymag.com
https://www.railwayage.com/news/
www.sgia.org (Specialty Graphic Imaging Association)
www.snipsmag.com
https://www.thefabricator.com/
www.tpatube.org (*The Tube and Pipe Journal*)
www.vision-systems.com (Vision Systems Design)
www.visionshow.org (For Vision Systems Integrators)
www.watertechonline.com

Food-related websites:
https://www.bakingbusiness.com/digitaleditions
www.foodengineeringmag.com
https://www.foodprocessing.com/
http://www.ift.org/knowledge-center.aspx (food technology)

www.meatpoultry.com
www.foodprocesssing.com
www.foodandbeveragepackaging.com
https://www.nrn.com/news (*National Restaurant News*)
https://www.pascalprocessing.com/blog/publication-international-meat-topics/
https://www.profoodtech.com/ (Food Equipment Trade Show
https://www.provisioneronline.com/topics/2228-meat-and-poultry-processing
www.specialtyfood.com

INDEX—ESSENTIAL GUIDE TO METALS AND MANUFACTURING

A36 Steel, 29
Aist.org, 3
abrasive saws, 170
AC Electric Motors, 218
ACME threads, 101
actuator for pneumatics, 236
adjustable Speed Drives, 219
air compressors, 233
air dryers, 234
air tanks, 234
air system components, 235
AK Steel, 10
Aluminum, 30, 55
Aluminum castings, 58
Annealing, 65
anti microbial coatings, 10
ArcelorMittal, 9
ASTM Specifications, 34, 35
austenitic stainless steel, 8, 33
ball screws, 213
band saws, 167
basic oxygen furnace, 5
bearings, 212
Cobalt, 30, 60 Ductile iron,
Coke, 3
cold forming, 102
common alloying elements, 29, 30
machining, 164
common steel alloys, 7
compression molding, 280

belts, 214
Bismuth, 30
Blast furnace, 3
Blown film extrusion, 274
Blow molding, 281
brazing, 146
Brinell, 48, 49
British screw threads, 98
Burnishing, 190
Buttress threads, 101
Calcium, 30
Capacitive sensors, 223
Carbon, 30
Carbonitirding, 65
Carbon affect, 16
Carpenter steel, 10
Cast iron, 15
centerless grinding, 187
centrifugal casting, 74
centralized lubrication, 264
chain, 215
Chromium, 30, 61
class of threads, 94
ductile iron, 19
dye penetrate liquid, 72
electric arc furnace, 6,17
electric discharge

electron beam welding, 144
electroplating, 199

compressive strength, 48
Computer numerical control, 159
CNC turret punch machine, 116
Control cabinet, 226
Control panel schematics, 225
Country of origin, 11
Couplings, 215
Cryogenic treatments, 67
Cutting fluids, 170
Cutting tools, 173
Cyaniding, 65
D Tool steel, 39
DC motors, 220
die casting, 73
Directional control valves, 245
Direct metal laser sintering, 191
Drilling, 164
Dry sand molding, 16
Gas welding, 143
Gray iron, 18
Grease, 260
Grease and oil lubricator, 263
Green sand molding, 15
Grinding, 186
Gold, 62
Hardness, 48
Hardenability, 64
Hard milling, 186
Heat treatment guide, 66
Hematite, 4
High carbon steel, 29
HDPE, 275
HMI graphics panel, 221
Honing, 190
Hot forgings, 102
Hot isostatic pressing, 73,103,121
Hydroforming 103, 120
Hydraulic components, 238

electromagnetic clutch, 214
elements, 1, 45
encoders, 224
extruder, 276
fabrication of sheet steel, 103
fatigue strength, 48
Ferritic stainless steel, 8,33
filler breathers, 244
filtering media, 244
fire resistant fluids, 242
flame hardening, 65
flow control valves, 245
Flux core welding, 138
friction welding, 141
Galvanizing, 200
gas carburizing, 65
Gas metal arc welding, 134
Gas Tungsten welding, 135
Hydraulic pumps, 246
Impact strength, 48
Inductive Proximity sensor, 223
Inductotherm.com, 6
Induction furnace, 6, 17
Induction hardening, 65
ingot handling, 7
injection molding, 279
inspection of castings, 22
International standards steel, 37
iridium, 62
investment castings, 71
knoop, 49, 50
laser alignment, 196
laser cutting, 81
laser heat treatment, 68
laser welding, 144
LDPE, 274
Lead, 30, 60
Lead screw, 213

Hydraulic fittings, 239
Hydraulic fluids. 240
Hydraulic hoses, 244
Hydraulic motors, 246
M-high speed steel, 40
Machine safety
Machinability of steel, 37
Magnetite ,4
Magnetic particle testing, 22
Magnesium, 60
Malleable iron, 19, 20
Manganese, 30
Manual milling, 187
Material certificates, 37
Medium carbon steel, 29
Melting of iron, 17
Metal injection molding, 77
Metal spinning, 103,122
Micro hole drilling, 166
metallurgy, 75
Molten Pig iron, 4
Molybdenum, 40
Nickel, 30, 60
Nitriding, 65
No bake process
Non ferrous metal prices, 61
Normalizing, 65
Nucor steel, 10
Quenching of steel, 66
Quality check for welds, 148, 149
Radiographic testing, 22
RFID tags, 224
Resistance welding 142
Return on investment 196
Rockwell, 49, 50
Roll forming, 120
Rolling of plates, 103
Rolling of thread, 102

Linear motion, 217
LLDPE, 275
lubricant selection, 260
LVDT sensor, 222
Oil filtration, 243
Oil hardening steel, 39
Oil lubrication, 261
Oil reservoir 243
Open hearth furnace, 5
Oxy-fuel cutting, 83
Photo electric sensor, 223
pig iron, 3
pipe thread, 95
Plate rolling, 117
plain carbon steel, 28
plasma cutting, 85
platinum, 62
plastic connectors, 236
Pneumatic systems, 232
pressure control valves, 245
Press brake, 119
production efficiency, 195
programmable logic, 226
polyamide, 275
polyethylene, 274
polypropylene, 275
polystyrene, 275
polyvinyl chloride, 275
Silicone, 30
sintering, 76
square thread, 101
stamping 102, 110
steel, 2.5
steel casting, 21, 34
steel plants, 8, 9
steel recycling , 12
steel stainless, 3,7,33
steel tariffs, 11

Rotational molding, 281
SAE, 31, 30
Sawing, 167
Screw thread terms, 97
Selection of welding electrodes, 139
Sensors, 222
Servomotors, 221
Shear strength, 48
Shock resistant steel, 40
Sheet metal presses, 111
Shielding gases, 136
Shielded metal arc welding, 137
Shotpeening, 69
Silver, 62
Torsional strength, 48
Tungsten tool steel, 40
Tungsten, 3
Turning on lathe, 177
Tuyers, 4
Types of iron castings, 18
Ultimate tensile strength, 47
Ultrasonic sensors, 223
Ultrasonic testing, 22
UNC/UNRC, 93
UNF/UNRF, 94
UNEF, 94
US Steel, 9
Vacuum systems, 238
Vacuum furnace, 67
Valves for pneumatics, 237
Vanadium, 30
Vickers, 48, 49
Viscosity, 240
Water hardening steel, 39
Water jet cutting, 86
Water quality, 172

stress and strain, 46
stress and strain curve , 47
Taconite, 4
tensile force, 46
tensile test, 47
thermoforming, 281
thermoplastic, 273
thermosetting
thread rolling, 116
tempering, 66
tin, 61
titanium 30, 61
tool coatings, 176
tool steel, 38

Welding cost, 147
Welding of iron casting, 22
white iron, 18
wiring, 225
yield point, 47
zinc, 60